Potboilers

Potboilers looks at the many forms of popular narrative – in print, film and TV. It considers the ways they have been analysed in literary criticism, sociology, communications, media and cultural studies.

The book introduces and summarises two decades of debate about mass-produced fictions and their position within popular culture. It assesses the methods that have been used in these debates, focusing both on narrative analysis and the communications process. It explores generic conventions, the role of commercial strategies, and the nature of the audience with reference to crime fiction, soap opera, romance and TV sitcom.

Distinctions between 'high' and 'low' culture have relegated many popular forms to the trash-can of 'great' literature. This book takes stock of the methods and concepts used to analyse popular culture and argues for a non-elitist approach to the study of literature, film and television.

Jerry Palmer's analysis of the debates surrounding popular fiction gives a clear account of existing work and provides an invaluable guide for students and teachers of literature, communications, media and cultural studies.

Jerry Palmer is a Professor of Communications at City of London Polytechnic. He is the author of *Thrillers* (1978) and *The Logic of the Absurd* (1987), and the wide range of articles he has written on popular culture indicates his lasting interest in the field.

Communication and Society
General Editor: James Curran

Potboilers

Methods, concepts and case studies
in popular fiction

Jerry Palmer

London and New York

First published 1991
by Routledge
11 New Fetter Lane, London EC4P 4EE

Simultaneously published in the USA and Canada
by Routledge
a division of Routledge, Chapman and Hall, Inc.
29 West 35th Street, New York, NY 10001

© 1991 Jerry Palmer

Set in 10/12pt Times by Selectmove
Printed and bound in Great Britain by
T.J. Press (Padstow) Ltd, Padstow, Cornwall.

British Library Cataloguing in Publication Data
Palmer, Jerry.
  Potboilers: methods, concepts and case studies in popular fiction.
  1. Fiction
  I. Title
823.91209

Library of Congress Cataloging in Publication Data
Palmer, Jerry.
    Potboilers: methods, concepts, and case studies in popular
fiction / Jerry Palmer.
      p.   cm. — (Communication and society)
    Includes bibliographical references.
    1. American fiction—20th century—History and criticism—Theory,
etc. 2. Popular literature—United States—History and criticism—
Theory, etc. 3. United States—Popular culture—History—20th
century. 4. Books and reading—United States. 5. Canon
(Literature) 6. Literary form. I. Title. II. Series:
Communication and society (Routledge (Firm))
PS374.P63P34 1991
302.23′0973—dc20   91–14013

ISBN 0–415–00977–4   ISBN 0–415–00978–2 (pbk)

To Berlin Walls, everywhere, and especially the one that separates low culture from high

Contents

Introduction

Popular narrative has not traditionally been well regarded in academic institutions.

The clearest expression of this disregard is silence. In 1982 the journal *Literature, Teaching, Politics* constructed a 'league table' of English literature by listing the authors who had figured on British public examinations syllabuses during the previous few years. If we count as one unit each occasion on which a given work appears on a syllabus, there were a total of 1,389 units on the syllabuses, of which more than half (699) were accounted for by the 'top 17 classic' writers (Shakespeare alone accounted for 190 units). In this pantheon only four units could be counted as popular narrative: John Wyndham, H.G. Wells, a collection of Gothic novels and Jules Verne. More recently, changes have occurred: the proliferation of courses in film and television studies, the reform of English literature public examinations, with syllabuses in part chosen by schools, all have encouraged the study of popular narrative. In the United States the traditional disregard was undermined at an earlier stage by the centrality of American literature, and the more developed interest in the mass media.

The reasons for traditional disregard are instructive. In broad outline, the literature syllabus consisted of a corpus of texts – the 'canon' – and a method of teaching, based upon the progressive refinement of aesthetic response. The two components were mutually reinforcing, in that the method made sense given the corpus of texts, and the selection of texts made sense given the method. Popular fiction challenges both, and we shall see that the choice of popular texts demands new methods of study. First, it is useful to explore the canon and its methods in more detail.

Part of the traditional disregard may be imputed to condemnation of popular narrative as unworthy of study. This judgement is typical, if more forthright than usual:

> Hardly anyone is unaware – at least viscerally – that 99 per cent
> of the material conveyed to us by the mass communication media
> is aesthetically and intellectually trivial . . . elevating worthless
> books to best-sellerdom, and endorsing TV imbecilities via the
> ratings polls . . . . Sub-art systematically unfits a person for art
> and vice-versa . . . heavy consumption of one eventually obviates
> the other.
>
> (Rosenberg, 1971: 7, 11)

The distinction between 'art' and 'sub-art' which underpins this
condemnation has a long and complex history; it is ultimately
political in nature. The arguments in question are commonplace in
all industrialised societies – for the sake of convenience I follow the
British version (cf. Bramson, 1967; Giner, 1976).

Coleridge was the first to claim, in Britain, the need for a 'secular
clerisy', a social stratum who would diffuse a set of values. Adherence
to these values would constitute a form of commonality akin to that
achieved by religion (or supposedly so) at an earlier stage in history.
In different post-Romantic thinkers the agency varied, and the tactics
to be followed too: but throughout the long nineteenth-century debate
on the nature of culture there is to be found at its heart an emphasis
on the need in our society for a common sense of values and some
agency to create and diffuse them. Within this process of value
creation the arts have been accorded varied importance, but a high
status is common. For Shelley, in a famous phrase, the poet was the
'unacknowledged legislator' of mankind. For Arnold too poetry, with
education and criticism, was an integral part of the 'best-self' of man,
that imaginary exemplar whose imitation would save mankind from
anarchy (Williams, 1958: 125–36). Subsequently, for F.R. Leavis
and the movement of which he is the best-known representative,
the appreciation and study of literature becomes the key feature of
the creation of a national culture (Williams, 1958: 246ff.; Mulhern,
1979: 35–40).

Within all of this tradition it is axiomatic that literature or the arts
means 'the best' within them; Arnold, for example, is quite explicit
that culture is the knowledge of 'the best that has been thought and
said in the world'. Central to the thesis of Q.D. Leavis' *Fiction and
the Reading Public* (1932) is the distinction between 'fiction' and
'literature': literary criticism is unable to 'take heed of the majority
of novels'; since they are not part of the 'moral community of culture'
they are in effect 'unrecognisable'.

The argument is clear: our society needs fine literature in order to help prevent it falling into anarchy or some other undesirable state such as philistinism; popular narrative cannot perform this function therefore it is best ignored, or only (briefly) noticed in order to be denounced. Only texts sufficiently fine to perform the tasks in question will be included in the 'canon' of literature to be studied. This argument seems to me to be false, for two reasons. Stated briefly and dogmatically, they are: firstly, literature has not in fact lived up to the task of civilisation; secondly, the distinction between 'art' and 'sub-art' is enacted via a supposedly universal canon of taste which is in fact a false universality.

It is perhaps unfair to reproach literature, or 'culture' in general, with the failings of our civilisation. Yet I am haunted by a scene from Munk's *The Passenger*, which takes place in Auschwitz. An orchestra composed of inmates, dressed in camp uniform, plays Bach and Mozart to an SS audience, while in the background a train unloads future victims of the death chambers; unfortunately, a taste for great art does not preclude personal and institutional bestiality (cf. Steiner, 1967: 81). And although it is conventional to refer to the Holocaust as proof of the failure of European culture, the excesses of colonialism are no less abundant a proof: the figure of Kurtz, in Conrad's *Heart of Darkness* (and its adaptation *Apocalypse Now*), is a summation of all that is best and worst in European civilisation, a man of culture and energy who is also a mass-murderer. These are references to fiction, of course, but the events in question are emblematic of realities.

It is basic to the capacity attributed to great literature that it is in fact great, that is to say, that its greatness is indeed a property of the texts in question, and that it is indeed objectively so that it is great. The objectivity of its greatness derives from the universality of its appeal, and this is necessarily so: great literature is such because it speaks to the universality of our experience; of course, this does not mean that it will say the same thing to each of us – perhaps the greatness of great texts is that they say different things to different people – but they must speak to all of us in some way. If the greatness is simply the judgement, the subjective collective taste, of a limited group of people, then its status is by no means so compelling.

Bennett (1987) shows how the universality in question is necessarily an imaginary postulate. According to traditional aesthetics, the claim that something is beautiful depends upon the person who recognises it as such being intuitively sure that the recognition proceeds from an appreciation of the object in question, not from some self-interest he or she has in the object. If this condition is fulfilled, the valuing subject is entitled to demand of everyone else that they accede to this recognition, and indeed must make this demand, for if they do not accede this casts doubt upon the disinterestedness of the evaluation and upon the location of beauty in the object. 'Taste' must be universal, or it cannot exist: not in the sense that everyone actually agrees on what is beautiful – such an accord is an ideal norm – but in the sense that 'the demand for agreement that accompanies aesthetic judgement presupposes the possibility of its eventual existence' (Bennett, 1987: 51). In other words, not everyone will agree with us, but everyone ought to agree with us, and once impediments to agreement have been removed – thus abolishing those disqualified to make such judgements – agreement will exist. That is to say, universality is always located in some hypothetical future.

At this point we may turn to a very different tradition of study of narrative, sociological in origin.

The act of communication has traditionally been conceptualised as a flow, in which a sender sends a message to a receiver, and its study is often seen as corresponding to a series of questions: who says what, to whom, in what channel, with what effect? That is, communication is always seen as a process involving more than one party, and some form of transmission. This model has been much criticised, and we shall return to some criticisms later; however, one of its features has survived this process: communication is a social act, which can be studied as can any other social act.

Here we may consider narrative as one such act of communication: A tells a story to B, and we may want to know what B thinks of the story, or what effect it has on B's feelings and perhaps behaviour (A and B are both likely to be collective entities, not individuals: say, a TV station and its public). In relation to the tradition analysed above, what is striking about this approach is that it ignores the question of aesthetic quality: instead of asking whether the story is a good story, it asks instead what impact it has on its audience; in Bennett's terminology, it refers not to a universalising taste, but to the judgements of a particular 'valuing community' (1987: 43).

Comstock (1983) argues that the text in television is never simply the content of what is broadcast but must always include the audience at which the text is targeted. For example, it is well established that daytime TV (in the USA) shows a cross-section of the population that is demographically closer to reality than the population of primetime TV; in this sense daytime TV is more realistic. But the essential demographic difference lies in the age-range of female characters, since primetime TV concentrates heavily on young women. The audience of daytime TV is disproportionately middle-aged and female, and this explains the different range of characters shown, not some putative truth (Cassata and Skill, 1983: 9–12).

Here lies an explanation of the difference between the methods employed on the one hand by literary critics and teachers and, on the other, by sociologists. The purpose of sociological analysis is always essentially to make inferences about some entity which is distinct from the communication in question. By starting from the notion of the communication act, however it is defined, sociological analysis insists on the distinction between source, message and recipient: this is what makes the process of inference possible and also what makes it desirable. In literary criticism the opposite assumption operates: that analysis of the artefact in question is a valid end in itself. This is because of the prior assumption that the cultivation of aesthetic sensibility in the individual will make that individual a better member of society, and the cultivation of such sensibility on the part of a substantial number of individuals will create a better society. The purpose of literary criticism is to participate in the process of aesthetic education, to educate both the critic and those who read the analysis in question, and thus through the building of a culture which incorporates sound aesthetic principles to improve the human world to some degree. Under these circumstances, inferences concerning the other elements of the communication process (source and recipient) are of little value, since the source is largely irrelevant and the whole purpose of the exercise is to change the nature of the recipient.

Focus on popular narrative entails a range of methods. The first half of this book is devoted to outlining several of them, and only brief introductory comments are required here. One way to open these considerations is through an analysis of methods which are not appropriate in this content: consideration of authors and texts, the central focus of literary criticism.

In the analysis of canonical literature, the text and the author are both absolutely central and taken for granted: it is 'obvious' that texts exist and that they are produced by authors, even if there are occasional difficulties of attribution (Shakespeare is a notorious example). It is worth remembering that in pre-Renaissance and non-European cultures, neither text nor author should be taken for granted in the same way. The medieval epics often existed in several versions, and in many instances are of unknown origin. In Winnebago society, storytellers buy the right to tell a story and then sell performances of it, but the story itself is traditional and no doubt varies somewhat with each performance (Radin, 1976). In post-Renaissance literature, the text is regarded as a self-contained entity which has a meaning contained within it, co-extensive with it. This meaning is the result of the activity of the author (influenced, of course, by his or her culture). Understanding the text consists of unveiling this meaning. The fact that there is an author is a guarantee of the unitary nature of the text.

In popular narrative, such considerations rarely apply. In many instances there is no single author: texts are assembled by a team, as in this contemporary description of a 'dime novel factory' in New York in the 1890s:

> This literary factory . . . employs over thirty people . . . [The first job in the division of labour is] to read all the daily and weekly periodicals in the land . . . . Any unusual story of city life – mostly the misdoings of city people – is marked by these girls and turned over to one of the managers. These managers, who are men, select the best of the marked articles, and turn over such as are available to one of a corps of five women, who digest the happening given to them and transform it into a skeleton or outline for a story. This shell, if it may be so called, is then returned to the chief manager, who turns to a large address-book and adapts the skeleton to some one of the hundred or more writers entered on his book.

> (Denning, 1989: 17)

Soap opera is created in the same manner. Although production methods differ somewhat from company to company (*EBU*, 1985), this outline seems typical: story-lines are created some fixed time in advance of broadcast and are then farmed out to scriptwriters; some large soaps may have as many as five levels of decision-making in scripting. In parallel, technical personnel (directors, camera-men, lighting technicians, etc.) receive scripts and turn them into production schedules. Actors too receive scripts and work on them both privately and in rehearsal; one person, or a small team, is charged with keeping a record of every fictional event narrated in order to achieve continuity. Only those at the top of the hierarchy have an overall view of the development of the story, but will not usually be involved in dialogue-writing or production details (Paterson, 1981; Podmore, 1984; Hobson, 1982; Cantor and Pingree, 1983: 57–68). All of these studies stress the extent to which technical exigencies – such as the number of sets that can be constructed in a given studio space, the number of camera crews available – influence the nature of the final broadcast 'text'. Such matters are ultimately controlled by budgets. In general, audio-visual media are produced by large teams, though it is usually agreed that in film, individuals such as well-established directors may exercise a high degree of control over the finished product. However, generalisations are unwise, since such matters are subject to considerable variation through time and space (Bordwell *et al.*, 1985).

Clearly, under circumstances such as these, 'authors' do not have the same kind of reality as they are accorded in traditional conceptions of literature. In the instance of soap opera there is no such thing as a text either, since the stories in question have no end: even when a given soap ceases broadcasting, the stories are not ended, in the usual sense, for it is impossible to resolve so many plot lines – they simply cease being told. This, however, is an exceptional case, and most popular narrative exists in forms where there are indeed texts, at least insofar as they have a distinctive physical existence, with a title, an end, etc. However, it is well known that the majority of popular narrative is produced according to tried and tested 'formulae' – the detective story, the romantic novel, the situation comedy, etc. – and where narratives are examples of such genres (see chapter 7), it may make more sense to study the genre than the individual text, since it is likely that the characteristics of the text that are responsible for impact upon the audience are in fact the characteristics that the text shares with other members of the genre, and which are only studiable on this basis. Thus the individual text is traversed by a layer of meaning that derives from outside it, and it is therefore not the unitary, self-contained entity that canonical criticism focuses on.[1]

In summary, therefore, what is needed in the study of popular narrative is some method(s) that will allow analysis of how such fiction has the impact that it has on whatever its audience is. In recent debates on the subject, several methods have found favour, and will be discussed later. One common starting-point is the relationship between narrative and sign systems.

The usual starting-point for a study of sign systems is the nature of the sign, which is conventionally defined as any entity which stands for something for somebody – i.e. a sign is always a representation of something other than itself, and is understood as such by somebody (Zeman, 1977).[2] The sign itself is usually seen as having three aspects:

(1) Its material existence (the phonic or graphic substance of a word, light imprinted on chemically coated paper for photography, etc.); this aspect is called the signifier.
(2) What it refers to, which is a concept: the word 'table' refers to the mental concept 'table' and via this concept to the class of objects thus classified; this aspect is called the signified.
(3) What it is used to refer to in any individual message, for example, a particular table; this is called the referent.

(Saussure, 1974: 65ff.)

Signs are further classified according to the way in which they represent: in other words according to the nature of the relationship between signifier and signified in each instance. In language this relationship is 'unmotivated' (sometimes the term 'arbitrary' is used) because there is no connection between the signified and the signifier other than the convention that the latter means the former: 'tree' is 'arbre' in French and 'Baum' in German, but the mental concept 'tree' does not vary significantly between the three cultures. These signs are called 'symbols'. In visual representations, however, there is normally a connection of resemblance between signifier and signified which 'motivates' the signifier – photography is the clearest instance; such signs are called 'icons'.

Signs are capable of bearing meaning because they are different from each other. Any message consists of a set of signs brought into proximity with each other, in the form of sentences, or scenes in a film, etc. The signs can only be articulated on to each other to form a message because they bear different meanings – a large number of identical signs, all bearing the same meaning, would not be capable of transmitting meaning. The set of signs is called a paradigm (or 'system', or 'langue', the French word for the language system – while these words are not synonymous, they all refer to the same feature of signs). Within any paradigm, signs are identifiable as such by the fact that when one is replaced by another, meaning changes.

It is important that here I have failed to distinguish between linguistic signs and visual signs, between symbols and icons. In symbols the relationship between signifier and signifed is unmotivated, as we have seen; another way of putting this is to say that language is a digital system, as opposed to an analogue system (Fiske, 1982: 69). Because there is no motivation of this relationship, meaning derives entirely from the place that a given sign occupies within a paradigm: the distinction between 'rain' and 'drizzle' derives from the place that these words occupy within a set of words referring to weather. But a visual image does not work in the same way, since it derives its capacity to bear meaning from the resemblance between itself and what it is an image of.

The analysis of language consists fundamentally of attempts to show how meaning is the product of a series of rules for the combination of signs, but the analysis of visual communication is difficult to pursue in the same terms because of the fundamental difference in the nature of symbols and icons. More exactly, semioticians have asked to what extent it is possible to pursue the two enquiries on the same terms, and attempts have been made to reduce the difference between the two types of sign.

These attempts have centred around the argument that visual signs are not exclusively motivated by resemblance, because there is a high degree of convention – i.e. 'arbitrariness', or unmotivation – involved in them too. Firstly, visual signs represent the three-dimensional world in two dimensions, and it is only within civilisations that admit the possibility of such a representation that these signs can be decoded by viewers; outside such a context they are not comprehensible. Secondly, there are strong elements of conventional coding within visual representations. Eco has argued that these conventions can be broken down into minimum units of meaning that could be assembled into something akin to a dictionary. However, he has since rejected this on the grounds that these units can only be established as such in the context of particular messages; in other words a piece of visual information which is a unit of meaning in one message may not be such in another (Lauretis, 1984: 42–8).

If we accept that there are indeed fundamental differences between iconic and symbolic systems, then it is clear that visual narrative cannot be analysed in terms deriving from the analysis of language. For example, if it is accepted that in film the individual shot (i.e. a segment of film which is continuous and discrete) is the minimum unit of meaning, then it is clear that it is significantly different from the word in language; the chief differences are these:

(1) Words are built up out of smaller units of meaning, i.e. individual sounds and letters, into which they can be analysed; shots cannot be broken down in this way.
(2) Shots are infinite in number, whereas the list of words in any language is finite.
(3) Shots are invented, whereas words are used.
(4) Shots contain a quantity of undefined information, in other words, information whose meaning is not in any way fixed outside the shot itself – for example, intensity of light.

(5) A shot is a unit in a message which has actually been composed, and has no existence outside this context, whereas a word has an existence in a lexicon, and is therefore part of an infinite number of potential messages.

(6) Language is fundamentally dialogic – i.e. all its structures are only comprehensible on the basis that it is spoken by someone to someone *who can reply*; cinema is fundamentally monologic – there is no mechanism of reply.

(See Cegarra, 1973: 112, 155)

Insofar as iconic systems resemble language, they resemble discourse – i.e. the connected flow constituted by a verbal message – rather than the language system considered as something which has a potential existence outside of any actualisation of it in a message (Lauretis, 1984: ch. 2). However, the subject of this book is not language or iconic sign systems but narrative, the telling of stories, and stories are not the same thing as language either even though they may use it: stories too are a form of discourse. If we reconsider the six differences between shots and words in the light of this new concern, we will see that the differences disappear, since shots are intrinsically narrative in their orientation:

(1) Although words in a verbal narrative can indeed be analysed down into their minimum units, as can any words, their meaning is dependent at least as much upon their place in narrative as upon their place in grammar and the lexicon.

(2) Narratives are infinite in number, like all discourse.

(3) Narratives are invented, not used.

(4) Narratives contain undefined information, in the sense that the meaning of bits of narrative cannot be established outside the narrative.

(5) Narrative is actualised discourse, and has only limited potential existence in the form of a grammar.

(6) Narrative is monologic (but see chapter 3).

That is to say, narrative is an entity whose structures do not depend entirely upon the signs out of which it is built up, and therefore it is legitimate to investigate it across a range of media. This possibility was noticed in the earliest European debates on the subject. Aristotle says:

[Different art forms] differ from each other in three respects: either they imitate different things; or, they imitate *with* different things; or, they imitate in different ways, not the same way.

(Aristotle, 1968: i.3)

Leaving aside the question of whether Aristotle is right to assert that all art is imitation, the principle underlying his analysis clearly has wide validity: the distinction by medium of transmission is only one of the ways of distinguishing between art forms. Thus, for Aristotle, the distinction between comedy and tragedy is clear, although both are transmitted by the same medium, namely theatre. Music and poetry, even though they may be used together in a joint work of art (song) are distinguished both by what they imitate and by what they imitate with – in semiotic terms, both their referents and their signifiers are different.

At the same time, it is clear that there may well be links between the elements in the structure of works of art which Aristotle differentiates in this schema: thus film 'imitates' by using an audio-visual medium (imitates 'with something different' from the novel, to use Aristotle's terms) and it is not difficult to demonstrate that certain differences in narrative structure between film and novel are dependent upon features of the medium of transmission. For example, in film, space and time are presented simultaneously, whereas in the novel this is not possible in quite the same way; verbal narrative has the benefit of tense structure to construct time sequences that film cannot – there is no direct filmic equivalent of 'While he was eating the meal I had already prepared'; and there is no real equivalent in the novel of the lighting effects which are fundamental to film.

In short, without necessarily taking Aristotle as the last word on the subject, there is good reason for taking his distinction seriously. Where it can lead us may be shown by a consideration of the distinction that both he and Plato make between diegesis and mimesis (Genette, 1966). Here mimesis is the direct imitation of an action, for example by an actor, or by an epic poet quoting the words of a character in direct speech; diegesis is the act of narrating by a poet speaking in his or her own voice. However, it is clear that even the pure recording of the speech of a character, which apparently involves no narrator (though it, of course, implies a 'transcriber' of the characters' words, i.e. an author) in fact implies also (by the same token) an act of diegesis, since the meaning of the words reported does not consist only of the sum of their signifieds, but also of their implications. They are (for instance) an indication of what their speaker is like, what (s)he thinks or feels about the situation in which (s)he is speaking. In other words, through their implications, they enter into the narrative structure of the story as a whole at the same time as they mean, through their signifier–signified relationship, whatever it is that they mean (Chatman, 1978: 167). This is especially true in that form which Aristotle held to be the very type of mimesis, the theatre.

Thus it is clear that in narrative there are elements of structure which are carried over between media of transmission. Although this book will very frequently focus on elements of narrative that do vary between media, its founding assumption is that it is meaningful to speak of features which are common to different media.

Part I
Concepts and methods

INTRODUCTION TO PART I

Part I of this book is devoted to the analysis of the concepts and methods necessary for an understanding of popular narrative. As soon as this topic is raised, a problem becomes apparent: it is axiomatic in traditional literary criticism that the meaning of a narrative text – any narrative text – derives from the shape of that narrative, whether such a shape is thought of as the shape of a single text, or the shape common to a whole group of texts, a genre of text. Modern analytic techniques encourage us to direct our attention elsewhere – towards the codes that constitute narrative, towards the position the reader or spectator occupies in the act of reading or viewing, towards disruptions of narrative form. However, we shall see that in each case the form of narrative is central even in these displaced emphases. In other words, what is found throughout these series of ideas is the presence, dominating the agenda, of the concept of narrative: for it is tantamount to the same thing to say that it is narrative shape (or the disruption of narrative shape, or the list of the components of narrative) that is responsible for the meaning of a text, and to say simply that it is narrative that gives meaning to the text in question.

Now it is not that this notion should be rejected: perhaps it is correct, perhaps not. But at least it is clear that certain forms of commercial narrative place a question mark against such an assertion. For example, soap opera (see chapters 10–11): in what sense can it be said that soap opera has any narrative shape at all? One of the essential components of narrative is closure: the certainty that the story has come to an end, and that, as a result, all that can be known about the characters and events in question has been told. Traditionally, literary criticism argued that it was the closure of the ending that gave final meaning to the events portrayed in the story

– after all, until that moment the possibility of an ironical reversal was always possible. But soap opera has no closure, at least not until the programme in question has been scrapped, and to this extent the meaning of any event in a soap is provisional. Typically, moreover, soap audiences do not attend equally to all the events in the serial: they may miss segments of an episode – because of attending to household duties, for instance – and even entire episodes; they typically focus on those events which concern the characters in whom they are most interested and simply ignore other segments of the story. It is rather as if Shakespeare's audience only watched *Hamlet* when Ophelia and Polonius were on stage, and the rest of the time chatted to each other or wandered off to the bar until their favourite characters were cued back on stage.

Similarly, Raymond Williams has argued that the form of television is characterised by a 'flow' of images that transcends the division between programmes (Williams, 1974; cf. Heath and Skirrow, 1977: 14ff.). This implies that in television there is effectively no single self-contained narrative at all; that all television narrative is characterised by the kind of fragmentation and lack of resolution that is commonly held to be typical of modernist narrative (Feuer, 1986: 103f.). An example of this approach is to be found in Newcomb (1988), where he analyses three hours of primetime American television output across three networks. If the spectator channel-hops at programme breaks, (s)he has 81 possible combinations of stories to watch, and watching some combination or other from this selection will change the meaning of the stories in question. For example, one of the shows is *Lady Blue*, a cop show featuring an extremely macho detective who is female; the extremity of gender inversion leads the viewer to 're-read' the versions of gender implied by other programmes in the 'viewing strip' (i.e. the sequence of programmes) (Newcomb, 1988: 90).

If this argument is correct, then there is manifestly a fundamental difference between television 'narrative' and narrative in the more traditional sense in which the term is applied to (for instance) the nineteenth-century novel. However, it is to be noted that nineteenth-century novelists who published in instalments were often published in miscellany-based periodicals, where the reader could read an episode of a novel in conjunction with other pieces of fiction and non-fiction writing: in principle, there is a similarity between this mode of reading and viewing in strips. The same would be true of serialised publication in contemporary women's magazines.

We may conclude from these introductory remarks that the

centrality of narrative shape is both subject to question, and crucial to this process of questioning, where the analysis of popular fiction is concerned. The first chapter is devoted to various approaches which largely ignore the question of narrative shape, or at least thoroughly displace it. Chapters 2–4 are concerned with recent techniques of narrative analysis and closely related matters. Chapters 5 and 6 are devoted to forms of analysis of the cultural frame within which narrative exists and has meaning, and chapter 7 is devoted to the notion of genre, the immediate frame of much popular fiction.

1 Approaches to popular fiction

QUANTITATIVE CONTENT ANALYSIS

Content analysis is a technique for the measurement of meaning. That is to say, it is based upon the argument that the meaning of texts is not accessible to analysis except through the intervention of some measuring instrument (Krippendorff, 1980: 71). At first sight, such a statement may appear nonsensical, since it is clear that anyone can read a newspaper, watch a soap opera or go to a Shakespeare play without the benefit of measurement. The logic of the insistence upon measurement is that there is a layer of meaning that is not accessible to ordinary reading and that is in some sense more important than the meanings revealed in an everyday manner.

For example, if we watched a single TV show featuring a young 'attractive' woman who was in love with a man and wanted to marry him, we would probably relate this to other relevant features of the story (say, his romantic involvement with another woman) and understand the woman's situation in these terms. Content analysis reveals a different pattern: the activities systematically associated with the genders in TV fiction stereotype women, for whereas only one in three male principal characters on American TV is shown as intending to or ever having been married, two out of three female principal characters are in this position; one in five male leads are in the 'sexually eligible age group', as opposed to one in two female leads (Gerbner and Gross, 1976: 183). Similarly, female characters are consistently shown in a more restricted range of occupational roles than men (Dominick and Rauch, 1972), while Gerbner and Gross comment that

> Men can act in any role, but rare is the female part that does not involve at least the suggestion of sex.
>
> (Gerbner and Gross, 1976: 183)

These assertions by content analysts tell us little about the immanent meaning of any individual text, since typically the type of meaning they look for is to be found beyond its boundaries. Specifically, content analysis seeks to make inferences that refer to some other feature of the world outside the texts. Such things might be: (a) something about the producer(s) of the texts – in the case of our example, analysts might have been asking whether TV producers were biased against women, and using the characteristics of the messages they emit as evidence in this investigation; or (b) something about the audience for such texts – perhaps American culture systematically places women in a particular position. In short, content analysis is based upon the assumption that meaning does not reside in texts, but in the interaction between texts and the rest of the world, and its purpose is to use the analysis of texts to reveal something about the state of affairs arising in the interaction.

Such concerns have often centred on the 'effects' of the mass media. From the earliest days of cinema, there was concern that it might provoke violent behaviour among the audience (Glucksmann, 1971: 11), and in the 1930s it was widely held that crime films actually caused crime to occur. Nowadays it is rare that such direct effects are alleged. By and large, the results of decades of such research produced very little reliable evidence, but this is probably because of the nature of what was looked for, and what was counted as evidence. Such studies were based upon the assumption that the 'effects' of mass media would be some observable change in behaviour on the part of the audience; correlatively, observation of such change would constitute evidence of media impact. Studies therefore concentrated on trying to observe correlations between media input into tightly controlled situations (often in laboratories) and subsequent behaviour which could be imputed to the influence of the input. Typically, two groups of experimental subjects might be shown some film: say, one group a 'neutral' piece of film, e.g. a travelogue, the other a clip of violent action. If the second group subsequently behaved markedly more aggressively than the first, this would be held to support the idea that screen violence caused real violence. The consensus among researchers is that such studies do not produce reliable evidence, since (a) if fiction does have an effect upon behaviour, it is likely to be long term and filtered through patterns of everyday activity; and (b) such effects are more likely to consist of the reinforcement of existing attitudes than of the inculcation of new ones, and here no behavioural change would be observable. Recent research has therefore concentrated more on two other features of the text–audience interaction: firstly, on what people do with texts (as opposed to what texts do to people) – this is discussed below; secondly, on what Gerbner calls the 'cultivation effect', i.e. those aspects of a population's value system – perhaps manifested in behaviour – that are imputable to long-term exposure to mass media (Gerbner and Gross, 1976: 175ff.). It is the second category of study that is our focus here, and especially the method used.

A single example will show what this tradition has achieved. In a series of studies, Gerbner and his colleagues examined the effect of heavy TV viewing upon Americans' conception of various law and order issues (Gerbner *et al.*, 1976; 1977; 1978; 1979; 1980). Among other things, they found that heavy TV viewers were more likely to overestimate the number of their citizens involved professionally in law enforcement, and were more likely to be afraid of real-life violence than light TV viewers (1977; 1980). Clearly, this finding – if correct – is important, since it is not difficult to see that such fears would have significant effects upon behaviour: avoiding being on the streets at night, for example. In the long run, this avoidance arguably has the effect of encouraging car use, emptying the streets of pedestrians and making them less safe, thus increasing the demand for the services of the (motorised) police and focusing attention upon their activities. We are likely to be in the presence of a set of self-fulfilling prophecies and a vicious circle of self-reinforcing cause and effect.[1]

Such conclusions are reached by the statistical analysis of both texts and audience response. Samples of TV output (100 per cent of TV fiction for two weeks a year on all national TV channels in the USA) were analysed to see what level of violence was portrayed, and who was portrayed as involved in acts of violence. The results were then compared with federal government statistics of relevant activities. Viewers were then asked to give their opinions about various matters, for example 'What percentage of all males who have jobs work in law enforcement and crime detection? One per cent? Five per cent?' The answers they gave were then correlated with the amount of television viewing they did. The results are these: in real life, 1 per cent of working males are employed in law enforcement, etc., but 12 per cent of all male TV characters are. Answering 5 per cent to this question is therefore the 'TV answer' to the question, and heavy TV viewers are more likely to give it than light viewers. Similar analyses underpinned the conclusion that heavy viewers are more likely to be afraid of real violence.

A similar method was used by Cassata and Skill (1983) to measure gender stereotyping in soap opera. This showed that a majority of 'powerful' occupational positions were occupied by men, and a majority of subordinate occupational positions by women. Interactions between men and women were roughly evenly divided between family, social, business and romantic activities. Male/male interactions were overwhelmingly in the arena of business activities, with less than 10 per cent of them in the family arena, and female/female activities were, in the majority, in the arena of social activities. These measures add up to a stereotyped portrayal of gender relationships, in which women are typically portrayed as primarily socially oriented, in subordinate occupational positions, whereas men are predominantly portrayed as business oriented and in powerful positions (Cassata and Skill, 1983: 149ff.). Even a primetime soap with an obvious commitment to the portrayal of the 'new woman' such as *LA Law* may maintain some similar stereotyping: a pilot study based on a small sample showed that while men and women interacted with each other across the full range of arenas of activity, and men interacted with men in business, family and social settings in roughly equal proportions, there were very few moments in which women were allowed to interact with other women in any of the arenas of activity: all-female activities appear to be nearly invisible in this serial (Terry, 1989).

Analyses such as these are based upon a device for turning text into discrete, enumerable units. This is essential, for unless text can be categorised in this manner it is impossible to compare it with some other information source. For example, Gerbner's comparison of fictional and real-life law enforcement is based upon the number of people involved in the two cases: it is the fact of enumeration which makes the comparison possible. Similarly, the analysis of soap opera into arenas of activity was only possible because the text could be represented in the form of a number of units of activity – one social interaction, one family interaction, etc. – and numerical distribution could be used as the basis of comparison and analysis.

Text is not naturally divided into such units. The choice of which units to divide it into is a product of what research purpose lies behind the investigation. If you want to ask the question 'Is TV guilty of stereotyped pictures of gender relations?', then many possible measures of stereotyping could be found. We have seen some of them: the percentage of women portrayed as sexually eligible and romantically involved versus the percentage of men; the distribution of the genders across occupational roles; the distribution of gendered interactions across different arenas of activity. Each of these is essentially a way of turning the non-numerical concept of stereotype into something that can be enumerated for the purposes of comparison.

Thus, as text is analysed, each relevant moment of it must be assignable to one category or another, and must be assignable to only one category – placing a unit in two categories would falsify the statistical inferences. For example, if you want to know what percentage of principal male characters are in law enforcement, then all male characters must be (a) either principal or not and (b) either involved in law enforcement or not. If you want to analyse gender interactions by arena of activity, each interaction must be clearly assignable to one and only one arena. This means that some decision must be made about how to assign units of text to a category and what constitutes one unit as opposed to more than one. This can best be illustrated by considering how Gerbner analysed the amount of violence on TV.

Gerbner assigns a piece of text to the category 'act of violence' if it accords with the commonsense definition of what violence means, and if it appears to be one continuous act involving a constant number of protagonists. The following problems arise: if two people are fighting and a third joins in, does this constitute one act or two? If the film cuts to another scene and returns to the fight, is this one or two? Does comic violence count? Does accidental violence? Regardless of the actual answers, we may remark that the answers selected will cause the amounts of violence on the screen to vary greatly, and any comparison between these figures and some other set will be affected by the decision made. Thus, for example, CBS surveys into TV violence used a different definition of a violent act to Gerbner's and reached very different conclusions to his (Blank, 1977). Such problems are exacerbated by the fact that the vast amounts of material analysed demand a research team, and a method must be created for ensuring that all members of the team apply the same criteria in the same way when assigning text to categories. This is done by training and discussion, and eventually testing a sample of members' assignments for compatibility; this method ensures that analysis is consistent across a research team, but is no guarantee that it is true – hence the disagreement between CBS and Gerbner.

Similar problems are revealed in the analysis of arenas of activity in soap opera. What constitutes one interaction (as opposed to more than one) is as problematic there as in Gerbner, but the assignment of interactions to categories of activity presented difficulties which seemed insuperable. I experimented with a class of students. They were divided into groups and each group was given a copy of the same tape (one episode of *Neighbours*, duration: 25 minutes); they were instructed to assign interactions to the four categories used by Cassata and Skill, on the same basis as the original study, and I spent half an hour discussing what the categories meant and showing how they could be assigned to segments of text. On completion we compared results: there was hardly any agreement on distribution, and variations of between 100 per cent and 800 per cent (using the smallest number of any category as the base-line for measuring deviation) were very frequent. When the discrepancies were revealed, we discussed what caused them, analysed particularly difficult examples, established what seemed like firmer guidelines for categorisation and repeated the exercise. Agreement was still very rare, and significantly large discrepancies were still common. We repeated the experiment a third time, with the same results. One student (Fenton, 1989) did an extended version of this experiment in which she alone did the analysis, trying to produce a set of results in which ambiguity was obliterated, in other words trying to achieve consistency across time by repeating the same analysis of the same extract of video (an episode of *Brookside*); she too was unable to achieve consistency, and significantly large variation was commonplace across her repeats.

The source of the problem is not difficult to locate. In soap opera it is usual for characters to be related to each other in a multiplicity of ways simultaneously – for example, members of the same family or romantic partners work together, ambiguous friendships between ex-lovers or spouses are commonplace. Any given interaction may well have more than one dimension: for example, a husband and wife who are business partners discuss the behaviour of a relative who works for them. In this instance there is no way of distinguishing between the business and family dimensions, and thus assignment to one category or the other is entirely random. Since such moments are rather frequent in soap opera, distribution of interactions by arena seems uncertain.

The problem that is observable here goes to the heart of the application of content analysis to popular narrative. These methodological difficulties derive from the fact of narrative: the assignation of pieces of text to categories is difficult because the meaning that these items of text have is settled in the structure of the narrative flow. Content analysts are well aware of such difficulties, for they distinguish between 'recording units' (those bits of text to be assigned to a category) and 'context units', which are the maximum-sized unit of text to be scanned in an attempt to determine the meaning of each recording unit (Holsti, 1969: 117f.; Krippendorff, 1980: 58ff.). However, for practical reasons deriving from the cost of managing large research teams scanning masses of fiction, it is virtually impossible to make an entire narrative the appropriate context unit.[2]

THE ACT OF READING AND THE READER

It has become a basic axiom of recent theory that narrative has only a potential existence until it is realised in the act of delivery to an audience. Narrative consists of an interaction between a text and its audience; recognising this principle leads to a question: to what extent is the audience's response produced by the text and to what extent do the audience's responses define what the text is? Put in other terms: does a text have a meaning, immanent to it, or does it have as many meanings as are attached to it by different audiences?

At one limit of possible answers lies the assertion of authoritative distinctions between valid and non-valid responses to a text (e.g. E.D. Hirsch, 1967); at the other the view implied by Douglas' judgement that a joke is not a joke unless it is *permitted* by its audience as well as perceived (M. Douglas, 1968; cf. Palmer, 1991). Viewed from within this dichotomy, differences between schools of interpretation – which assert apparently incompatible criteria for the validity of interpretation – are *relatively* unimportant, since all have in common the desire to demonstrate its possibility and importance; opposed to them is the belief in a plurality of meaning (Michaels, 1980). Answers which are formulated in terms of some interaction between audience and text largely disregard the first alternative, since it is based upon the supposition that audiences must subordinate themselves to the structure of the text. Studies of interaction with which we are here concerned fall largely into two categories: those according to which texts produce active collaboration from their potential audience in the realisation of their structures; and those according to which meanings are attached to texts by actual audiences – rare are the studies which deal with both.

It is convenient to begin with the first category, often referred to as 'reception aesthetics'.

In this tradition the real reader is distinguished from the 'implied reader'. The real reader has a distinctive biography and a physical existence separate from the text; the implied reader on the other hand is the embodiment of all those predispositions necessary for a literary work to exercise its effect – predispositions laid down not by an empirical outside reality, but by the text itself. Consequently the implied reader as a concept has his roots firmly implanted in the structure of the text; he is a construct and in no way to be identified with any real reader.

(Iser, 1978: 34)

However, we should not imagine that the real reader is irrelevant to the act of reading: without the real reader's beliefs and dispositions no communication would be possible, since there would be nothing to communicate with, as the reader would be a blank space. That is to say, Iser's focus is on the act of reading itself, not the reader (real or implied), and this act is situated between the text and its actualisation by a real reader (Iser, 1980b). Thus the text is always a 'virtuality': 'fictional language provides instructions for the building of a situation and so for the production of an imaginary object' (Iser, 1978: 64). For example, the opening words of Clavell's (1981) *Noble House* are:

Prologue

11.45pm

His name was Ian Dunross and in torrential rain he drove his old MG sports car cautiously around the corner . . .

These words invite a series of speculations on the part of the reader: if this is the prologue, what are the main events? Why is the precise time important? Dunross has an old sports car and drives it cautiously: are these things related to his personality, or just to the force of circumstances? We probably also judge that this person is a central character rather than peripheral, since he is introduced in this way: the opening 'his' normally suggests reference to someone previously identified, but here it does not; the implication of status is clear. Obviously he is on his way somewhere: where? Why is he going anywhere at 11.45 pm in torrential rain? etc., etc. (Compare Eagleton's analysis of the opening sentences of Updike's *Couples* (Eagleton, 1983: 74f.).)

The activity of reading typically follows this pattern: at any point in the text the reader has a certain knowledge of what is past, and uses this as the basis of a set of expectations about what is to come. That set of expectations is also a set of retrospections, since the movement forwards through the text is always at the same time the reconstruction of the pathways that have led to the current state of affairs; the past of the text is whatever has led to the construction of the set of expectations with which the reader confronts the future of the text.

> This whole process represents the fulfilment of the potential, unexpressed reality of the text, but is to be seen only as a framework for a great variety of means by which the virtual dimension may be brought into being.
>
> (Iser, 1980a: 54)

We must therefore fill in the gaps left by the text itself, make connections, for the text always demands completion by the reader.

On the second page of *Noble House* we read that Dunross takes an elevator to a penthouse over an office block. On entering he says

> 'Evening, tai-pan' . . . with cold formality.

The text continues with a brief description of the man to whom he is speaking, who

> had ruled Struan's for eleven years. 'Drink?' He waved a hand at the Dom Perignon . . .

The phrase 'cold formality' gives added meaning to the word 'ruled': it implies some level of enmity between the two men, and the autocratic implications of 'ruled' perhaps help to explain it. Similarly with the gesture: we may impute the 'lordly' wave of the hand and the fact that he doesn't offer to pour the drink to the same feature of their relationship; or we may write it off as the result of long acquaintance, or the manners of the rich. Whichever way we read the words we make a connection, across the space of the text, between 'cold formality' and the later phrases. Note that not only does 'cold formality' inflect our reading of the subsequent words, but also 'ruled' and the gesture give us retrospection on the earlier phrase. Do they imply that the dislike is shared? And this opens up a prospect for the forthcoming sentences, which we may well scan for indications of mutual enmity. In Iser's words:

> These gaps have a different effect on the process of anticipation and retrospection, and thus on the gestalt of the virtual dimension, for they may be filled in different ways. For this reason, one text is capable of several different realisations . . . it [is] always the process of anticipation and retrospection that leads to the formation of the virtual dimension.
>
> (Iser, 1980a: 55f.)

An extended example of this approach is to be found in Jauss (1974). Traditionally, one fundamental distinction between literary texts has turned on the relationship between the hero and the world in which he (and occasionally she) moves: the hero is either better, worse or of equal stature to this world (which implicitly includes the reader). This schema is to be found in Aristotle, and an influential recent version is in Frye (1971) (see chapter 7 of this book for details). Jauss reworks this schema in terms of different forms of implied reader, or – as he calls it – different 'levels of identification' between hero and audience. That is to say, the existence of the hero has traditionally been thought in terms of a relationship between hero, action and 'the world'; it should be thought as the relationship hero–reader, through the concept of identification. Specifically, the nature of this relationship varies with the historical circumstances of the reader.

We should note that the historical differences between conditions of reception in Jauss are very broadly drawn, and coincide roughly with traditional divisions between one period of history and another. Those studies which start from meanings attached to texts by actual audiences make finer distinctions between different acts of reception of texts. The usual method is to select one or several audiences which have some distinctive feature(s) and to study the meanings they attach to some text or texts.

Liebes and Katz (1986) studied the range of meanings found in *Dallas* by a series of ethnically distinct audiences. They showed an episode of the serial to groups of viewers who were collected by asking a couple to invite some friends to a viewing and discussion in their home; this was to create as close an analogue as possible to the 'natural' viewing situation (it was easily established that discussion of the serial was normal in ordinary everyday life). The ethnic groups from which viewers were chosen were: second-generation Americans in the Los Angeles area; second-generation Israeli kibbutzniks; recent immigrants to Israel from the USSR; established immigrants to Israel from Morocco; and Israeli Arabs. While the choice of ethnic groups was clearly dictated by the researchers' location, they argue that the range of ethnicity is sufficiently large to give meaningful contrasts. Discussions – led by a researcher – were recorded and analysed for the presence or absence of recurrent themes, which could then be correlated with the ethnic origin of the discussants. Consistent correlations were taken to indicate that different ethnic groups saw different meanings in the text.

The themes which were observed were these:

(1) The extent to which statements reflected the belief that *Dallas* referred directly to some recognisable feature of the real

social world; at one extreme statements would indicate that the speaker accepted an unproblematic relationship between the text and the real world ('referential' statements); at the other they would be based upon an appreciation of its status as fiction ('critical' statements). For example: 'JR is a rich egotist' vs. 'JR is well-acted'.

(2) Where statements were referential, they were distinguished by theme:
   (2a) motivations for action
   (2b) kinship and its norms
   (2c) moral dilemmas
   (2d) business relations

(3) Referential statements were further distinguished by the degree to which they referred directly to some aspect of the real world ('realistic' statements) or to which they alluded to it 'playfully'; for example, 'wealth like JR's makes people do such-and-such' vs. 'If I was in JR's shoes, I would . . . '.

(4) The grammatical person in which statements were made, which is taken to indicate whether discussants identify *Dallas* as referring to themselves and the group with which they identified, or to some other group.

(5) The extent to which statements were normative, or judgemental, as against objective and descriptive.

When these themes are distributed by ethnic origin of discussant, the resulting distribution is taken to indicate differences in meaning attributed to the text. For example, the distinction referential/critical gives this distribution:

	Americans	*Moroccans*	*Arabs*	*USSR*	*Kibbutzniks*
Critical	27%	10%	11%	37%	28%
Referential	72%	90%	88%	62%	72%
Totals: n = 100%	293	264	167	251	187
Approx ratio	2.5:1	9:1	8:1	2:1	2.5:1

This table is typical of the results obtained: while all discussants are more likely to make referential statements than critical, it is clear that Arabs and Moroccans are far more likely to make them. This disproportion indicates a difference in attributed meaning, the difference being that Arabs or Moroccans are less able or willing to discuss the programme as 'only fiction' than the other groups; or are more interested in discussing it in terms based on its assumed reference to some feature of the real world. The distribution of other themes revealed that:

(a) All groups except Arabs gave prime consideration to questions of motivation; Arabs focused on kinship. Only Americans talked about business relations to any appreciable extent.
(b) Americans and kibbutzniks were significantly more likely to make playful statements.
(c) Arabs made significantly more comparisons between *Dallas* and their own communities than other groups.
(d) All groups were more likely to make value-free, descriptive statements about the programme, in the ratio of 9:1, except the Arabs who made such statements in the ratio of 1.5:1; in other words, Arabs were far more likely to evaluate the programme (in terms of its real-world implications).

What general conclusions does this analysis permit? The authors combine the various measures we have seen into an index of distance from/involvement in the programme, and conclude that Americans and kibbutzniks are least involved in it, and that Arabs are by far the most involved. They offer two hypothetical explanations for this.

(1) They argue that Arab culture is more based on the extended family than western culture, and that in Arab society the extended family is the real locus of both wealth and power; this is also true of *Dallas*.
(2) They argue that *Dallas* represents western modernity, which is a challenge – both an opportunity and a threat – to the Arab way of life, indeed to 'traditional' societies in general.

What can such a study be taken to indicate about the relationship between texts and audiences?

Firstly, if its method is reliable, it shows that different audiences do indeed attach different meanings to texts (not that there was much doubt about that in the first place). Such doubts as attach to its method are twofold. We have already seen the difficulties involved in accurate coding of segments of fictional texts into categories and units of meaning; although non-fictional statements do indeed create less difficulties in categorisation – since their meanings are arguably less dependent upon a holistic context (i.e. an entire narrative) than are fictional meanings – unitisation is no less problematic. Moreover, in this study the meaning perceived in the text is assumed by fiat to be identical with the meaning that is attached to it in subsequent discussion. We shall see shortly that this assumption is problematic.

Secondly, the variation in meanings has been shown to correlate with ethnic or cultural difference; although the division between the discussant groups is based on ethnicity, the significant correlations appear to indicate cultural distinctions: crudely speaking, the 'westernised' discussants have relatively homogeneous responses compared with the 'nooon-' or 'less-westernised' groups. If we compare this conclusion with the approach favoured by 'reception aesthetics', we see that the 'reader in the text' is by no means identifiable with any particular 'real reader'. Implied readers are either universal in that they are no more than properties of the text (e.g. Todorov, 1970), or only localised by the most generalised historical processes (Jauss, 1974). The real readers studied by Liebes and Katz (1986) are highly sociologically specific.

Thirdly, we should note that there is a distinct methodological link between the discussion-based format of the study and the concept of the real reader as outlined here. In Liebes and Katz's study, the intrinsic meanings that *Dallas* may have are not systematically related to the meanings that are attached to it by viewers. Indeed, this separation is what permits the clear sociological conclusion that the study reaches, for if *Dallas* had some immanent meaning, that was *ex hypothesi* related to viewers' responses, then it would be difficult to distinguish between those meanings attached by viewers that derived from their sociology, and those that derived from the programme. For example, the conclusion about Arab viewers and the extended family: if *Dallas* systematically represents the family in this light, why do other viewers not perceive it? Clearly because their sociology does not predispose them to. But in that case, in what sense can we say that this view of the family is 'in' the text? Yet this is what Liebes and Katz assert of the Arab response to it, that the Arab response is not something randomly attached by the meeting of Arab culture and some western text, but that it arises in an interaction with a text which has this immanent meaning. In general, this difficulty seems to arise from the pursuit of the positivist method, with its clear insistence upon factual observability as the only valid basis of evidence. The clearest statement of this link is to be found in Silbermann:

> the artistic life . . . is characterised by *the experience of art*. It is this meeting – resulting from conflict or contract – between the producer and the consumer, these social processes and these social actions, which concretise and assume a definite shape. Around

them the art groups assemble; they alone, *in accordance with the methods of empirical sociology*, may and can, as sociological facts, be the centre and starting-point of observation and research.

(Silbermann, 1968: 583 (emphasis added))

One of the rare studies which deals with both implied and real readers is Radway's (1984) *Reading the Romance*. The details of this investigation are sufficiently interesting to demand extended treatment elsewhere (chapter 11); here we are concerned with method. Radway got access to a group of women readers of romantic fiction who frequented the same bookshop, and was able to interview them, at length, and to administer a questionnaire based upon their responses to the earlier interview. The material covered here refers to readers' motives for reading and to the qualities they ascribe to both the texts they read and the act of reading itself. Here the method is not essentially different from Liebes and Katz's, since it consists of analysing a set of self-reported attitudes to narrative, albeit not quantitatively.

In crude outline, the interview material reveals that readers find in romances a form of 'emotional nurturance', both in the texts themselves and in the act of reading them. Radway then argues that in order to pursue the investigation further, what is needed is an analysis of the characteristics of the texts which the readers themselves nominate as particularly satisfying. That is to say, the readers themselves nominate texts and also describe why such texts are the source of satisfaction; the descriptions all centre on the form of the interaction between heroine and hero. By comparing what readers say about this set of texts with the texts themselves, Radway is able to construct a model of them which both conforms to what readers say and to an analysis of immanent features of the text (the method she uses here is closely akin to that used by Wright and analysed below in chapter 2). In outline, what readers nominate as a good romance is based upon a set of psychological characteristics attributed to 'good' and 'bad' characters, and a narrative structure which distributes these characteristics clearly between characters who are the object of readers' empathy and those who are not. In other words, there is clear link between what readers see in a text and the types of textual feature which structural analysis would look for in them.

It is important to note what Radway has achieved here. By constructing a textual analysis based upon readers' responses, she is able to demonstrate two points: firstly, that the meanings described by readers are not attributed at random to texts, that they derive from an interaction between text and reader; secondly, that the analysis of textuality advanced by the critic is firmly based in what readers themselves have seen in the text. In a further stage of the analysis she is able to construct a speculative model of the elements of our culture which are responsible for women seeking the forms of satisfaction that they do seek in such texts; the model in question is a feminist analysis of female gender roles in a patriarchal society. In so doing she has dealt with various problematic areas in earlier audience and response-oriented research.

In Iser and in Jauss, no attempt was made to ascertain the actual responses of real readers: response was a product of textual structures and typical predispositions based upon broadly conceived characteristics of historically defined audiences. In empirical studies such as Liebes and Katz, audience response is held to be whatever emerges in subsequent discussion and only connected in the loosest of ways with any textual structure; meanings thus appear to be attributed randomly to texts. In Radway, these two types of process are brought together and the interaction between them is firmly demonstrated by the explicit linkage between textual structure and empirically observed response; this, in its turn, is placed in the context of cultural forces – ideology, in short – that shape readers' responses even if they are not aware of them.[3]

PERFORMANCE

As popular narrative crosses the boundaries between media, any account of it must refer to its performance elements: the incarnation of characters by actors and actresses (use of camera and other technical apparatus is usually considered part of the narrative structure). Indeed, popular accounts of popular fiction rarely make any firm distinction between character and the performance of the actor or actress in question. The reason is probably that, despite the continued existence of theatre, the majority of performed popular narrative takes the form of film and TV, and in these media the preservation of performance on film promotes a greater identity between performer and role than was the case in theatre (just as the production and direction is preserved by the same token). This principle has many effects upon the structure and reception of popular narrative, some of which are easily seen in debates about the nature of character.

In modern literary theory, character is seen primarily as a function of narrative. However, everyday reading experience contradicts this: we speculate endlessly on what characters are 'like', on what they would do in various situations; and we frequently have a very clear sense of what a character is 'like' without being able to remember a single sentence, even approximately, of the text(s) they appeared in, or very much of the narrative, even in summary form (Chatman, 1978: 117–18). It is clear that in soap opera some viewers only watch those parts of the story that contain the characters they are interested in, simply ignoring the rest (Ang, 1985: 46ff.). The implication is that characters transcend the texts in which they are rooted. This is anathema to traditional literary theory too, for which questions such as 'How many children did Lady Macbeth have?' are close to meaningless.

Now in popular narrative this principle has two applications. Firstly, where audio-visual media are concerned the performance dimension of character is an intrinsic part of character, especially in serial modes (soap opera, cop show series, sitcom, etc.). Secondly, popular fictional characters do indeed prolong their lives outside the confines of the text in which they originally appeared, in a variety of ways. For example, newspapers comment frequently on developments in popular serials, especially if there are parallels between fictional events and some element in the lives of the performers: such material is a direct incitement to increase the speculation that is anyway a normal feature of the reading process. When novels are turned into films – or any other process of adaptation occurs – the characters are 'extended' beyond their original existence: for example, they are given a specific appearance.

The 'all too visible player' (e.g. Olivier as Heathcliff) may restrict the reader's conception of what the character 'looked like' by narrowing down the possibilities that verbal description allows to proliferate – Flaubert never allowed his novels to be illustrated in order to avoid this possibility. Choosing an actor to film a well-known novel character may well be a difficult decision: 1,400 actresses were interviewed for the film part of Scarlett O'Hara in *Gone With the Wind*, and 90 were screen tested, before the British actress Vivien Leigh was eventually chosen, a decision that outraged many Americans, but pleased Southerners who had feared a Northerner would get the part (Taylor, 1989: 82ff.). Similarly, the disagreement between Ian Fleming and the producers of the Bond films is well known: Fleming wanted David Niven to be Bond, the producers wanted Sean Connery; casting Connery modified Fleming's conception of Bond (Bennett and Woollacott, 1987: 55f.). On the other hand, it is well known that several other actors have in fact incarnated Bond, and such multiple incarnations are normal: Dr Who, in the successful and long-running English TV serial, was incarnated by a series of actors, and this is common also in American daytime TV serials (Hennessee, 1978: 16). All of these phenomena illustrate the general principle that performance extends the existence of narrative characters in various ways, and that this process is especially marked in popular fiction.

The process of interpenetration of role and performer is seen at its clearest in the case of stars, who have an existence which is quasi-independent of the narratives in which they appear. Firstly, they exist in a dimension which has other determinants: they open supermarkets and are interviewed in newspapers under their own names rather than character names (even if their 'real' names are in fact assumed). Indeed, an entire category of publications (fanzines) are devoted to their existence as real people, again even if many of the events, attitudes, etc., which are reported exist only in order to fill the pages of such publications and in that sense are 'pseudo-events' (Boorstin, 1962). These restrictions on the reality of stardom in no way reduce the fact that the social dimension of stardom has a high degree of independence from the originating narratives: popular interest in stars is entirely premised upon the fact that these are indeed real people, who have an extra-textual existence.

Secondly, the characters that they play in narrative are usually relatively consistent across time: John Wayne's screen persona (at least after *Stagecoach* in 1939) scarcely changed at all; Marilyn Monroe was condemned to play dumb blondes for most of her life despite struggling against this type-casting. Indeed, as is well known, the Hollywood studios carefully constructed film narratives to provide 'vehicles' for stars, narratives whose structure was based on the creation of a character in line with a star's screen and public persona (Dyer, 1979: 70). Equally, the existence of a public persona for a star may be used for other purposes: Greta Garbo was so well known for her tragic roles that when she eventually played in a comedy the contrast with her previous roles was in itself interesting, and studio publicity for the film was based on the emphasis that 'Garbo Laughs!'. Similarly, Fred Zinneman cast Deborah Kerr completely against her type-cast roles when she appeared as a promiscuous wife in *From Here to Eternity*: in so doing he ensured that the audience would consider the character in a different way, that is to say, audience expectations about the star's persona became part of the horizon of expectations played on by the narrative (Zinneman, 1990).

This quasi-independence indicates clearly the problematic relationship between character and performance. As Dyer points out (1979: 149f.), in the western tradition performance means the incarnation of character (despite occasional exceptions such as *commedia dell'arte* or Brecht); that is to say, performance skills are overwhelmingly oriented towards producing character. Character is constructed primarily by textual elements that are independent of performance: by script, by the actions that the character is required to perform, by the story-line, and by *mise-en-scène* (Dyer, 1979: 143f., 162f.).

Character as defined in these elements is then given incarnation by an actor's performance; that is to say, despite the fact that on occasion actors succeed in redefining character, in general performance is based upon pre-existing textual elements, which the actor uses as the basis of the character (s)he will build in his or her performance. In general, lack of fit between such textual elements and an actor's performance is considered bad acting. However, where a character is played by a star with a well-defined persona, there are reasons for lack of fit between text and performance which may not be the result of inadequate acting ability, but may be due to the inertia of the star image in question: the star may not be allowed to modify performance style to fit the text because the modification would be incompatible with the star persona. Dyer discusses the example of Marilyn Monroe's performance in *Gentlemen Prefer Blondes*, in which she plays the part of a cynical golddigger; the dialogue as written is clearly intended to show that the character is aware of her manipulation of men while she is playing the *fausse naïve*. However, Monroe's persona strongly emphasised another dimension of sexuality:

> The weight of the Monroe image is on innocence. She is certainly aware of her sexuality, but she is guiltless about it and is moreover presented primarily in terms of sexual narcissism – i.e. sexuality for herself rather than for men.
>
> (Dyer, 1979: 147)

In this film the result is massive disjunction between Monroe-as-character and Monroe-as-star. In another example of the same process, Kaplan (1974) discusses the way in which Brando's persona arguably disrupts the intentions of the director in Bertolucci's *Last Tango in Paris*. How such disjunctions are read by individual audiences may be very varied, subject to the kinds of processes outlined in the previous section. In less dramatic disjunctions, other textual elements can stress one aspect or another of a star's persona to bring it into line with the narrative in question: Dyer gives the example of the different ways in which Robert Redford has been lit in various films, stressing either the romantic appeal or the political side of his persona (Dyer, 1979: 143f.).

Such proof of the impact of a star persona upon textuality leads us to ask what is their source. Many different theories of the phenomenon have been offered, of which the most plausible is that stars are the incarnation of social stereotypes, given added plausibility by their individuality (Dyer, 1979: pts I and II, esp. 109ff.). Specifically, Dyer argues, stars illustrate problematic, fractured points in ideology, aspects of culture where values conflict and uncertainty arises; it is their capacity for apparently overriding such conflicts in their personal lives, as well as in their performances, which is the source of their charisma (ibid.: 95).

This charisma is most visible in the star–audience relationship known as 'para-social interaction' (Horton and Wohl, 1956). As Tudor shows, audiences identify with stars in various forms, under different circumstances (during performance/outside performance) and to different degrees (Tudor, 1974: 79f.); the most profound form of identification leads to confusion between performer and role. At its outer limit, such confusion is demented: the story is told that in the nineteenth century a member of the theatre audience shot Othello on-stage in order to prevent him killing Desdemona; it was clear that the killer was not intending to shoot the actor, but the character. Happily, most para-social interaction is less confused than this. A US soap featuring 'Dr Welby' received around 250,000 letters in five years addressed to the doctor, asking for medical advice (Gerbner and Gross, 1976: 178). When Ena Sharples was sacked from her job as a caretaker she received many job offers from viewers. The British soap *Crossroads*, set in a motel, regularly received enquiries about how to book a holiday there – including one lady who came to the audience relations department at the TV studios to make the enquiry (Hobson, 1982: 100). Such stories abound in informal accounts of film and television, and even if the reliability of many is open to question, there is little doubt that identification at this level does occur. This phenomenon seems to be restricted to audio-visual, performance-based forms of narrative and indicates that performer and performance easily transcend the texts in which characters are created.

BESTSELLERS

The title of this book refers directly to the notion of narrative as a commodity, as something produced directly and explicitly for sale. Indeed, to talk about 'popular' fiction in a capitalist society necessarily refers us to this dimension of culture, for here popularity is primarily measured by audience size and sales figures. In this section we will consider the extent to which discussion based upon the commercial dimension of narrative is helpful in analysing it.

Clearly any object which is the product of professional activity must be paid for: in this sense narrative, in a capitalist society, is a commodity like any other. However, it is a commodity which has certain unusual features in relation to other commodities. Many commodities (foodstuffs, transport facilities, etc.) are consumed repetitively: each item we consume is a repeat of the previous one. In principle, narrative is capable of being 'consumed' in the same way: we might be induced to pay for repeated tellings of the same story. People repeatedly go to the cinema or rent videos in order to see the same film, and may well re-read favourite novels (see e.g. Taylor, 1989: 12, 22f.). However, this is a relatively unusual activity nowadays, and the commonest consumption of narrative is based on a non-repetitive rhythm. Thus the production of the commodity 'narrative' necessarily includes a higher degree of unpredictability than the production of literally repeated commodities. To be sure, narrative is not unique in this respect – any commodity sold on the basis of its design features (clothing, for example) shares it. But narrative (in common with other art forms) has a higher quotient of design input than most commodities – it has no function other than appeal to our desire for design features, whereas clothes, cars, furniture, etc. all have other functions too. (It has become a standard comment on the culture of the last twenty-odd years that the centrality of the design feature has constantly increased and the relevance of functionality has concomitantly decreased; this is a key element in definitions of post-modernism.) This increased element of unpredictability poses particular problems for the marketing of narrative (Compaine, 1978: 145; Schick, 1958). Two ways of dealing with the situation are common: to maximise the points of contact between narratives and potential readers; and to make narratives close to repetitive without sacrificing all individuality in them (Radway, 1984: 24ff.). As we look at these marketing techniques, we see how the demands of commerce have a direct impact upon the nature of narrative.

The multiplication of contact takes many forms. In pre-print civilisation, contact with narrative was restricted: it took the form of theatrical performance and oral recitation, where payment obtained the right to only a single representation of the story. Libraries held handwritten copies of texts, but access was very restricted, both by illiteracy and by control over entry to the libraries. The advent of print fundamentally changed relationships to narrative (Eisenstein, 1979). Indeed, it is arguable that the novel as a form was made possible by print, and especially by its commodification (Lovell, 1984). In the nineteenth century, books were made available through 'circulating libraries' and subsequently public libraries; they were sold predominantly through bookstores and in the form of serial publication in magazine format (Williams, 1961: 189ff.). This situation was fundamentally changed by the 'paperback revolution', which brought book prices down to a level where reading and ownership were easily linked (Schick, 1958: 79).

However, the logic of cheap paperback production demands that each book sell a very large number of copies. Where narrative is concerned, this raises the problems outlined above, which are conventionally solved by two techniques: by selling books through supermarkets, newspaper stands, etc. – anywhere with a large number of customers; and by producing narrative according to successful formulae. In combination these reintroduce a high degree of predictability into marketing fiction.

Much of this book is premissed on the centrality of 'formula' to an understanding of popular narrative; the impact of marketing routines upon the creation of narrative is partly understandable in these terms. However, it is clear from marketers' terminology that formula occupies an ambiguous position in their practices. This terminology distinguishes between 'lead title', 'filler', 'blockbuster' and 'genre product' (Sutherland, 1981: 33). These terms clearly reveal a series of different ways in which narratives are given commercial existence, and are therefore thought to relate to public interest in them. In general, the implications of these distinctions is that formula by itself is not enough to describe how texts acquire their publics. This is particularly clear in the case of the 'bestseller'.

What does this term mean? As Sutherland acidly points out, there can be only one bestseller, if one takes the term literally. As most commonly used – in the *New York Times* or *The Sunday Times* lists of bestsellers – it means whichever books are selling most copies in a list of representative sales outlets during the duration of the listing, usually a week. However, this tells us little about the social phenomenon lurking behind the ever-changing sales figures, and various ways of describing the meaning of the term have been evolved. Firstly, it may mean an annual aggregate of books appearing in bestseller lists, based on sales returns from a sample of bookstores (Hackett and Burke, 1977); this sense is not substantially different from the journalistic one. Secondly, F.L. Mott (1947) defines a bestseller as any book that sells a number of copies equivalent to 1 per cent of the US population in the decade in which it is published; this definition allows slow sellers to be included, which are excluded from press lists based on a week or a month's sales. The most thorough discussion is to be found in Escarpit: a bestseller is a book that sells fast and that becomes a steady high-volume seller through regular reprints; he estimates they are 2–3 per cent of books published (Escarpit, 1966: 118). However, even this definition fails to deal with the bestselling author, whose individual books may not sell exceptionally well, but whose cumulative sales are enormous, for example, Barbara Cartland (Sutherland, 1981: 6). However, at this point we are effectively returning to the subject of 'formula', in the form of the individual author's stamp.

Regardless of difficulties in reaching a precise definition, we can see what is of interest here: the process by which individual texts are selected out from the mass of formulaic fiction for some form of special attention on the grounds that they are more likely to be profitable than their fellows. What forms does this special attention take?

In the late 1970s, Penguin Books experienced a disturbingly large drop in profitability, and hired P. Mayer – a publishing executive who had established a reputation at Avon Books in the USA as a successful and aggressive marketer – to remedy the situation. He set out to do this by concentrating resources into a massive publicity and marketing campaign to sell a single book (M.M. Kaye, *The Far Pavilions*). Clearly, such individualised attention is one way of marking a book as different from other popular fiction (Sutherland, 1981: 18f.).

Another feature of the potential bestseller is that it may well be subject to commercial calculation before it is written; for example, the outline of a book or a series may be developed by someone who then commissions the actual writing by someone else (Sutherland, 1981: 30, 137f.). As is well known, James Bond novels have continued to be written after Ian Fleming's death by 'Robert Markham' and John Gardner. Mario Puzo wrote *The Godfather* because the publishing world expressed interest in passages of an earlier, commercially unsuccessful novel which dealt with the Mafia (Puzo, 1972: 34–40).

Another feature of the bestseller is that it is very likely to be a multi-media phenomenon: basing a film on a novel may produce a far greater interest in the original; successful films may be 'novelised' (e.g. Leone's *Once Upon A Time in America*, D. Seltzer's novel version of his script of *The Omen*). *Star Wars* seems to have been conceived from the outset in these terms: a film which would sell souvenir programmes, book versions, toys, posters, games based on the story, even ice-lollies in the form of the characters (Sutherland, 1981: 88ff.).

Yet it is clear that much bestselling fiction is not substantially different from formula fiction; is there any systematic relationship between the two categories? Radway demonstrates that there is a common structure in the stories which are consistently rated as best by the women readers she studies (and which are frequently bestsellers, e.g. K. Woodiwiss' *The Flame and the Flower*); this suggests that here at least there is some close relationship. But in other instances it is more difficult to see such a close relationship. For example, all of Arthur Hailey's novels have been consistently high-sellers, and have figured frequently in bestseller lists. Yet they do not seem to have any clear-cut relationship to any of the common 'formulae' of popular narrative. According to Sutherland, they are characterised thus: each novel 'centres on a renewal crisis, an interregnum, a succession struggle' and the process is always brought to a successful conclusion by the adjustment of personalities learning from experience; this is a very social-Darwinist conception of the world: it is the up-to-date and adaptable who survive and manage the transition (Sutherland, 1981: 56f.). Of course, it is also true that Hailey – in common with most popular novelists – works within the tradition of melodrama, but it is questionable whether this can be considered a 'formula', since it encompasses such an enormous breadth of narrative forms (Brooks, 1976; see also chapter 11).

On the other hand, Sutherland's analysis of *The Thorn Birds* makes it clear that it is related to various conventional plot sequences (1981: 78ff.): firstly, it has the epic sweep of national development portrayed in the form of individual lives, like traditional family or dynastic sagas; secondly, it is a portrait of the manners and morals, the grand passions, etc. of the rich, in the manner of *Gone With the Wind*; thirdly, it is concerned with the forbidden loves of two women, for which they suffer (a traditional theme of novels aimed at 'the mature married woman reader'); fourthly, the succession of heroines becomes progressively more 'emancipated', since as Sutherland points out elsewhere, the women's novel produced a series of radical and articulate bestsellers during the 1970s (e.g. French, 1977; Jong, 1973).

Another example of an analysis of the relationship between a 'unique' bestseller and its formulaic roots is Taylor (1989), which shows that *Gone With the Wind* is firmly rooted in various traditions of fiction about the Confederate South. For example, it is related to the work of Southern women writers who self-consciously wrote about the South as a historical entity, fighting the civil war over again; in this context, claims of meticulous historical accuracy are a way of 'trying to control the impact of the novel' (Taylor 1989: 64, 69). A group of enormously popular novels defending the record of the Ku Klux Klan by T. Dixon presented a version of Southern history largely in tune with the version found in *Gone With the Wind*. One of these novels, *The Clansman*, served as the basis for Griffith's film *Birth of a Nation* (1915), which was in its turn a constant reference point for films about the South (ibid.: 161). At the same time, the South was the setting for traditional 'moonlight-and-magnolias romances' about the *ante-bellum* period, for example by Thomas Nelson Page, which had come to be regarded as an out-of-date representation of the Confederacy (ibid.: 75). *Gone With the Wind* 'plays upon and transforms' such tales – 'the Southern Gothic and Victorian Southern belle saga'. Such tales had been taken up by Hollywood in a large group of films which

> presented to Depression audiences nostalgic and idealised images of a feudal 'paradise lost' of large plantations, white columned mansions, beautiful Southern belles and chivalrous beaux, against a backdrop of loyal and humorous slaves. *GWTW* was the last and most celebrated of [them] . . . and it followed the by then well-known, indeed, clichéd patterns of setting, costume and characterisation.
>
> (Taylor, 1989: 165)

However, Taylor also reads *Gone With the Wind* against a series of other features, for example the reactions of English readers and filmgoers, for whom its American antecedents and especially its overtly political and historical meanings were largely irrelevant. For these readers, it is evident that it was the version of womanhood presented in the film, and especially in the figure of Scarlett O'Hara, that was the focal point of their experience. Clearly, here what is inflecting the act of reading is both the everyday experience of womanhood and the body of women's fiction that such readers would have experienced, for example the costume melodrama that was the speciality of Gainsborough Studios in the 1940s. This dimension of Taylor's reading of *GWTW* follows the methods outlined in section 2 of this chapter.

Such examples reveal clearly that bestsellers such as this exist in a space defined by relationships with other texts, but also defined by readers' experiences of the real world. Many bestsellers would appear to use formulaic elements in different ways to their predecessors, or to use them in combination with something else; but it is near-impossible to generalise about such processes, which must be studied on the basis of examples.

2 Narrative grammar

The next three chapters consider an approach to popular narrative based upon presuppositions that are very different from those under-pinning the approaches dealt with in the previous chapter. Those approaches were based upon the model of communication flow; these are based upon the notion that narrative texts have an immanent structure, and that the meaning of those texts is derived from that structure, which is independent of meanings derived from other positions in the communication flow. We shall see as we investigate this approach that its proponents have been obliged to move outside the strict confines of textuality in their search for meaning, and that this has created a certain convergence with the approaches discussed above; nevertheless, it is always the structure of textuality that is the starting-point, and it is the nature of the questions asked of textuality that determines the way in which convergence has occurred. Thus it is textuality and the problems that its analysis has raised that are the focus of these chapters.

Our starting-point is Will Wright's *Six Guns and Society* (1975), a study of the Hollywood Western using the structuralist method, which reveals with exemplary clarity both the method's strengths and weaknesses. The basis of such analysis is that the surface of the text, the story as it unfurls before our eyes, is produced by a mechanism which is hidden beneath it, and the purpose of the analysis is to reveal this hidden layer. Since it is the latter that is responsible for the nature of the story, demonstrating what it is amounts to an explanation of the story, and once it has been revealed there is nothing more for the critic to do. As is well known, this is based upon the analogy of linguistics, where the infinite proliferation of actual acts of speech is to be understood by reference to a limited number of linguistic rules which, between them, explain the existence of any potential statement: the rules are said to 'generate' the statements. In the case of the Western, what has to be analysed is in fact a large group of stories, and it is by locating the similarities between the individual stories that compose the group that Wright proceeds. Since there are many accounts available of how structuralist theory became the basis of a critical method, I will deal only with those themes that are directly relevant to Wright's *Six Guns and Society*.[1]

The mechanisms which Wright isolates beneath the surface textures of the Western are these:

(1)   certain common sequences of events;
(2)   a common matrix of evaluative norms in the form of binary oppositions (eg good/bad);
(3)   a common set of characters, a 'cast list'.

When these elements are combined, we have an account of any Western story:

> In this way we can reveal what the [story] is communicating – what types of people are taking what kinds of actions with what results.
>
> (Wright 1975: 114)

There is no single sequence of events which is common to all Westerns. Instead there are four sets of common sequences, which between them give four Western plots; there are, therefore, four types of Western where plot sequence is concerned – as opposed to the detective story, which only has one plot (Cawelti, 1976: ch. 4). However, the other root elements of the Western – the cast list and the matrix of norms – are to be found in all such stories, and therefore the different plot sequences are part of a deeper unity, the unity of a genre (see chapter 7 of this book).

The notion of a common plot derives from a fundamental structuralist idea about narrative: that specified elements of narrative which are accounts of different events are functionally equivalent to each other. To that extent they are the same event. For example:

(1)   A king gives an eagle to the hero. The eagle carries the hero (the recipient) away to another kingdom.
(2)   An old man gives Sucenko a horse. The horse carries Sucenko away to another kingdom.
(3)   A sorcerer gives Ivan a little boat. The boat takes him to another kingdom.
(4)   The princess gives Ivan a ring. Young men appearing from out of the ring carry him away into another kingdom.

(Propp, 1968: 18)

Undoubtedly the four events described here are 'functional equiva-lents': the role that they play in the story, as well as their internal structures, are the same. Each of these events can therefore be summarised under the common headings 'Control of a Magical Agent' and 'Transference to a Designated Place' (Propp, 1968: 40ff., 132); what we have here are thus two narrative 'functions'. The link of narrative succession implies the relationship of causality: the recipient leaves because of the gift.

Here we can see several basic principles of structuralist analysis of narrative. Firstly, the meaning of the events narrated is given not by any resemblance they may have to real world events, but by their function in the story: this is a point to which we shall have to return later. Secondly, the nature of each individual story is derived from the way in which it incarnates the series of functions into which it is analysable; if the story were not representative of a large group such as the folk-tale, it would still have a 'skeleton' of nameable events. Thirdly, all events in all the stories that Propp analyses are similarly reducible to some function or other, and a list of all the functions is a representation of the common narrative structure.

Wright's analysis of the set of evaluative norms which is to be found in all Westerns derives from other ideas which are fundamental to the structuralist method. At the deepest level, the origin is the idea that meaning is composed of differences, that words are able to have meanings solely because they are different from each other (Jameson, 1972: 15ff.). It also stems from an idea fundamental to many semantic theories, that meaning derives from a relatively limited set of concepts, which when combined provide the meaning of individual words; such concepts are always organised in the form of binary pairs, such as young/old, male/female, animate/inanimate, etc. (the ultimate model for this is the digital device on/off). Thus the meaning of the word 'woman' is 'animate' + 'human' + 'female'; the meaning of 'girl' would be the same, with the addition of 'young'. The advantage of such a scheme is that in theory, if it works, it can demonstrate how meanings are attached to words in a systematic and objective way: the enumeration of a limited number of basic attributes enables one to demonstrate the semantic structure of a large number of words (Culler 1975: 77ff.; Lyons, 1981: 75–97).

In the case of the Western, Wright argues that all characters and actions are composed of some set of attributes deriving from a combination of these four oppositions: good/bad, inside/outside society, strong/weak, and wilderness/civilisation. Thus, in one version of the Western plot, the hero consists of the qualities good + strong + inside society + wilderness, whereas the villain consists of bad + strong + inside society + civilisation; society consists of good + weak + inside society + civilisation. This analytic set describes the mechanism whereby a story such as *Shane* is produced: the hero comes from outside society, from the wilderness, and saves the settler group from greedy ranchers who hire a gunman to terrorise the farmers. By referring this story to a 'generative mechanism', Wright is able to show what it has in common with other such stories, and in so doing is able to argue that the mechanism is indeed what is responsible for the production of the story: it determines the nature of the story. In another version of the Western plot, Wright shows that the coding of the characters is different: the hero is good + strong + wilderness, but he moves from being inside society to being outside it; the villain is the same as before, bad + strong + inside society + civilisation, and society too is coded in the same way as the villain: in other words, in this version of the Western, society and the villain are essentially the same (Culler, 1975: 80).

The reader will have noticed that in outlining the four sets of semantic oppositions that structure the Western, the third element in their structure, the cast list, has already made its appearance. This is because the characters are fundamentally no more than the list of attributes that derives from these semantic functions. Here is another fundamental feature of structuralist analysis of narrative, and the locus – as we saw in the introduction – of major disagreement in literary theory in general. Characters, like events, do not derive their meaning from some resemblance to people in real life, but from the functions that they perform in the story, functions which derive from their positions on these axes of values. Characters, in other words, are no more than the sum of their actions, and these actions can only be understood in terms of the values which structure them. In structuralist theory, the term 'character' is commonly replaced by the term 'actant'. An actant is the textual entity that is composed of a set of attributes attached to the actions it performs: thus all of the characters in the four folk-tale events listed above would be examples of the actant 'donor', because essentially they are no more than the function of giving the hero the magical object in question. Similarly, the central male characters in the Westerns are all examples of the actant 'hero', defined as we have seen. This idea is commonplace in a less rigorous form in non-structuralist criticism (Hawkes, 1977: 90).[2]

At this point the strength of such a form of analysis should start to become apparent. Here we have various different films – say, *Shane*,

The Far Country, High Noon, and *Johnny Guitar* – all of which are in some obvious, commonsense way classified as Westerns: reviewers, studio executives and fans would all agree that they are Westerns. Wright's analysis is original and satisfactory in three ways: firstly, it shows how each story is built up; secondly, it accounts for why they are Westerns (or, better, *how* they are Westerns); and thirdly, it shows how they are significantly different from each other where there are in fact such differences.

A common criticism of Wright is that there are many films, or groups of films, which fail to fit his schema. Such criticisms are only partially valid for the reason given by Jameson in a review: 'deviation from a given sequence is meaningful and can only lead to further analytical activity' (Jameson, 1977: 550). For example, Ella in *Heaven's Gate* is good + weak + wilderness + outside society, a combination which does not appear anywhere in Wright's lists; but the fact that it does not appear is irrelevant: there is nothing in Wright's schema to prevent it appearing, and indeed the application of his schema immediately sheds light on the character. Unlike many women in Westerns, she is directly (visually and narratively) associated with the order of the wilderness: bathing naked against a backdrop of magnificent scenery, living on the edge of town, associating with two men who are both ambiguously related to the divided social order that the town is located within, etc. Whereas the conventional good woman's role in the Western is to represent stability and settling down within society, her role is more ambiguous and unsettling, and her association with the order of the wilderness is part of this role.

Another example: at the end of *Shane* the hero rides off alone again into the wilderness. In Wright's interpretation this is because at the end of this type of Western, the hero is accepted by the society and loses or abandons his special status (Wright, 1975: 47). For Cawelti, the end of the film shows that Shane is still a gunfighter, who is incapable of being part of that community (Cawelti, 1976: 249). Frayling argues that these two interpretations are incompatible, which would imply that if Cawelti is right, Wright must be wrong at a very central point in his analysis, since he says *Shane* is absolutely typical of this type of Western (Frayling, 1981: 48). In reality, the disagreement derives from the chosen framework of analysis: although Cawelti works with a notion of formula that is apparently similar to Wright's schema, in fact it is much looser. Here variations found in individual texts remain largely unrelated to the concept of formula; thus he can interpret the ending of *Shane* in terms that derive largely from that film itself, whereas Wright, because of his larger framework of analysis, refers the ending to something that transcends the individual text. To look at it from Wright's point of view, of course Shane is still a gunfighter and of course he feels that he cannot live in the community (for reasons that the film does not make entirely clear); but the point about the hero's special status in the world of the Western as a whole is that it can only be conferred by the community against the background of which the hero defines himself as an exceptional man, and therefore by quitting the community the hero necessarily abandons his status. This status is a relational thing, not a property of the actant in isolation from the set of relationships in which he exists. The relationships are, in their turn, part of the network that constitutes the determinant layer of meaning in the Western. For Wright, the meaning of individual films is always subordinate to what is allowed by the matrix of elements that constitute the Western as a whole.

My purpose is not to defend Wright against his critics: it is to show what his method is capable of, and to seek its limits. These can be seen by examining the question of sequence. In Wright, the narrative functions that constitute plot are arranged in sequence, but it becomes apparent that this sequence is variable. This is significant because narrative succession is usually taken to indicate causality: in the example taken from Propp, an actant is transferred from a to b *because of* the preceding acquisition of a magical agent. The ways in which Wright's sequence is variable are: (a) some functions or groups of functions are missing in some films; (b) some functions appear out of place in sequence – especially function 3, the hero's special ability; (c) individual functions appear more than once.

Wright's system of narrative functions is complex, and a complete analysis is beyond the scope of this book. Each function is capable of appearing in various places because individual functions are organised into sequences. For example, in the 'classical' Western, the hero at some stage becomes committed to the community he is in. This sequence ('commitment') consists of three functions: 10, staying aloof; 11, threat to the hero's friend; 12, the hero fights the villains. Similarly, the sequence 'fight' consists of functions 12, 3 (the hero's exceptional ability) and 13 (hero defeats villains). These two sequences appear at various points in the list of sequences that constitute any individual plot, and may combine with other sequences (Wright, 1975: 146ff.).

The problems that this causes can best be seen through two examples. Firstly, function 12 is situated at the junction of two subsequences; this suggests that something in its internal structure is capable of entering into relationship with more than one other unit in the narrative: specifically, something in it makes it the concluding unit in the subsequence 'commitment' (in which the hero decides he cares enough for the community to fight for it) and the opening unit in the subsequence 'safe' (in which he fights and defeats the villains because of his exceptional ability – function 3). In relation to the preceding units, function 12 involves his relationship with the community; in relation to the subsequent units, it involves his relationship to the villain. Although it is therefore in a sense a unit, which is nameable as such, delineatable within the narrative flow, etc., it also clearly has sub-components itself, which cannot be specified within Wright's schema (cf. Holloway, 1979: ch. 1).

The curious behaviour of function 3, the hero's special ability, is the locus of the second inconsistency in Wright's method. This function appears in the sequence of functions close to the beginning, where it consists of the *revelation* of this ability. It appears again at the point where he fights and defeats the villains, and Wright places it between these two functions. But why should it be between them? The audience already knows about the special ability, and this affects our reaction to on-screen events: the type of suspense we feel depends upon the degree of confidence we feel in him – compare the type of suspense typical of a horror film, in which we know the central characters will not be competent to deal with threats. For the audience, function 3 is in the same place as function 12, where he fights. From another point of view, we could say that the exceptional nature of the hero's ability is only truly revealed by the fact of his defeat of the villains, in which case function 3 ought to follow function 13 (the defeat), not precede it. In truth, the hero's special ability is something which is present in all of the film once it is revealed, since it colours the way in which the audience views events on screen (Palmer, 1978: 62–5).

What these two analyses of inconsistencies in Wright's text have demonstrated is that at the heart of his method are two lacunae: firstly, the reading processes by which meaning is transferred along the text; secondly, the subject position that the reader is invited to adopt towards the events that (s)he views on screen. The first point derives ultimately from the fact that the set of meaning creation elements that Wright uses is essentially static: the elements do not differ according to placement in the sequence of the text, and there is no mechanism for transition from one function to the next. The second point is more complex, for Wright in fact assigns two mechanisms to enforce some position on the reader *vis-à-vis* the text: one is the evaluative complex good/bad and strong/weak, the other is the reference of the meaning of the Western as a whole to the field of ideology, that ulterior instance of meaning which lies beyond the text and is ultimately rooted in the institutional structure of society itself (see below, chapters 5 and 6). That is to say, the ideology of our society assigns meanings to the various events and processes that constitute the story, and the story gets us to see events through the values that constitute the ideology in question; but this does not in itself tell us much about how the story positions us *vis-à-vis* these events – for example, by getting us to admire the hero's exceptional ability, which then inflects the way in which we view subsequent events.

It so happens that these two occluded processes in Wright are the site of many of the major debates in narrative analysis that have occupied the last two decades. While these debates certainly extend far beyond the bounds indicated by the notion of reading processes and subject positions in the text, none the less these two foci involve reference to all the major matters involved. The following pages will use them as a guideline through these debates.

3 Narrative and connotative processes

What these inconsistencies in Wright's schema suggest is that there are some features of textuality which link together the functions into which narrative is divided. Among these is what Barthes calls 'connotation', in the enlarged sense which he gives it in *S/Z*:

> a feature that has the power to relate to previous, subsequent or exterior terms, to other places in the text (or in another text)
>
> (Barthes, 1970: 14)

It is therefore any expansion of meaning beyond the limits of the individual sign. Using a word in a narrative context necessarily involves linking it with other words, and meaning immediately starts to proliferate, both along the sequence of sentences ('like the sucker on a plant') and in an

> agglomerative space, places in the text correlating with other meanings external to the text and forming with them sorts of nebulae of signifieds.
>
> (ibid.: 15)[1]

This process can be borne as well by visual images as by verbal, and therefore applies directly to film (Barthes, 1971).

Behind this brief and apparently anodyne remark on the two ways in which meanings proliferate in texts lies a complex debate on the different dimensions in which meaning expands. On the one hand, the 'agglomerative space' to which Barthes refers returns us to the 'classical' conception of connotation as it is defined in introductory texts on semiotics.[2] On the other hand, the image of the sucker of a plant, representing meaning as expanding through the text in a linear fashion, creating new links in that text, suggests a way of creating meaning that is incompatible with the classical definition of connotation. It suggests that combinations of signs do not merely incorporate – in the etymological sense of 'give body to' or 'incarnate' – meanings derived from elsewhere (i.e. from the language system) but that the combinations *produce* meanings; whence the slogan 'the productivity of the signifier'. Both of these definitions of connotation demand further exploration.

In the first of these definitions, the 'classical' definition of introductory textbooks, all signifiers are defined on the basis of an unequivocal relationship with a signified, the relationship of denotation; this meaning process then becomes in its turn the signifier in a second-order system, where 'extra' meaning is added to the original: connotation. Thus, for example, the *Oxford English Dictionary* definition of 'rain' is 'The condensed vapour of the atmosphere, falling in drops large enough to attain a sensible velocity', in other words what commonsense tells us, by and large. Meaning can be expanded from this basic, denotative meaning in various ways. Firstly, 'rain' is part of a set of words referring to similar weather phenomena: 'drizzle', 'sleet', 'hail', perhaps 'fog' and 'snow' too. By implication, therefore, 'rain' refers us indirectly to the set of words denoting the range of phenomena of which it is a part (water falling); this form of reference is the conceptual base of a poetic image such as Verlaine's 'There are tears in my heart/Like the rain on the town' ('Il pleure dans mon coeur/Comme il pleut sur la ville'). Further, lurking behind the set of words implied by rain is the concept 'weather', and behind that, in turn, is the whole order of 'nature', which can be opposed to the order of 'culture' and 'civilisation', or be seen as part of the opposition 'animate/inanimate'. This is the basis of T.S. Eliot's metaphor implicitly comparing fog to a cat: 'The yellow fog that rubs its back against the window-panes', where the image is composed on the basis of the incompatibility of 'fog' and 'rubs its back', the incompatibility of the inanimate and the animate. In both of these examples, meaning is expanded by the mechanism of the word which is the starting-point of the process (tears, fog) referring us to the set of words and concepts of which the first one is a part.

The second way in which meaning can proliferate, according to the classical definition of connotation, is this: the real-life phenomenon rain causes a specifiable range of experiences – wetness, discomfort, etc. – and this range of associations, which is infinitely large and therefore indefinable, creates a range of expanded, connoted meanings for the word. The expanded meaning derives from the various associations that everyday life leads us to make between the signified in question and other phenomena. In the classical definition these two processes are frequently not thoroughly distinguished.

Now it is clear that this analysis is inadequate, as two simple examples will show. In the case of a word, the possibility of a dictionary entry for it gives the impression that a word has a specifiable meaning, which is fixed and which is 'its' meaning, in the sense that it possesses it, so to speak. But as soon as that word is used in a context, the context invites us to focus on some specific feature of the meaning of the word: the word 'rain' has the signified of water falling in small drops from clouds; but to say 'I hate the rain' focuses our attention on some limited specific features of rain – what rain feels like, probably; if I continue 'but I expect the farmers are happy', different features of rain are evoked (fertility, etc). In these examples, the zone of meaning associated with a word is highlighted by the context in which the word is used, and other areas of meaning potentially associated with it are left inactive.

Similarly, a photograph of me has the signified (and referent) J. Palmer, but also the obvious 'additional' signified 'human male'. We have already seen in the introduction the problems raised by analysing verbal and visual signs in the same terms, deriving among other ways from the fact that a photograph is more like a sentence than a word; allowances made for this, we may still ask why I have specified that its signified is male as well as human. Why not add 'adult' to the list? Or 'adult' + '(badly) dressed'? And since the photograph was perforce taken somewhere, why not call the signified all these things about me plus 'in surroundings x'? In each of these instances we might guess that there is some feature of the photograph that indicates which parts of it are worthy of note and which are not. Clearly, meaning proliferates in a way that makes it impossible to specify what the 'basic' meaning of a photograph is.

What has happened in these brief allusions is that we have moved from the classical model of connotation to a model in which two things have occurred: firstly, connotation is produced as much in the flow of syntagmatic relationships as in paradigmatic ones; secondly, there is no longer any clear distinction between connotation and denotation, for the way in which meaning is determined in syntagmatic relationships disrupts the boundary between 'literal' (i.e. lexical) meanings and 'extended' (connotative) meanings. This process can be illustrated further by considering C. Metz's analysis of meaning in the cinema.[3] Metz repeatedly uses the example of the balloon in Fritz Lang's *M*: in this film the central character, the child murderer, kills a little girl and her death is indicated by the balloon she has been holding drifting away and getting caught in some telephone wires. The question Metz addresses is: by what process does the balloon come to 'mean' 'death of the girl'?

At the most basic level, cinematic meaning depends upon a process of 'semantic induction':

> in a Western: we are shown a stagecoach going through a pass and then a group of Indians high up on the cliff, just watching. The idea of menace and imminent attack, which is not contained in any of the images, is nonetheless clearly communicated to the spectator through . . . the 'current of signification' circulating through the elements of the film, transforming the photographic analogon into a narrative.
>
> (Metz, 1973a: 44)

That is to say, in the transition from one shot to another, in a camera movement, or in the juxtaposition of the coach and the Indians in the frame, we perceive a link: the semantic induction leads us to infer backwards along the signifying chain a meaning that is only retroactively present – or, as Metz puts it, is not given in any of the individual images. This is done partly on the basis of commonplace cultural codes (settlers and Indians), partly on the basis of experience of a particular genre, the Western.

Subsequently, Metz debates the nature of 'cinematic metaphors' such as the implied comparison between rush-hour crowds and a flock of sheep in Chaplin's *Modern Times* and the girl's balloon in *M*. In *Modern Times*, the comparison stems from the commonsense knowledge of our culture about sheep, and from the juxtaposition on film. In *M* the connotation of brutality and death attaches itself to the girl's abandoned balloon because: (a) we know it was hers; (b) seeing it in the telephone wires tells us it has been abandoned; and (c) there is some shared quality between the balloon and the girl – playfulness, helplessness, pathos because abandoned and trapped, etc. The signifier (the balloon) 'is partially motivated [and] carries something of the experienced reality and human resonance of the signified event' (Metz, 1973a: 74).

Here the principle of semantic induction is expanded: in the first example (Westerns), commonplace cultural codes and cinematic juxtaposition create meaning. In the example of the girl's balloon the same elements are used, but in a more complex fashion: (a) the juxtaposition is a multiple one, viz. (i) girl – balloon, (ii) balloon – wires – abandonment; (b) the juxtaposition is over a greater space, since it involves remembering that the balloon is the girl's; (c) the abandoned balloon demands an effort of interpretation – perhaps she got fed up with it? – and thus a further element of juxtaposition is involved: girl – abandoned balloon – murderer. Here we can see how the semantic induction operates as the basis for the transfer of meaning over potentially large spaces of text; we shall see further examples of such large-scale transfers of meaning below.

At this point, Metz is content to mix together forms of explanation which refer to commonsense background knowledge, external to the text in question, and forms of reference internal to the text (juxtaposition), without analysing how they interact; in a later article (1982) he returns to this topic in a more rigorous fashion. Here he distinguishes four principles by which meaning may be transferred between signifiers:

(1) Similarity

In metaphor, the relationship between the word or image chosen as a metaphor, and what it (metaphorically) represents is one of similarity. In *Hamlet*'s 'slings and arrows of outrageous fortune', it is the similarity between how bad luck inflicts unpleasantness on us and how we may be assaulted with slings and arrows that provides the conceptual basis of the metaphor. In the case of the little girl's balloon in *M*, it is the 'childish' connotations of the balloon, as we have seen.

(2) Contiguity

In many forms of linguistic and cinematic substitution, x substitutes for y because they are in some sense 'next to' each other. For example, 'steel' has often been used as poetic substitute for 'sword', as in the expression 'cold steel': the principle is clear, it is because swords are made of steel. Similarly, the guillotine was named after its inventor, Dr Guillotin, as a reduction of a phrase such as 'Dr Guillotin's machine', or perhaps via an invented word such as 'guillotined'. In *M*, the girl's balloon can come to indicate her death because we know it was hers. In Eisenstein's *Battleship Potemkin*, the mutinying sailors throw one of the officers overboard: in the following shot we see his pince-nez (which have been heavily emphasised) dangling in the ropes, thus substituting for his ejected body.

(3) Discourse

Discourse is the sequence of linguistic or cinematic elements, ie elements arranged in a particular order (see chapter 4). We know that the balloon is the girl's, in *M*, because we have already seen her with it. If I say that a house is 'pretty' rather than 'beautiful', clearly the choice of word depends upon the lexical distinction between the two terms, which pre-exists my choice between them (this is the traditional explanation of statements by referring them back to the language system); however, it also depends upon my perception of the house in question, and my decision to associate 'house' and 'pretty' in the chain of my discourse. More importantly, it is the consistent juxtaposing of terms in discourse like this that is responsible for changes in their meaning, and the meaning of words is constantly (though slowly) changing – dictionary entries are always temporary, although the existence of dictionaries, schools, and other institutions slows down, perhaps the pace of linguistic change. The process being discussed here is not essentially different from that discussed above, in the critique of the traditional concept of connotation, and arriving at the slogan 'the productivity of the signifier'.

(4) Reference

All language and representational visual imagery refers to something that exists outside itself. At the most literal level, a photograph refers to whatever it is a photograph of. Words refer not only to the concept that is their signified, but also to the range of objects subsumed under that concept, and when they are used in speech they refer to whatever object is being spoken about. If I say 'sit in that chair', 'chair' refers both to the concept 'chair', to the class of objects 'chairs' and to the particular object in question. All these external objects come to us already associated with a set of attributes, which are responsible for the signs that refer to them having a meaning: the meaning of a sign *is* the set of attributes associated with the object. Thus the meaning of the word 'lamp' refers us both to the notion of light, and to the notion of manufacture, electricity, etc. (as opposed to 'candle', which refers us to light and handicrafts), thereafter to the various circumstances in which lamps are commonly used: streets, drawing rooms, offices, etc.[4]

It is important that the same example occurs more than once: Metz is showing that the meaning of a cinematic metaphor such as the girl's balloon in *M* is dependent upon several processes simultaneously, and that these processes are analysable. In one process, the girl's balloon can carry the meaning of her death because the discourse of the film has established that it is hers. In this instance the contiguity that was established as part of the basis of its meaning is established in the discourse, as opposed to outside it, whereas the contiguity that makes 'steel' mean 'sword' is established outside the flow of any particular discourse: here the contiguity is referential, since it is the nature of swords as real-life objects that makes this transfer of meaning possible. In another process, the balloon can mean the girl's death because it was abandoned; here the transfer of meaning is based on discursive contiguity – the fact of being abandoned – but is also referential – the behaviour of balloons on being abandoned is to float away. In a third process, the balloon means her death because it has something pathetic and helpless about it: this is the realm of similarity, but also of referentiality, since it is features of balloons in general that make it appropriate for such a meaning (small, float helplessly when abandoned). At the same time, this meaning is also discursive, for the imputation of helplessness and pathos derives in part from the fact that we make the link with the girl's death – otherwise its drifting on the wind might seem fun, or exhilarating.[5]

These examples demonstrate some dimensions along which meaning can be transferred in narrative, more than one of which are usually present in any individual instance. It is these processes which Barthes has in mind in *S/Z* (1970).[6] Here Barthes sets out to achieve two things: firstly, a reading of an individual text which will be 'exhaustive' in the sense not of saying everything about it that can be said, but in the sense of showing all the forms of linkage that constitute it as a text; secondly, the demonstration of a method which is adequate to its object – a conventional (i.e. non-modernist, non-experimental) narrative. By implication, therefore, the method should provide an exhaustive reading of any other similar text. However, rather than present us with an analysis of what the meaning of the story *is*, Barthes chooses to show us *how the story achieves meaning*; in his terminology, he analyses not its structure, but its structuration. Put in terms derived from Metz, he aims to analyse the interaction of the various dimensions of meaning (similarity, contiguity, discourse and reference) in the production of a meaning. This meaning will appear to the reader (the casual reader, the ordinary reader who merely seeks 'a story', with a beginning, a middle and an end) to be fixed and stable; but Barthes' analysis will reveal that behind this apparent fixity and stability lies a process of production of meaning which is itself profoundly unstable, because composed of a set of elements whose relationship to each other is non-specifiable, and which do not, in their turn, rest on any firm basis.

These elements Barthes calls codes. They are not codes in the linguistic sense of code: a paradigm, part of a system, which guarantees that such-and-such a sign has a fixed meaning which is ascertainable by referring it to this code (or paradigm, or system: these terms are more or less interchangeable in this context). In Barthes each code is no more than the place where there is some form of transfer of meaning, of interaction between signs: each sign certainly has some element of its meaning determined by its place in a linguistic code, but further elements of its meaning are determined by the way in which it interacts with other signs in the flow of the discourse of which it is part, just as the network of discursive relationships in which the girl's balloon is situated are responsible for the meanings which are transferred onto it in *M*. Barthes conceives of code on the analogy of a set of stages on a route: each member-sign of the code is one stage on the way, and indicates the route to be followed; but we can never actually complete the route, since there is always some further transfer of meaning which lies beyond the stage we are at, even when we have come to the end of the text (para. XII). Elsewhere he says that in narrative, connotation does not refer to any single meaning (one signifier $->$ one signified), but to a 'synonymic complex, whose common kernel we can guess', whose dictionary would be more like a thesaurus than a lexicon, based on echoes and transformations rather than reduction to a single fixed meaning (para. XL). This synonymic complex, like the little girl's balloon, is organised discursively: if a character is said to be 'one of those strong-willed people who brook no obstacle', and is subsequently called 'energetic', we perceive a link which derives from the contiguity (reference to the same character) of the two references in the text and from the similarity of what is said.

Barthes demonstrates the operations of five codes:

(1) Hermeneutic code

This is all those processes in the text which make us wonder what is coming next. The clearest example would be the discovery of a dead body at the beginning of a detective story, which makes us want to know 'whodunit', but in general anything which makes us seek an answer to a question would also be part of this code. In romantic fiction, it is commonly the case that the hero is brusque and offhand, even cruel, towards the heroine, in inexplicable ways; this device invites the reader to question his motives, and provides the opening to a series of enigmas and partial answers that are only finally resolved in the conclusion (Radway, 1984: 128ff.; Modleski,

1982: 42ff.). Such questions will be answered by the end of the story, and although the average reader may have forgotten that (s)he asked them, the way in which (s)he followed the story will have been in part dictated by the fact that they were evoked. The kernel of this code is thus the sequence of questions and answers.

(2) Proairetic code

The sequence of events of which the story consists; it is very similar to the list of functions which Propp and Wright make the basis of story structure. The kernel of this code is thus a sequence of named actions.

(3) Referential code

This is the inclusion in the text of any reference to some feature of the outside world which is presented as common knowledge, such as 'Here in Berlin Wannsee, where furs and cashmere are everyday clothes' (Deighton, 1986: 1) – a piece of 'worldly' knowledge about the social structure. It may be revealed in a choice of words: 'The trawler plunged into the angry swells of the dark, furious sea' (Ludlum, 1980: 11), where the adjectives clearly depend upon traditional notions of danger at sea deriving from a mixture of literary sources, news stories, collective memories, etc.

(4) Semic code

This represents the totality of connotative references in the text. Thus the reference to furs and cashmere in the opening paragraph of Deighton's spy story *London Match* is part of a large series of references in the novel to the theme of expensive living, which is in its turn connected to the major theme of treachery in high places. In this instance, 'riches', or some such label for the set of references in question, would be one kernel of connotation in the text *London Match*; the semic code would be all such references in the text, in other words the process by which such references are possible is the kernel of this code.

(5) Symbolic code

This is the set of references to those features of the interpersonal social order that have to be assumed by the individual in order for him or her to have an identity. Here Barthes is relying on a psycho-analytic account of the notion of identity, in which acceptance of the set of objective meanings which constitute the social order is both the pre-requisite of the individual's identity, and simultaneously intensely problematic because of the psycho-analytic process which is necessary in order for this acceptance to occur.

We may distinguish two levels at which Barthes' method in *S/Z* works:

(1) The processes by which codes operate within his example can be borrowed for application to other texts: in this sense it is the 'superior formal method' that Coward and Ellis want to avoid it being reduced to (1977: 46).

(2) The overall process by which a text comes to have a meaning which appears to inhere naturally in it, to be 'its' meaning as if it was a natural property of it. This naturalisation of meaning refers us to one of the central concerns of recent post-structuralist debates, and we shall return to it in the next chapter.

The processes of coding can be divided into two categories: those codes which depend upon linear sequence in the text for their efficacy, and those codes which do not: i.e. sequential/non-sequential codes. The sequential codes are the hermeneutic and proairetic codes; the other three are non-sequential. Thus, if we take the example of the phrase from Len Deighton's *London Match*, we can see that the presence within in it of both the referential and semic codes is in no way dependent upon the place that it has in the narrative – such references can occur at any point in the sequence of events, and link up with other ones in a way that does not depend upon the sequence. On the other hand, this phrase also plays a part in the hermeneutic code, since we are led to ask ourselves why the narrator is at an expensive party in Berlin, and this function is inextricably linked to narrative sequence: he is there to arrest a senior West German official suspected of spying for the USSR, and the ramifications of this arrest will be responsible for various subsequent features of the plot. Here we can also see how the proairetic code is inevitably sequential too: at this point the narrator is waiting for the spy's contact to arrive, and thus this moment in the text forms part of a sequence which could be called 'arrest', and which consists of the three sub-sequences 'lying in wait', 'arrest' and 'interrogation'.

The fact that narratives must necessarily proceed in a linear sequence is one of the means by which they achieve the kinds of effects they do. In other words, narratives achieve meaning in many different ways – as Barthes clearly demonstrates – and one of them is by arranging events in a linear sequence. It has often been said that in narrative, sequence implies causality. For this reason Hayden White (1980) makes narrative the founding principle of historical writing, since absence of narrative implies inability to understand the interactions between events, and it is this ability which is the basis of historical understanding.

We may start by considering the kind of elements in narratives that do *not* depend upon sequence for their effects; our example is the notion of fictional character.

In structuralist criticism, character was reduced to actant, in the way that we have seen when discussing Wright's *Six Guns and Society*: Shane is 'the hero' and nothing more, other people are 'the villain(s)', 'the townspeople' and nothing more, etc. Features of text that commonsense would see as referring to psychological traits analogous to the psychological traits we see in everyday life were treated as no more than functions of narrative (these theories are summarised in Chatman, 1978: 108–16).

In *S/Z*, character is treated differently: it is a collection of references in the semic code, of the type mentioned briefly above ('energetic, brooks no obstacle'), which cohere around a name. That is to say, all the various features of personality that make up a 'character' are each produced by a process of connotation: we see this person do such-and-such actions and say various things, and we are told various things about them. Each piece of information is associated – through commonplace cultural codes – with relevant personality traits. What unifies these various traits into a character is the fact of a proper name, which creates a point around which traits can cluster (in film the name is given the adjunct of the actor: to psychological traits we can add physical appearance, costume, etc.). This process depends upon the linear sequence of events which constitutes a narrative to the extent that the actions characters perform must take place at some point in time, and therefore form part of the sequence; but they contribute to character only to the extent that they cohere into an entity that transcends the sequence of events. The proof of this is that the attribution of certain traits to a character may well be what makes it comprehensible that (s)he behaves in such-and-such a way (*S/Z*: para. LXXVI; Chatman, 1978: 123–32).

Martin (1986: 119–21) criticises this account of character, suggesting that our ordinary experience of fictional characters involves 'projecting' on to them a range of potential actions and attributes that go beyond what we know of them from the fiction in question. This level of potentiality is perhaps especially clear in popular fiction characters, where the public speculate endlessly on what x would/will do under such-and-such a set of circumstances. Martin suggests that this process is more fully elaborated with characters who have depth rather than the flat predictability of mass media fictions, but observation of audiences suggests the opposite, since the form of fiction that most readily fosters such speculation is soap opera, where it is aroused not by fictional depth in the traditional sense, but by the serial form.

In general, the approaches analysed here suggest that traditional literary conceptions of character as deriving their value from imitation of the real world of everyday experience are misleading. While both Martin and Chatman defend the traditional argument, they ignore the extent to which 'character' is produced in the mechanisms analysed in the next chapter.

Barthes' two sequential codes are the proairetic and the hermeneutic. The hermeneutic code is essentially the mechanism whereby the reader is led to want to know what is happening; we shall return to this subsequently. The proairetic code is the mechanism whereby narrative represents a sequence of what commonsense recognises as actions. This is easiest to understand on the basis of an example: the opening of Forsyth's (1971) *The Day of the Jackal*.

The first chapter concerns a series of assassination attempts made by a French right-wing organisation against President de Gaulle. The opening page recounts the execution of one of the conspirators, and this is followed by the failed assassination for which he was convicted: de Gaulle's motorcade leaves the presidential palace, it is followed by one of the conspirators who works out which route they are taking to de Gaulle's helicopter and phones the information to the hit squad. They take up their positions, de Gaulle drives into the ambush, but the attempt is bungled and he escapes. This is followed by the narration of various other attempts on his life.

This summary of the plot of the first eight pages is entirely conventional: it is approximately what any reader would give. At the same time it is based on the recognition that the story has, so to speak, a skeleton, which is the sequence of the most significant actions, each of which can be labelled by using the commonsense names for actions or events, and which are labelled by anybody who summarises plot. This skeleton of labellable events is what Barthes calls the proairetic code; in Aristotle, proairesis is the process of consideration or debate which precedes taking action: it is thus what stipulates the logic of any action. Barthes argues that the skeleton of a story is a series of actions linked together in significant sequences such that one implies the other – each action is the proairetic prelude to the next, and to understand as a reader why one action follows from another is to reconstruct this logical linkage (1970: paras XI and XXXVI).

If we analyse this passage in more detail we find this sequence of events:

(1) execution of conspirator;
(2) departure of de Gaulle's motorcade;
(3) setting up the ambush;
(4) ambush takes place;
(5) de Gaulle survives the attempt.

But we should note that each of these events is in fact composed of a series of smaller events. Thus (1) execution is composed of tying the victim up, blindfolding him, and firing; in (2) departure we have (a) the drivers waiting, (b) all the ministers departing, (c) de Gaulle departing and (d) the conspirator following his motorcade. Thus a more detailed breakdown of the opening pages would give us this plan:

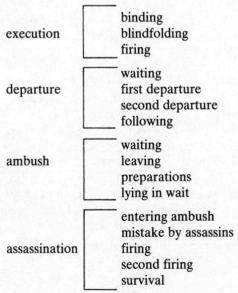

execution	binding blindfolding firing
departure	waiting first departure second departure following
ambush	waiting leaving preparations lying in wait
assassination	entering ambush mistake by assassins firing second firing survival

If we compare this plan with the actual text, it is clear that the attribution of labels is far from obvious. To take only the first: the conspirator is bound in the first paragraph, but this paragraph also contains the information (a) that it was very cold, (b) where the event is taking place and (c) that he only partly believed what was happening to him. Why therefore call this event 'binding' rather than 'disbelief'? Because the following paragraph describes the blindfolding (among other things), the next one the moment of execution, etc., and it is the sequence of the three which enables us to see what is being narrated in each instance: without the sequence to guide us, the attribution of labels cannot be certain; in other words it would be difficult to know what is happening, and indeed that is our experience as readers. We read what is coming next in order to find out (among other things) what it is that is being narrated: it is in the flow of events that their meaning resides. Disagreement about how to label sequences is likely to derive from the connections between events that individual readers make.

This is why the embedding of sequences within each other is important: each time we say that such-and-such a sequence is embedded within one another, we are asserting a particular connection between events, rather than some other one. The more complex a text, the more connections there will be between events, and the more difficult it will be to arrive at agreed labels for sequences. Such complexities are often alleged to be the source of the value of great literature; however, serial fiction such as soap opera and sitcom also produces multiple readings of this kind because of the multiple relationships that serial form allows.

At this point we may return to the question of coding as it is developed in the tradition of empirical content analysis (see above, chapter 1). We saw there how difficult it is to arrive at an adequate set of labels for the research team to apply to the texts under scrutiny; and how difficult it is, even when a set of labels has been agreed, to apply them in a systematic way, avoiding random or subjective attribution of segments of text to different labels. We saw too, that these difficulties resulted in the statistical data that such analyses typically produce being questionable to the extent that different encodings produce dramatically different data. As a result of the analysis of the opening of *The Day of the Jackal* we can see why: we know that the naming of sequences of actions is the result of the application of commonsense cultural codes, in just the same way as the connotative processes discussed earlier have their roots in such codes. But we have also seen that this can only be done when we understand how a given event fits into a sequence of events: in other words, when we see how large segments of narrative shape our perception of the small-scale events of which they are composed. Empirical content analysis – perhaps because of its emphasis on the 'manifest content' of communication acts – only uses the first of these processes (commonsense cultural codes) as the basis of its labelling procedures, whereas we can see that even the simplest narratives demand the second one as well.

One further feature of sequence demands analysis. In *The Day of the Jackal*, Forsyth is precise about dates: the execution on the first page took place on the 11th March, 1963; the assassination attempt which caused the execution – described on the following pages – took place on 22nd August, 1962. Thus the 'real life' sequence of events has been reversed. And within individual bits of narrative the verb tenses used tell us that bits of different time sequence are intercalated: as the ambush is described we are told in detail how the conspirators had already spent days working out exactly where to position themselves long in advance. This device – which is of course absolutely commonplace – refers us to one of the fundamental tools of structuralist and post-structuralist analysis, the distinction between 'story' and 'narrative' (Genette, 1972).[7] 'Story' is the sequence of events narrated in a 'narrative', but seen not as they are told in the narrative but as they happened in real life, or would have happened if the narrative is fictional. In the opening of *The Day of the Jackal* the 'real' order of events has been inverted in the novel: in 'story' A precedes B, in 'narrative' B precedes A.

The relationship between 'story' and 'narrative' is useful because it enables us to analyse the way in which sequence is the embodiment of fictional meaning. For example, at the beginning of Chandler's (1948) *The Big Sleep*, Marlowe is hired by General Sternwood to investigate the disappearance of his chauffeur and the origin of some gambling debts incurred by his younger daughter. Both the debts and the disappearance occurred before the novel opens with Marlowe's arrival at the Sternwood house; as in Forsyth, the order of events has been inverted. More exactly, in this narrative B is followed by *a report of* A, where of course the report of A by the General follows Marlowe's arrival. The General's report of the events shows why he has summoned Marlowe and proposes to hire him; in general, such devices at the beginning of detective stories show that the detective is not dealing with his own problems, but with somebody else's, which is fundamental to the meaning of such stories (see below, chapter 8).

In this instance the difference between story and narrative is one of order, but the difference may be based upon other features: frequency and duration.

In the case of duration, obvious examples would be entire events from story which are completely removed from narrative, or referred to only briefly. In *The Big Sleep*, Marlowe goes from the Sternwood's house to the bookstore owned by the man trying to collect gambling debts. On the way he stops at the Hollywood library to do half an hour's research, which is narrated in two brief sentences, whereas the scene that follows is narrated *in extenso*. In story – or if you like in 'real time' – the interview in the bookstore lasts for a few minutes, but in narrative it occupies several pages: the difference in the rhythm of narrative is striking. The measure of the two different time-scales, story- and narrative-time, cannot be exact in the novel, but it is none the less possible. Comparison with cinema will illustrate this point.

In film, the time that narrative takes to unfold is measured precisely by the time that film takes to project or TV to broadcast (the interruption, freeze-frame, skipping boring bits, etc., that video-recorders allow does not really change this); thus narrative-time can be precisely measured and this can serve as a base for the comparison between the duration of an event in story and the same event's duration in narrative. For instance, it is common in film for time to be expanded by showing two events one after the other which would, 'in reality' (in story-time), have happened simultaneously: somebody says something, with the camera focused on him or her, and the next shot moves to the listener to record their reaction to whatever was said, a reaction that might well, in story-time, have been simultaneous with the words spoken. The nearest equivalent in the novel to this precise measure of narrative-time is the time it takes the reader to read a particular passage. However, readers read at very different speeds, and the same reader's speed may well vary from moment to moment, and thus no precise basis for comparison between story and narrative exists in these circumstances. However, this is unimportant, because what matters is not the absolute time of story versus the absolute time of narrative, but a comparison of the two in different sections of the same text. When we observe the compositional difference between the two scenes from *The Big Sleep* quoted above, we can see the different types of importance accorded to the different events portrayed.[8]

Frequency refers to the different number of times a given event is portrayed in narrative compared with the number of times it happens in story. In theory one can:

(1) narrate once what happened once;
(2) narrate once what happened more than once;
(3) narrate more than once what happened once;
(4) narrate more than once what happened more than once.

(Genette, 1972: 146ff.)

In practice, it is (1) and (2) that are most common, although (3) is far from unknown: in a court different witnesses recount the same event, a commonplace in detective fiction; the quasi-entirety of Kurosawa's film *Rashomon* consists of the same event narrated by four different witnesses. In the novel the commonest form this distinction takes is the alternation between the extensive reproduction of the events to be narrated, and the brief summary of events which in story-time were often repeated. In Chandler's (1959) *The Long Goodbye*, Marlowe makes friends with an alcoholic called Terry Lennox, who one day makes a point of taking him out for a drink to a bar called Victor's, and this establishes a routine:

> From then on it got to be a sort of habit with him to drop in around five o'clock. We didn't always go to the same bar, but oftener to Victor's than anywhere else.
>
> (Chandler, 1959: 19)

In cinema this form of narration is less frequent than in novel, since any event that is filmed is an individual event: film lacks the built-in capacity for summary that language provides through many mechanisms such as the ones in *The Long Goodbye* ('it got to be . . . not always . . . oftener . . .'). None the less something similar is possible in film: a sequence of shots may be accompanied by a voice-over stating that these events were typical of a series; in *The Godfather I*, a period of gang-warfare is summarised by a series of disconnected shots with a continuous sound-track of jangling, out-of-tune piano music: men in shirt-sleeves playing cards, gunfights, newspaper stills of bodies surrounded by police, etc. It is clear that the brief sequence of shots is to be taken as a summary of a far more extensive set of events.

Analysis of the differences between story and narrative allows us to understand the relative levels and types of importance assigned to different events in and by a narrative. This is perhaps clearest in the case of duration. If we consider the events in *The Big Sleep* referred to above, it is clear that the half-hour's library research narrated in two sentences is in some sense less important than the interviews that precede and follow it, and that its low level of importance is indicated by its brevity. Yet, at the same time, it is far from insignificant. Marlowe's library visit gives him some information that enables him to establish that the bookshop he is about to visit is a fraud. This is only retrospectively clear, revealed in the interview in the bookstore that follows the library visit. Marlowe, both hero and narrator, has deceived us by wilfully withholding relevant information so that his strategem in the bookstore will surprise us, and thus the brevity of the narration of the library visit is in a sense a false indication of unimportance, since there are clearly other factors at work too. What the brevity indicates is two things. Firstly, it tells us that the details of how Marlowe acquired his information (what books he used, who the library assistant was, etc.) are unimportant – whereas the details of his interview with the phoney rare-books sales assistant will be very important. Secondly, it tells us something about Marlowe as narrator/hero: he likes to surprise us with his ingenious strategems, which can easily be referred to the context of his status as hero, as someone to be admired. Thus the brevity of this incident, easily established by comparing story and narrative, indicates to us both its degree of importance and the type of importance that it has: on both counts, it assigns a role to it in the narrative structure.

Similar considerations apply to order and frequency. At the beginning of Mario Puzo's (1969) *The Godfather*, three disconnected incidents are narrated, each of which leads one of the participants to ask a favour of Don Corleone, the godfather, and thus to reveal their dependence on him. In the next section of the book Corleone is directly portrayed; as a result of the opening incidents we see him as someone to whom people turn. In this instance the order of narrative is the same as the order of story; elsewhere in the story – primarily in the extensive use of flashback to Don Corleone's youth – it is different. Evidently the decision to narrate incidents in their chronological sequence in the opening pages is done deliberately to set up a point of view in the text, a relationship between the reader and one of the main characters.

Perhaps this sounds excessively obvious: perhaps we do not need the distinction between story and narrative to make simple points about the rhythm of fiction. What are the advantages of using this framework? Firstly, it enables us to be more systematic: if we want to compare the narrative structure of this novel with another, we have a common framework to use. Secondly, if we can demonstrate that a given group of works systematically has the same relationship between story and narrative, then we have learnt something valuable about that group. Perhaps Marlowe always hides this type of information from the reader, which would tell us something about the themes of Chandler's novels; perhaps all detective narrators/heroes always hide such information, in which case what might appear to be specific to Chandler would turn out to be a characteristic of the genre in which he works. Thirdly, we might observe that such extreme variations in rhythm are missing in other types of novel: indeed, quick reference to the *Arabian Nights* or the *Decameron* would reveal very different rhythms of story-telling. This would direct our attention to major historical questions about the development of narrative forms, and perhaps lead us to ask questions about their audiences too. All of these matters are easier to pursue using a systematic framework, and all of them are matters which are significant when trying to understand popular fiction; we shall have occasion to return to them.

4 The speaking/reading subject

The easiest way to demonstrate the necessity of analysing the subject (the speaking or reading or viewing subject, i.e. the person who uses language or a text) is to give an account of certain fundamental features of language.

Benveniste (1971) demonstrated that the tense system of verbs can only be understood by reference to the act of speaking. The difference between 'I saw him' and 'I have seen him', for example, lies not in the time in question (since both could easily refer to the same moment in time), but to a difference in the relationship between then and the moment of speaking. Similarly, an entire category of words (commonly called 'deictics' or 'shifters') can only fully have meaning when used in specific contexts: words such as 'I', 'here', 'now', etc. Such words do have dictionary entries: 'I' means 'the one who is speaking', 'here' means 'where the speech act is occurring', and so on, and these definitions are indeed valid definitions, thus demonstrating that the words in question are fully part of the language system insofar as they are definable without reference to anything outside this system. But at the same time, it is clear that their meaning is significantly and fundamentally different from the meanings of nouns and verbs, in the sense that the meaning of nouns and verbs can be established on the basis that they classify objects and events into categories (it is the category that is the meaning of each individual word: 'chair' means 'that category of objects used for sitting') independently of the application of such words in the flow of actual spoken or written language. Shifters' definitions, on the other hand, are empty spaces which can only be filled when the words are used in actual speech or writing (Benveniste, 1971: ch. 19; Kerbrat-Orecchioni, 1980: 37f.).

These examples should be taken as brief indications of a general point: that there exists a dimension of meaning which is not reducible to language considered as a system ('langue', or 'competence'), and yet which is not the arena of the free, spontaneous combination of units from the language system by a speaking subject – who would thus be the unconstrained 'author' of his or her own speech – since it is clear that (for example) the use of both pronouns and tenses is rule-bound; many other examples can be given (Smith and Wilson, 1979: ch. 8; Kerbrat-Orecchioni, 1980: Foreword and ch. 1). This dimension of meaning – which is a dimension of every 'communication act', or every speech act, of all creation of meaning – is conventionally called 'discourse'.

In this dimension, language is considered primarily as an act, an act in which meaning occurs. Of course, meaning occurs in all acts, simply because that is part of the nature of human action. All acts have some meaning or other; the purpose of semiotics, the general science of signs, has been to investigate how (or, more modestly, whether) the meaningful nature of all human activity is subject to systematic rules in the same way as language and other formalised communications systems. Whether such a general science is possible remains open to question (Coward and Ellis, 1977: chs 2 and 3; Cherry, 1980; Leach, 1980). In formalised communications systems, meaning occurs at the intersection point of two entities: the communication system, based on a set of rules which constitute it as a system; and the subject who produces meaning through the application of the rules of the system to a particular situation.[1] What is central to the study of narrative in this theory is the way in which it demonstrates that the subject who uses a communications system necessarily creates him or herself in the process, in the form of creating a series of places from which, by implication, (s)he is speaking. This, in its turn, is best illustrated first with examples from everyday speech.[2]

It is easy to find examples of statements that do not make sense because they are self-contradictory: 'I think he is honest, but I am wrong', 'I do not know that Peter has left', etc. In each case the statement does not make sense because its implication is that the person who is making it has two incompatible attributes: to say that you are wrong in a belief is tantamount to saying that you do not believe it, and to say that someone has left is tantamount to saying that you know that this is the case; therefore the statements are self-contradictory. In other words, these statements – in common with all statements – commit the person who utters them to certain propositions. This simple basic principle has profound implications. If I say 'Peter has gone', this implies that I – although not linguistically present in the sentence – none the less am asserting the truth of the statement. In traditional grammar, the subject of the sentence is 'Peter', since it is he who has performed the action described by the verb; but clearly it is the speaker who is taking responsibility for this assertion – as is recognised in the law of libel, for instance.

Thus contemporary linguistics distinguishes between the subject of the statement (Peter) and the subject of the act of speaking (the speaker); this distinction allows us to stipulate who is committed to what by the various components of any utterance.[3] If I say 'John knows that Peter has gone', I (the subject of the utterance) am asserting the truth of three statements, even though I am still not linguistically present: I am asserting the truth of 'Peter has gone'; the truth of 'John knows p' (the proposition that Peter has gone); and this further implies that John too is asserting that Peter has gone. Thus I have committed myself to asserting two things, and have also committed John to asserting something – I have implicated John in my statement. This clearly demonstrates the difference between the subject of the statement (in this last instance, John) and the subject of the utterance (me, since it is me who is asserting these various propositions).

The advantage of these distinctions is that they allow us to analyse, with a considerable degree of precision, the different positions that are adopted by the various parties involved in any proposition. Consider, for example, the statement 'Susan said she was in love with that beast': who is responsible for the various attributions here? Clearly it is Susan who is responsible for the assertion that she is in love with x; clearly it is the speaker (say, JP) who asserts that she said so: but where does the attribution of beastliness to the object of her affections come from? Is it Susan who is saying that she is in love with a beast ('despite everything', perhaps)? Is it JP who is claiming that x is a beast? Or is JP claiming that Susan called him a beast – which Susan (justifiably or otherwise) may subsequently deny, especially if x is present at the time.

So far these considerations have been based on the assumption that the role of the listener is irrelevant: the propositions analysed could have had a listener or not, but the meaning process presented did not depend on their presence. But in fact this is fallacious: all language is *essentially* dialogue, and the presence of the listener is written into it in various forms. Consider the sentence 'John doesn't read detective novels'. This can have many different meanings:

(1)   John, at least, doesn't read them (even though all my other stupid friends do).

(2) John and John alone doesn't read them (what a strange chap).
(3) John doesn't really read them, he just skips through them.
(4) John doesn't read detective novels, he only reads literature.
(5) John refuses to read detective novels on principle.
(6) I am not going to allow John to read detective novels, so there's no point in giving him one.[4]

Minimally this demonstrates the variety of different subject positions that can be taken up by the subject of the utterance in this single case. More importantly, the variations in meaning can only be established on the basis of the place of this statement in a dialogue, where each of the cases listed above is with a different imaginary interlocutor (or at any rate a different conversation). Thus, (1) presupposes a context in which detective novels have been blamed, probably by both participants (a minimum of two, but of course there might actually be any number) and their widespread appeal has been regretted; (2) is more or less the obverse of (1), where their universal appeal is no longer regretted; (3) suggests a conversation about how different people read detective novels, or about John's way of reading various types of book, etc.; (4) implies that someone has just suggested (horror of horrors) that John reads junk; (5) suggests a context in which John's habits and personality in general have been the topic of conversation; (6) suggests that someone has just offered to lend John one, but his wife/mother/lover/lawyer/tyrannical manservant won't let him read them, among other interferences in John's life. Of course, these different meanings could be suggested by inflexions of the voice – it is easy to imagine some of the different tones in which they could be spoken – and such tones could be regarded as part of the language system, something codified and interpretable independent of the situation in which they were used; but this would not affect the argument pursued here, for the inflexions used would still depend upon the position in the dialogue that the statement occupied.

Similarly, consider the sentence 'I know if Susan got the 10 o'clock train'. This sentence is grammatically impossible, since the rule is that 'know' is followed by 'that' if it is positive, and by 'if' or 'whether' if it is negative or interrogative. However, this form would be perfectly possible in such a circumstance as this: someone asks me 'Do you know if Susan got the train?'; I reply 'Of course I know if Susan got the train'. In these circumstances, it is the breach of grammatical normality that is responsible for the meaning of the reply, i.e. the implication that there is some feature of the relationship between questioner, me and Susan which ought to have indicated to the questioner that this was a stupid question. In other words, in a reply of this nature the speaker is adopting a very specific stance *vis-à-vis* the questioner, namely an aggressive stance, and in so doing is (a) revealing something about him/herself; (b) revealing what (s)he thinks about the question and questioner; (c) showing something about his or her (and perhaps their joint) relationship to Susan. This reply is meaningless outside the flow of a dialogue, and the process by which it has meaning necessarily allocates defined positions to the various parties to it.

These considerations about everyday language tell us the following:

(1) All statements necessarily represent their speaker: (s)he is the position from which the statement is made.
(2) All language is fundamentally dialogic: that is to say, the addressee is a necessary and intrinsic part of all statements.
(3) The addressee is thus also a position 'inscribed' in the statement, the place where the statement is to be heard.
(4) These positions necessarily implicate the speaker and listener in whatever identifications are suggested by the utterance. Of course, this does not mean that listeners are obliged to accept whatever is said to them – that would be self-evident nonsense (that they do not is anyway empirically observable, as we have seen earlier); but it does imply that if a listener rejects something that is said (or modifies it, or understands it in only a partial way, etc.) then the process of rejection, mis- or partial understanding is predicated in part upon whatever was in the statement that is being rejected, as well as upon the attitude of the listener. For example, it is well known that jokes (and comedy in general) sometimes fail to amuse: predictability, childishness, incomprehensibility, offensiveness and embarrassment, all are forms of failure of humour and comedy. It is clear from the terms themselves that it is the interaction between some feature of the humour and some feature of the audience that is responsible for the failure, not just some feature of the audience acting at random (see Palmer, 1987: 21ff., 181ff.).

These conclusions are based upon an analysis of everyday language; but the subject matter of this book is narrative: do these conclusions apply here too?

If narrative is indeed a dialogue, it is dialogue of a special kind: one in which the interlocutors are not physically present to each other; where the speaker is represented by words (and images); and where the listener cannot reply – it is worth recalling the traditional definition of a mass medium of communication as one source, many receivers and a one-way information flow. This places the 'listener' (reader, viewer) in a place which has its own special characteristics, characteristics which derive from the relationship between the two parties to the transaction involved. The parties are the (listening, viewing, reading) subject and the structure of the narrative: both its internal characteristics, as outlined here, and its characteristics as an institution, in other words as a phenomenon with a material and social dimension to its existence. What is involved is best approached through a consideration of how the basic apparatus of the cinema functions.

For J.-P. Oudart (summarised in Dayan, 1976) the privileged position of the viewer is set up in the apparatus of perspective and the transition between shots. Relying on the analysis of monocular perspective in post-Renaissance painting, he argues that the technology of the lens necessarily places the viewer of the cinematic image (at this stage in the analysis the image can be static) in a certain place in relation to the image. He shows that the codes of representation used in such paintings produce an illusion of the direct imitation of reality provided the painting is viewed from the right place, the place of the viewer. The codes inscribe the viewer as the place of coherence of the representation, thus producing a double effect: firstly, the viewer is assured that his or her place is indeed a meaningful place, since it is the place at which meaning is produced; secondly, the codes (which are in reality constructs, the product of a particular work achieved in a particular civilisation) appear to be totally natural, to be no more than the fact of imitation. Thus the perception of the imitative image achieves two fundamental things: it gives to the viewing subject the sense of coherent meaning, and in so doing gives the impression that the highly artificial, coded 'imitation' of reality is in fact no more than a copy, thus the natural bearer of some meaning or other which is already fixed in the world as it is imitated. These two processes are mutually supportive: it is insofar as one is achieved that the other is also.

However, in a second moment, Oudart argues, the viewer perceives the frame, perceives that the image is bounded, shut off from the rest of the world, and that it is the fact of framing which enables the image to have meaning; this simultaneously reveals that the meaning is, after all, the result of a process of meaning creation, and therefore the result of work, by somebody. Thus the point from which the image is seen becomes a point which is already occupied, but occupied by someone who is not there, whose presence is merely implied but not constituted in actuality, whereas the presence of the viewer is real: his or her body actually is where it is. This presence-in-absence threatens the secure 'possession' of the image by the real viewer, for the coherence of the image is now guaranteed by the 'absent-one'. But a third moment in the constitution of the filmic image restores the real viewer to the threatened pride of place: the transition between shots, of which Oudart takes the shot/reverse shot pair to be emblematic. Say a film represents a scene between two characters, A and B, sitting on opposite sides of a table, talking – an absolutely banal example of film narrative. In shot 1 of this scene the camera is positioned behind and slightly to one side of A; in frame we see A's shoulder and back of head, beyond him we see B looking at A, therefore looking roughly towards the camera. At this point all the preceding analyses of codes and frame obtain. By cutting the film and moving the camera, we can now move, in shot 2, to a complementary position behind B, where we see his shoulder and A's face. In shot 2, the camera reveals that the position of the absent-one, which threatened the viewer's supremacy, is in fact the position from which A was looking, i.e. the absent-one is in fact simply a character in the film, whose position thus comes to be the guarantee of coherence of the image, and thus this threat to the primacy of the real viewer is obliterated by the filmic mechanism in question.

Of course, not all film editing consists of this particular technique; but it is a commonplace of film history that the type of editing 'rule' of which this is an unproblematic application was intended to achieve the impression of continuity and direct imitation of reality (see e.g. Bordwell *et al.*, 1985: part I). What Oudart is arguing, in effect, is that the techniques commonly used to ensure continuity in film are all based on the same fundamental principle: obliteration of the absent-one, reinstatement of the viewer as the principle of coherence of the (succession of) images. This analysis of the basis of cinematic narrative is linked directly to a conception of the viewing subject – i.e. the viewer, conceived of as the place in which meaning and coherence reside, therefore something akin to the 'subject' in the traditional philosophical sense. How this subject is conceived can be seen in Metz's 'The Imaginary Signifier' (Metz, 1982).

The basis of this account is a metaphor, the metaphor of the mirror. This is doubly a metaphor. In the psycho-analytic account of the development of the child, the child's perception of itself in the mirror is the basis of its recognition of itself as a unity before its control of its own body is in fact sufficient to give such a unity in reality (Lacan, 1949; Wilden, 1972: 463ff.). Here the mirror is a metaphor in the sense that it summarises all those experiences of the outside world which reveal to the child that it is indeed a unitary entity. In its mirror image, the child recognises an 'ideal' version of itself with which it identifies, and which will become the basis of all subsequent identifications. This ideal version and all its subsequent identifications constitute the Ego and are responsible for its attributes of permanence, identity and substantiality. But because the ideal version that the child sees is 'out of step' with the child's real development, this inaugurates a kind of rupture within the psyche, since the child experiences this ideal version as simultaneously there and not-there, as something passionately desired and yet outside himself, an image that he 'fixes on himself . . . which alienates him from himself' (Lacan, 1966: 113). The attributes of permanency and identity, etc., are thus both illusory and real simultaneously: they are illusory in the sense that they are based upon the rupture constituted by the unbridgeable divide between desire and reality; they are real insofar as the assumption of their existence is a major form of the orientation of behaviour.

This metaphor is then applied to the cinema. Previous metaphors for the cinema screen had been 'window' and 'frame'; both of these metaphors focus on what is on the screen, whereas the 'mirror' metaphor focuses our attention on the spectator, and especially on the unconscious processes involved in perception (Altman, 1985: 521ff.). But, of course, the screen is not a mirror: what the spectator sees is not him or herself, but a representation of the outside world. In what sense then can the metaphor of the mirror be said to work? The screen is like the mirror of the child's imaginary identification in that the apparatus of the cinema installs the spectator in a position where looking and identifying with what is seen places the viewer in a position of mastery in relation to the world – mastery in the sense that (s)he is the place where coherence occurs. Of course, says Metz, the identification with the characters on screen is different from the child's identification with his or her own image in the mirror, since the latter is a primary identification, which is the foundation of all perception of the outside world; whereas looking at the screen is secondary. But although looking at the screen is not the foundation of perception, the psyche, identification or any of the other manifold processes described in psycho-analysis, it is the foundation of cinema as an activity. In it are constituted processes such as 'identifying' with a character 'so that he benefits, by analogical projection, from all the schemata of intelligibility that I have within me' (Metz, 1982: 57).

This is a very incomplete account of psycho-analytic theories of the relationship between audience and narrative, but constraints of space prevent further development. In general, such theories have been applied to narrative in a way that produces a general conclusion: the nature of the human subject is that there can never be any completely coherent sense of identity; all human beings suffer permanently from psychic processes which undermine it; subjectivity is irremediably 'split' between the different levels that compose it. However, narrative – and especially 'realist' narrative (to be defined below) – gives the temporary illusion of a coherent identity through the mechanisms described above: the imaginary signifier installs the viewing subject in a position of coherence, in other words of a plenitude of meaning – since what is there is coherent, it must be unified; since it is unified, it must be unsplit, therefore characterised by plenitude. That is to say, the imaginary signifier institutes a process which disguises or palliates the fundamental anxiety which derives from the universal process of splitting. The process of cinematic narrative gives to the viewing subject the illusion that (s)he really is the principle of coherence that the film proposes.

What are the implications of these psycho-analytic accounts of the fundamental narrative apparatus of the cinema? How do they relate to the accounts of textual processes that preceded them? The line of thought we followed through Barthes' text extracted from it the 'superior formal method' that Coward and Ellis wanted to avoid it being reduced to. Put at its simplest, this method consists of showing how meaning is built up in a text by a system of something akin to cross-referencing. As the narrative progresses, the process of connotation produces an ever-increasing number of 'echoes' across the space of the text. Taking again the brief example from Len Deighton: 'Here in Berlin Wannsee, where furs and cashmere are everyday clothes' (1986: 1), we can see that the process of connotation produces (at least) the following meanings:

(1) 'Here' calls our attention to the first-person narration; we are reminded (as we constantly are) that we are seeing everything through one particular set of identified eyes.
(2) The person who makes the statement about clothing is characterised as the sort of person who has such knowledge at his disposal, thus further identifying the set of eyes through which we see everything.
(3) The geographical location is precise, defining 'here', and thus giving reality to it.

(4) The location places the story in relation to a commonsense set of geographical knowledge – Berlin as the frontier between 'our' world and the Communist world, for example.

(5) The choice of fabrics refers us, via commonsense identifications, to the notion of 'riches'.

(6) The narrator is placed as someone watching these rich people: Why? What will happen as a result?

No doubt more could be seen in this brief passage. What is important for our purposes is not that even such an anodyne phrase contains so much, but that this plurality of meaning is what grounds the reader's position and the illusion of mimesis: recognition of the 'natural' correct use of a first-person speech form implicates us in the recognition of the narrator; the recognition of the commonsense identifications (Berlin + fabrics = money on the frontier) implicates us in the activities described – we place ourselves as people who also 'know' this kind of thing; the interaction between the two makes us recognise the narrator as someone who 'knows' this kind of thing, and what their significance is; etc. In short, in these recognitions the illusion of naturalness is created: the mimetic illusion. All of these meanings appear to inhere naturally in the world represented on the printed page, insofar as we – equally naturally – intuit ourselves as what all this meaning is addressed to. In just the same way, the camera movement from behind one participant in a conversation to a position behind the other one (motivated perhaps by a change of speaker, perhaps by recording the listener's or speaker's reaction) will also appear to be no more than a 'natural', imitative representation of what is already there in the real world.

What we have seen in this brief example is how three processes are fused. In the first place – as we saw earlier – texts actively produce meanings, they do not merely reproduce meanings that already pre-exist elsewhere. Secondly, these meanings have to be sought out by a reading subject, who follows the chains of association that are activated in the text. In doing so – the third process – the subject brings the meanings in question to inhere in the text: the meanings that the text produces give the appearance of being naturally there, of belonging there as by right, simply from the fact of imitating the world, of being a true reflection of some pre-existing reality. At the same time, such recognitions implicate the reader in self-recognition as the place where these meanings are recognised.

A similar argument about the source of the mimetic illusion is to be found in Heath (1976). Summarising Oudart, Heath argues that when compositional arrangements within the frame are disrupted by motion, in other words by the sequence of frames, it is narrative that in fact contains them, restoring both sense to the arrangements and unity to the viewing subject:

> Frame space . . . is constructed as narrative space. It is narrative significance that at any moment sets the space of the frame to be followed and 'read', and that determines the development of the filmic cues in their contributions to the definition of space in frame (focus-pull, for example, or back lighting). Narrative contains the mobility that could threaten the clarity of vision in a constant renewal of perspective; space becomes place – narrative as the taking place of film.
>
> (Heath, 1976: 83)

In other words, at any point in a film narrative, the way in which objects are disposed in the frame is a product of where the narrative is moving to: if the focal length is changed, so that the camera appears to get nearer someone (or vice-versa), it is because the logic of the story demands that we should see that person more clearly. The most obvious application of this principle is the shot, repeated to the point of banality in TV serials such as *Dallas*, where mounting emotion is accompanied by a move into close-up on the face of the character most centrally involved. Narrative, in short, explains changes in composition within the frame:

> What is crucial is the conversion of seen into scene, the absolute holding of signifier on signified: the frame, composed, centred, narrated, is the point of that conversion.
>
> (Heath, 1976: 83)

What is central here, for our purposes, is the signifier–signified relationship that Heath proposes: the signifier is held onto the signified, ie the apparently natural and unequivocal relationship between signifier and signified which is the basis of the impression of realism, is produced by the flow of the narrative.

This principle is especially important where popular fiction is concerned, since popular fiction presents us with narratives that are simultaneously highly implausible (non-stop drama, in other words) and yet are felt by their audiences to be highly plausible. The thesis about realism advanced by Barthes and Heath demonstrates how this is possible: the fictional audience does not react in the same way as a scientist does to a proposed new theory, checking it against empirical examples to see if it is possible to falsify it; the 'reality effect' does not derive from a comparison between the events portrayed and some version of the known everyday world, it derives from the way in which the mechanism of representation is deployed, from the arrangement of signifiers, in fact.

The principles outlined above are capable of further application. Beneath the details of the arguments that have been pursued here there is a consistent line of thought, which can be summarised in these terms. Meaning is produced in chains of signifiers, but in such a way that it appears not to be the result of an act of production but to inhere naturally in the artefact in question as an effect of its imitation of the real world. In the same process, a position is created for the reader or viewer in which they perceive the meanings produced in the chain in question and simultaneously intuit themselves (or better, intuit their selves) as the point at which the coherence of the meaning is produced, and therefore as constituted by coherent selves. This dual process constitutes realist narrative: as meaning unfolds along the text, following all the processes we have been describing, so the implied reader and the real reader are brought together in the intuition that this is indeed true. More exactly, this is the immanent logic of the process: whether it actually works or not is an entirely different matter, for as we know already, readers and viewers in fact re- or mis-interpret texts, or simply reject them. In a variety of ways they refuse or modify the position of the implied reader and either do not allow themselves to be constituted as the principle of coherence of the text, or selectively read it in order to constitute another coherence – we shall see another example of this process shortly.

It is important to realise that this process is only one layer of a narrative, but it is the layer which provides a framework within which all other identifications take place, and which is therefore the condition of possibility of those identifications. For example: in a film, A is talking to B, shown in the shot/reverse shot process described above. It is an emotional confrontation, and as the camera moves between shots the participants' faces show us the range of emotions they are experiencing. If we feel the same emotions as we impute to one of the participants, we 'adopt their point of view'; or we may feel neutral in the encounter, sorry only that two people should tear each other apart (for example). Either way, our attitude depends upon our assumption that the camera is revealing the truth of the occasion. Each participant sees the encounter in his or her way, but the camera sees it objectively, we implicitly believe: if we see the face of a participant register rage, we believe that that character feels rage, even though we may not feel it ourselves.

MacCabe calls this process a 'hierarchy of discourses' (1974: 8ff.), by which he means that one discourse – the narrative instance itself – is superordinate to the discourse of each of the characters. Thus in *The Day of the Jackal*, we meet an official in de Gaulle's entourage, a stuffy, pompous, self-satisfied man, who has a young mistress who is part of the conspiracy to murder de Gaulle. The narrative makes it clear that she has prostituted herself in order to help the conspiracy and that the official's self-satisfaction rests upon very thin ice; it thus enables us to judge the man's self-image against a wider framework – the narrative of the events of which he is part. The narrative is therefore the truth of this character and the capacity that it has for convincing us of this truth is one of the things that convince us that what the narrative shows us is real.

This model of realist narrative, in its simplest form (as in MacCabe, 1974), implies only two layers: the narrative-discourse, which is the truth of the events narrated; and the subordinate discourses of all the participating characters. In reality, such narratives are multi-layered, and in the interplay between the different layers they set up a series of positions to be (potentially) occupied by the 'speaker' of the narrative (the real or implied narrator) and the addressee, the reader or viewer. For example, in the case of de Gaulle's easily deceived aide, the 'truth' of this narrative depends in part upon the stereotyped belief that men are easily deceived by sexual desire and that women play on this fact. Although a comprehensive treatment is far beyond the scope available here, some brief examples will indicate the significance of this principle (see also the case studies in part II).

These examples are based on the procedure that is usually called 'focalisation' or 'point-of-view structure'. By this is meant the way in which objects, characters and events are perceived 'through the eyes of' one or other of the characters in the text, or through the eyes of a narrator when the narrator is not also a character (as in first-person narrative in the novel). For example: 'Bailey walked into Minny's hash-house . . . . His mouth felt like a bird-cage' (Chase, 1977: 7). Here it is clear that what is seen is seen through a defined set of eyes: it is Bailey who feels that his mouth is like a bird-cage.

In film and TV a similar process occurs when the camera occupies a position which we know to be the position of one of the characters (point-of-view shot). In *Coma*, the heroine escapes from a gunman by hiding in a row of frozen corpses suspended on a rail; as the gunman approaches the end of the row she pushes the line of corpses so that they fall off the end of the rail on top of him. We see the line of corpses moving down the rail from the side, i.e. they move across the screen, from right to left; the film then cuts to the position of the gunman as the corpses move towards him and the camera, on top of which they appear to fall. This is often called 'subjective camera'.

At the other end of the spectrum of subjectivity and objectivity is a passage such as the opening words of Dashiell Hammett's *The Maltese Falcon*:

> Samuel Spade's jaw was long and bony, his chin a jutting V under the more flexible V of his mouth . . . . He said to Effie Perrine: 'Yes, sweetheart?'
> She was a lanky sunburned girl whose tan dress . . .
>
> (Hammett, 1930)

Here it is clear that everything is seen from a point which is outside the perspectives of the characters, from the point of view of a narrator who is not a character in the text. As we shall see, focalisation is often a more complex and ambiguous process than this simple contrast implies; yet the core of the concept is indeed this contrast.[5]

Of course, a character's point of view can be incorporated in narrative in other ways than overt focalisation. A simple example is the presentation of the villain in the James Bond novels. Here we often see things from the point of view of the villain in the sense that we see what (s)he is doing apparently without the mediation of the hero's perspective. In chapter 21 of *Thunderball* (Fleming, 1961) the villains are discussing whether to torture the woman Bond has induced to betray them:

> 'There are certain uses of electricity of which I have knowledge. The human body cannot resist them. If I can be of any service . . .?'
> Largo's voice was equally polite. They might have been discussing remedies for a seasick passenger. 'Thank you. I have means of persuasion I have found satisfactory in the past.'
>
> (Fleming, 1961: 205)

Here Bond's point of view is not represented. But cultural commonplaces indicate to us that the narrator finds this behaviour revolting, and we are likely to find it revolting too. That is to say, the narrator induces us to adopt a perspective in which our sympathy for Bond is increased, even though Bond's own perspective on events is entirely absent at this point. As has often been said in studies of point of view in the cinema, adopting a character's point of view may mean placing the camera directly where the character is, or it may mean placing it roughly where (s)he is – say, looking over their shoulder

– or it may mean presenting things in the light in which (s)he sees them (for example, see Metz, 1973a: 46f.).

Clearly 'seeing things through the point of view of a character' involves a series of different narrative procedures, which are represented in this diagram:[6]

		Focalised	
		Within	Without
	Internal	A	B
Focaliser			
	External	C	D

Here we can see that focalisation in fact has two dimensions: one is based on who sees something, the other on what is seen – the focaliser and the focalised. Within each of these dimensions, two more can be distinguished. The focaliser may or may not be a character in what is being narrated: if (s)he is, the focalisation will be called internal; if not, external. What is seen, the focalised, may be seen from the inside or only from the outside. In box A, a focalising character will have insight into what other (focalised) characters are feeling, thinking, etc. In box B, the focalising character sees actions, events and objects, but without any particular insight into other characters' minds. In box C, a narrator who is not a character in the text sees into the minds. In box D, a narrator who is not one of the characters sees everything from the outside only.

We are now in a position to see how these procedures create subject positions for the reader or viewer.

> 'Cheer up, Werner. It will soon be Christmas,' I said. I shook the bottle, dividing the last drops of whisky between [us] . . .
>
> (Deighton, 1986: 1)

These are the opening words of Deighton's *London Match*. Given the conventions of realist narrative, we assume that it is indeed true that Bernard Samson (the central character and narrator) said this to Werner, and did pour the whisky. But how about the 'truth' of what he said? He evidently believes that Werner is sad (or bored, or something), and believes or pretends to believe that the approach of Christmas will cheer him up. In any event, the character Bernard has an attitude towards Werner, revealed in these words, which the narrator Bernard still thinks (since he is reporting something that is past, using the past tense – 'I *said*') is worth reporting to us. But is character-Bernard's assessment of Werner's mood as reliable as narrator-Bernard's report of what he said? Clearly not: if it was, character-Bernard would already know what is going to happen in the novel, and would be able to avoid the series of agonising decisions and disasters that befall him and the British Intelligence Service. Because the narration is in the first person, we are inside a character, or more exactly we are inside an entity that has the same name as a character: in fact there is a sliding between the positions of box A and box C. The form of pleasure that derives from both empathising with the narrator cum central character and depending upon him for information plays constantly upon the fact that the narrator is all-knowing (revealing the truth of events), thereby creating empathy, but the character of the same name does not know everything and is constantly, as a result, put in precarious positions. In short, much of the pleasure of such stories derives from the device of deliberately conflating two distinct narratological layers, and it is clear that this conflation sets up a subject position for the reader, a curious mixture of dependency and empathy.

Another example is to be found in an analysis of narrative that apparently contradicts MacCabe's (1974) argument. According to this analysis (Lodge, 1981), there is no such thing as an objective and therefore reliable presentation of events by a narrator, which is the truth of those events: the way in which the narrative presents events always implies an attitude towards them. For example, the opening lines of Le Carré's *A Perfect Spy*:

> In the small hours of a blustery October morning in a South Devon coastal town that seemed to have been deserted by its inhabitants, Magnus Pym got out of his elderly taxi-cab and, having paid the driver and waited till he had left, struck out across the church square. His destination was a terrace of ill-lit Victorian boarding houses with names like Bel-a-Vista
>
> (Le Carré, 1987: 13)

The conventions of realist narrative lead us to believe that it was indeed early in the morning, that there was indeed a taxi-cab, the houses were ill lit, and so on. But note how connotation works here: A 'windy' night, the choice of 'desertion' to describe emptiness, the fact that the cab is elderly, the placing of events in the church square, the names of the ill-lit boarding houses – all of these coalesce to create a certain atmosphere, evoked in a somewhat ironical mode: isolation or desolation, but what an unlikely place for events of international significance to occur! The event of Pym's arrival is not just reported, it is commented in the act of reporting it. Is this atmosphere part of the truth of the events, a truth against which the characters' behaviour and version of events can be measured?

As Easthope (1988: 48f.) points out, the problem with MacCabe's theory is not that the voice of the narration is less than 100 per cent reliable, but that he presents this position of reliability as static and stable throughout a narrative, whereas in reality it is something that has to be constantly renegotiated and achieved in the process of constructing the text. In narrative, there can never be a 100 per cent 'fit' between what the narrative represents and some state of affairs in the real outside world, because all sign systems are based on the principle of difference and therefore all signification involves positioning in discourse, the taking-up of a position *vis-à-vis* whatever is represented. (The same conclusion is also reached by the distinction between 'story' and 'narrative'.) But within any given text, there is a hierarchy of reliability, some things are more reliable than others; in realist texts, the narration itself is the point of the greatest reliability available, even though it is never total. The hierarchy of discourses is not something which is fixed in place by one absolute reference point, but is a network of relationships, the possibility given to any one discourse to contain, to 'be the truth of' any other discourse. We shall see a more extended example of the application of this principle when we consider the subject of gender in crime fiction in chapter 9.

What can we learn from this range of material about focalisation procedures? Essentially this: in the analysis of such procedures we have been able to see that in each case a range of discourses are in play – for example, the 'slippage' between narrator and character in first-person narrative, or the representation of a character's point of view by an implicit evaluation of events that is in accordance with his. That is to say, we can see that below the level of the acceptance of realist narrative as the truth of events there are always several layers of meaning that are, in their turn, arranged hierarchically – the system of discursive hierarchy is multi-layered. In this layering process a series of positions for readers and viewers to adopt is delineated.

At this point we are in a position to see where the arguments of the last three chapters have taken us. Our starting-point was certain inadequacies in classical structuralist accounts, which led us to focus on two features of post-structuralist developments of them: firstly, the nature of reading processes; secondly, the position of the reader or viewer *vis-à-vis* the text. It should be stressed that the two processes are not separable, and to that extent Coward and Ellis' hope that *S/Z* would not be reduced to a 'superior formal method' has been realised, for the formal method in question reveals the necessity of implicating the reader. Following the logic of these processes has enabled us to see how readers are led towards positions *vis-à-vis* what is represented.

Considerations about the mechanisms of everyday language showed that all statements inscribe the listener in them through the strategy of address adopted. Statements depend for their intelligibility both on the language system (or whatever semiotic system is relevant for the medium in question) and on the set of entities (objects, social roles, etc.) that are referred to. Of course, those objects are in a sense part of language (or other semiotic systems), since words have meanings by referring to features of the social world of their users; but it is clear that objects and social roles do not depend only upon language for their definitions, although language is intrinsic to their representation, and to that extent they may be considered an independent system. At the same time, statements are only comprehensible in the context in which they are made. Thus there are three levels of intelligibility involved:

(1) the semiotic system, in which the relationships between signs are defined;
(2) the system of objects and social roles and relationships, each of which has a definition of some sort, incorporated in definitions of words, but also in connotative associations of every variety – 'character' in the traditional sense is part of this layer of intelligibility;
(3) the situation of utterance, in which both the various participants to the dialogue involved and the objects referenced appear in the form of strategies of address.

In narrative (at least realist narrative) we are invited to adopt a position, or series of positions, *vis-à-vis* the components of the second system: they appear in such-and-such a light, depending upon the connotations evoked in the text. We are also invited to adopt a position or positions *vis-à-vis* the other participant in the situation of utterance (the author); but whereas in real life this person is physically present, identified, etc., in narrative he or she is usually absent, and anyway may not be a person at all, but a corporation (as in the instance of film and TV). To all intents and purposes, in narrative the utterer is the narrative itself. To take an obvious example: the first words of Melville's *Moby-Dick* (1972) are 'Call me Ishmael'. In this apostrophe, the narrator identifies himself; but he is no more than an element of the text, the way in which the text addresses the reader; Ishmael is no more than a textual strategy. (These words have been written on the assumption that the audience is a single person; for reasons of simplicity I am omitting considerations of collective or multiple audiences here.) All the processes of connotation analysed above invite us to adopt positions with regard to objects in the second system; use of this method of analysis enables us to be more precise about how such processes occur (the 'superior formal method'). But in recognising such meanings, we also take up a position *vis-à-vis* the narration (the position of imaginary coherence already analysed); and at the same time we place ourselves in relation to the hierarchy of discourses that the text proposes, negotiating that place using all the schemata of intelligibility we have adopted from our experience of the world.

However, it is important to remember – as has been pointed out already – that the subject implicated in the act of enunciation is not by any means a blank place, a neutral space, to be filled by whatever identifications the text proposes. So far we have seen purely empirical evidence of this fact. However, it is clear that the theory of subjectivity that subtends the previous pages demands in any case that the subject should not be a blank space. The subject that reads is always already constituted in the proliferation of discursive acts in which subjectivity is set up in the first place; there is no blank subjectivity which then awaits exposure to a series of discursive 'inputs': the constitution of subjectivity takes place in discursive activity and there is no space that precedes this activity (Heath, 1979; Willemen, 1978). Thus the act of reading is always a meeting between a set of subject positions implied by the coding of the text (in the case of realist texts, these positions are always hierarchically arranged) and the subject position or positions in which the reading subject is already present. The resulting interactions do not in any way have a determinate outcome, and there is no general mechanism which would permit a description of such processes independently of particular readings of particular texts (for good examples, see Clark, 1980; Bennett and Woollacott, 1987). The arena in which all of these acts occur is called ideology; it is the subject of the next chapter.

5 Narrative and ideology

In this chapter we turn to the question of the relationship between narrative and the social structure. Why is this a task which is worth undertaking?

There are many obvious links between art forms and the structure of the society in which they are produced and consumed (Wolff, 1981: 26–48). For instance, and most obviously of all, artists must be trained in their craft, trained to produce whatever artefacts they will produce. If they are to devote a substantial proportion of their time to art they must be sufficiently rewarded for their efforts to enable them to live. Of course, not all societies conform to this pattern: many tribal societies do not have formal, institutionalised training programmes for their arts and not all societies have artists who make a living from their art. In general, the lower the degree of division of labour in a society, the less the likelihood of the arts being a distinct sector of it. Nor should these points be taken to infer that only those who follow such training programmes and make a living from art can be called artists, whatever the nature of the society in which they live. But in general, art uses skills, which have to be acquired, and frequently but not universally those skills are rewarded. This process necessarily involves the artist occupying a place in the social structure, albeit that the place in question will vary enormously from society to society.

Similarly, the 'consumption' of the arts involves an audience and the allocation of time: the audience must have whatever skills are necessary for such consumption (say, literacy in the case of print media) and there must be some process whereby the decision is made that such-and-such a portion of time is to be allocated to listening or watching. Such processes are inevitably part of the social structure to the extent that they will be regulated by the norms and values of the society in question. This should not be taken to indicate that the production and consumption of art are necessarily separated: in art forms such as collective singing (church services, work songs, etc.), there may well be no audience; none the less, there must be agreement that the occasion is appropriate for the art form in question. This may extend to quite detailed prescriptions about stylistic appropriateness: when Ray Charles started using vocal techniques traditionally associated with religious music by black Americans, and applying them in the performance of totally secular songs, he scandalised many of his audience. The blues singer Big Bill Broonzy said: 'He's got the blues, he's crying sanctified. He's mixing the blues with spirituals; I know that's wrong.'

Similarly, the use of playful, post-modernist sculptural styles would probably strike most of our contemporaries in England and the USA as scandalously inappropriate for a war-memorial. In Winnebago society, there were stories that were appropriate for different seasons of the year (Radin, 1976: 118). Until the nineteenth century, aristocrats refused to dance the waltz, since it was a peasant dance and involved an 'unseemly' degree of bodily contact (Groves, 1954: article 'Waltz'). Some sociologists make a rigid distinction between those aspects of the arts which are a part of the social structure and those which are not. Talcott Parsons, for example, distinguishes between the 'timeless symbols' that the arts consist of (which are independent of any social structure) and the 'creation and maintenance of symbol meaning systems', which are part of given social structures (Parsons, 1959: 249f.). However, such a distinction fails to account for features such as a sense of stylistic appropriateness, where the symbols are anything but timeless.

These rather simple sociological generalisations and examples at least demonstrate that there is indeed, always and necessarily, some relationship between the social structure and the arts. However, they do not in any way specify what that relationship is, and to what extent it is variable in different societies. We have already seen, in the introduction, the outline of the most influential theory of the last two centuries – the Romantic-based theory of culture – and the extent to which that theory has been the basis of policy and has therefore become a self-fulfilling prophecy. A book on popular narrative is no place to offer a general theory of the relationship between culture and society, and our focus will be certain features of the relationship between popular narrative and its social framework. This chapter and the next will examine one influential group of theories about this relationship in our type of society, Marxist theories.

A convenient starting-point is the theory of realism in Lukács.

Lukács' aesthetics are inseparable from his theory of history, a summary of which is not possible here. What follows is a brief summary of one strand in a complex body of thought (for a good introduction, see Jameson, 1971: ch. 3).

The focus of Lukács' method is the 'typicality' of characters in realist narration: they stand for something larger and more meaningful than themselves, they are concrete individualities and yet at the same time maintain a relationship with some more general or collective human substance. They are not summaries of some social group – the rich banker, the exploited worker, etc. – because, if they were, this would presuppose that the author knew what the basis of the social structure was before constructing a narrative, and could then create representative characters in accordance with this knowledge. However, it is basic to Lukács' theory that such knowledge is not possible. Lukács' reasons for this assertion are complexly linked to his theory of history; in essence, he asserts that under capitalism adequate independent knowledge of the social world is well-nigh impossible to attain. Where authors do in fact write in this way – as is the case with Zola and with much Socialist Realism, especially under Stalin – they fail to produce characters who are 'typical' in Lukács' sense. For Lukács, 'typicality' refers to the relationship between the character and the reality of the social, historical situation in which they are fictitiously portrayed. Instead of being fixed as the representative or incarnation of some static social entity, the 'typical' character summarises through his or her actions, which constitute the narration, the process of history which occurred at a particular moment: a character such as Nucingen in Balzac is not a representative of a social category, but summarises, in his activity, the social processes which constituted the historical moment through which he would have lived if he had been a real individual. Thus 'typicality' is in fact a way of being true to history, and narration can be said to be a form of understanding of the world.

This form of analysis does not at first sight seem very promising for application to popular, commercial narrative, for realism in Lukács' sense is certainly not one of its strong points. For example, we shall see later that the forms of verisimilitude that typify popular narrative are variable according to the type of story being told: what is plausible in a crime thriller is not so in a romantic melodrama, and vice-versa. This implies that such verisimilitude is not based on a 'true' understanding of the world that is referred to in the story, but depends upon some set of expectations on the part of the audience for the genre in question, or upon some preconception that they or the population at large have about their world. Whereas it is central to Lukács' theory that 'typicality' is a form of truth. One implication of such a theory is that the whole of popular culture (and especially popular narrative) is worthless, nothing more than the incarnation of false consciousness; once this position has been adopted, the only possible response is denunciation. This attitude was shared for many years by certain Marxists (notably the Frankfurt School) and non-Marxist 'high-culture' critics, but nowadays is not taken very seriously. (For a brief summary of these positions and a dismissal of them, see Bennett, 1982; 1986a.)

A good testing ground for the applicability of the theory of typicality to popular fiction is Robert Warshow's 'The Westerner' (1974).

Warshow contrasts the hero of the Western with the gangster hero. The gangster story is typically a story of successful enterprise followed by dramatic failure; although the enterprise is criminal, even evil, the final failure is presented not as punishment but as defeat. His commitment to enterprise is total: his 'unceasing, nervous activity' seems almost an end in itself, and it is understood that if he decides to try to rest on his laurels he is about to be destroyed. He is lonely and melancholy, but this is not authentic; he is not so because life demands these qualities but because his career and his own nature make it inevitable. He is incomplete because he 'cannot accept any limits or come to terms with his own nature', and his career is a

> nightmare inversion of the values of ambition and opportunity. From the window of Scarface's bulletproof apartment can be seen an electric sign proclaiming 'The World is Yours', and . . . it is the last thing we see after Scarface lies dead in the street.
>
> (Warshow, 1974: 402)

His failure is a central part of his attraction, for it shows that the will to succeed is nugatory.

The Westerner too is lonely and melancholy, but these qualities are 'organic', in other words a genuine product of his situation: in his world, killing is endemic and love is an irrelevance – hence the only women who share the Westerner's view of the world are prostitutes, and if the Westerner prefers a respectable woman he is in fact giving up a way of life (cf. Tompkins, 1989). Against the restless ambition of the gangster, he is 'a figure of repose'; he essentially has no possessions beyond the minimum of his guns, horse and clothes, and no desire for any more: the commodities that are fought over

– land, cattle, gold – are merely the occasions for confrontation. Whereas the gangster's strength lies in his lack of self-control, his immediate willingness to shoot, the Westerner's lies in his control: he will only shoot when it is right to do so. He is overtly defending justice and order, of course, but really what is at stake is his honour. Whereas the gangster's final defeat entails the admission that his whole life has been a mistake, it does not matter whether the Westerner wins or loses:

> he fights not for advantage and not for the right, but to state what he is, and he must live in a world which permits that statement. The Westerner is the last gentleman, and the movies which over and over again tell his story are probably the last art form in which the concept of honor retains its strength.
>
> (Warshow, 1974: 405)

But the Westerner is also a figure of moral ambiguity, because he is, in the end, a killer: recurrently, the obligation to shoot results in his isolation and the sense that although he 'did what he had to', he cannot be any the happier for it. This gives him, as a fictional figure, a 'mature sense of limitation' and a tragic dignity different from the gangster's. The gangster's tragedy is romantic, deriving from the impossible demands he makes on the world; the Westerner's derives from the fact that even the limited demand he makes – to assert his personal worth – cannot be fully met. Thus the Westerner is never the bearer of some social order – he is neither pro- nor anti-social – he just is himself, and must play the part that this sense of individuality assigns him. In this sense of individuality, violence is central: the Westerner lives in a world where it is unavoidable. Yet this is not a world where violence is the product of cruelty; the Westerner in a sense believes in violence, yet his dominant quality is self-restraint. In the end it is not so much violence itself that is the subject matter as 'a certain image of man, a style, which expresses itself most clearly in violence' (Warshow, 1974: 415).

Is Warshow saying, or implying, that these fictional figures are typical – in Lukács' sense – of some piece of history? Clearly they are not typical of the actual moment of history that they are taken from: Warshow is quite explicit that the Western is not realistic in the sense of having a relationship of truth with the history of nineteenth-century America (ibid.: 406, 410), whereas for Lukács the great realist writers did describe the truth of the historical situations they represented. But at the same time, what Warshow is seeing in his fictional figures is truth to a particular experience of the world. The gangster, he says, is the negative side of American official optimism: he represents the truth of trying to live the American dream – isolation, distrust, defeat – not in the sense that everyone who tries to live the American dream becomes a gangster, but in the sense that trying to live the American dream when you are powerless leads to experiences which can be translated into the dramatic events of the gangster's rise and fall. Similarly with the Westerner: he is the person to whom possessions mean little, they are at most the proving ground on which commitment to one's own sense of worth and identity can be tested; implicit in this presentation is an assessment of how men live the relationship between economic activity and their sense of self-definition. In this intense description of what these figures stand for, Warshow is analysing elements of an experience of the world, an experience which he postulates as the audience's experience. When he asserts, in the opening lines of his essay, that the gangster and the Westerner are the 'two most successful creations of American movies', he is implicitly making a claim for the 'truth to experience' of the narratives he is describing.

Certainly this is different from Lukács' emphasis on truth to the reality of underlying historical processes. We have already seen another version of this debate, in the question of metaphors for the cinema screen: is the screen a window, a frame or a mirror? Broadly speaking, to consider the screen as either a window or a frame implies considering the cinema as essentially a realist medium, in a sense akin to Lukács': if the screen is a window it gives us access to a world beyond it by revealing it to us in a way that is not essentially changed by the act of revelation. To consider it as a frame implies subordinating the revelation of the outside world to its interpretation in the act of representing it, but insofar as the film uses iconic signifiers, it inevitably reveals as it represents. Compared with either of these two metaphors, the metaphor of the mirror implies a radically different perspective, since it refers us not to how the screen reveals the real world, but to how the screen has impact upon the spectator, how it 'positions' the spectator in the process by which meaning is created. It is this metaphor which is at the heart of the new Marxist aesthetic of the late 1960s and 1970s; its potency derives as much from its relationship to the traditional Marxist theory of ideology as from its mobilisation of psycho-analytic arguments.

In the Marxist tradition, the purpose of the theory of ideology is to explain the relationship between human consciousness and the social structure.[1] In a famous metaphor, Marx compared society to a building, in which some activities constitute the base (or 'infrastructure'), and others the 'superstructure'. The base consists of the production of the materials of everyday life, and especially the social relationships that people must enter into in order to carry out these activities (for example, the relationship of employer and employed). Other activities, such as law, politics, religion, the arts and so on, make up the 'superstructure'. Of course, this is a metaphor, and its purpose is to indicate a type of dependency: the products of consciousness such as religion, the arts, the law and political activity have the effects and the meanings that they have within a context defined primarily by the activities of the 'base', the production of the materials of everyday life. In a stronger formulation, nowadays usually regarded as false, the 'base' may be said to 'determine' the superstructure, or the latter may be said to 'reflect' the base; in either case, the ascribed relationship between the two 'levels' is virtually one of cause and effect, since what happens in the superstructure is always seen as subordinate to what happens in the base.

In societies that are divided into classes, the Marxist tradition argues, one class dominates the others (the ruling class), and part of the way in which it rules is through gaining consent to its rule from those over whom it rules. If this argument is put in terms deriving from the base–superstructure metaphor, then the ruling class is said to control the base directly (through ownership of the means of production) and thus to control the activities that constitute the superstructure, including the way people think about the world. As Marx and Engels put it in one of their early works:

> The ideas of the ruling class are in every epoch the ruling ideas: i.e., the class which is the ruling material force of society, is at the same time its ruling intellectual force. The class which has the means of material production at its disposal, has control at the same time over the means of mental production, so that thereby, generally speaking, the ideas of those who lack the means of mental production are subject to it.

> (Marx and Engels, 1965: 61)

Here we see very clearly the core of the Marxist theory of ideology: the forms of association between people that constitute any society are rooted in the act of production; at the same time, production can only take place within a set of relations between people. These relations are historically variable, and within societies which are divided into classes (such societies constitute the overwhelming bulk of human recorded history), they are exploitative and hierarchical, dominated by one group within the population. This domination must be constantly secured, since it does not occur automatically, and influence over people's ideas is part of this process. Since the exploitation and domination in question are distinctly to the disadvantage of the dominated, securing consent involves convincing those on the receiving end that it is in their best interests to accept being exploited and dominated; ideology contributes to this process by presenting such inequitable arrangements as natural, equitable, inevitable, etc. – or some combination of these – in other words, presenting them in a false light. Hence ideology is a form of miscognition, which functions to maintain exploitation and domination.

In the passage from *The German Ideology* quoted here, this influence is ascribed to control over 'the means of mental production': those who lack the means of mental production are thereby subject to such control. This is an extremely vague phrase, and the well-known difficulties of interpreting it with any degree of precision are in fact the location of the many different theories of ideology produced within the Marxist tradition during this century. One of the things that Marx certainly means is that in class-divided societies, it is commonly the case that there is a section of the population whose task it is to direct the labour of others – he calls this the 'division between mental and manual labour'. However, it is obvious that all tasks, indeed all activities, involve the mind: there is little that human beings do that is entirely independent of it. Therefore, unless we assume that this specialised section of the population has total control over the minds of their subordinates, we cannot use this sociological observation, correct though it is, to explain what Marx set out to explain, and we are back with the difficulties of interpreting Marx's dictum.

These difficulties revolve fundamentally around this question: what are the 'means of mental production'? A brief, probably partial list would include: the mind, language and other sign systems, education, the means of communication such as telephones, newspapers, etc. Some of these things can obviously be directly controlled: if education is institutionalised it is controlled; telephone systems are owned and their use can be limited; newspapers are owned and can be censored; etc. But it is not clear in what sense sign systems such as language can be controlled, even if the occasions on which they can be used (newspapers, political meetings and broadcasts, for example) clearly can be. If we include the mind itself, it is silly to say that anyone has the human mind 'at their disposal', unless you can show that they in some way control thought processes; but this is exactly what the notion of 'the control of the means of mental production' was meant to explain. On the credit side, it is at least clear that 'mental production' is partly a question of various social institutions and insofar as these institutions are owned or controlled, their contribution to 'mental production' is also subject to control. But it is equally clear that vast areas of social experience are not directly subject to these forms of control: we might summarise these as 'the experience of everyday life'. Is Marx trying to say that everything in our experience of the world around us results from control over our minds exerted by the ruling class? If not, what is he trying to say?

The simplest way out of these dilemmas is to return to the heartland of Marxist theory. All activity, for Marx, is material activity, not in the sense that the mind is 'only matter', but in the sense that the mind is part of what he often calls 'human sensuous activity'; it is part of the process by which the human species appropriates what it needs from nature (for Marx, there is no fundamental difference between 'need' and 'desire' – see Heller, 1976). But this activity must always take place within the network of social relations that constitute a society, and which has an independent existence. Thus experience of everyday life is always an experience which is structured by the network of social relationships within which it occurs. As Stuart Hall says, 'You cannot learn, through commonsense, *how things are*: you can only discover *where they fit* into the existing scheme of things' (Hall, 1977: 325).

The act of appropriation of what nature places at our disposal is always the appropriation of things which are defined by the place that they occupy in the network of relationships that constitute the society in question; similarly, the experience of (relationships with) other people is always the experience of a relationship that has a place within this overall network. Experience, in short, is always experience of a world which is structured in advance of the experience. Moreover, if Marx's thesis about the role of class in social structures is correct, the world is always (in class societies) hierarchically structured: the network of social relationships is always dominated and controlled by a group from within the population. For example, in our society the relationship of employer to employee is fundamentally of more benefit to the former: it gives to both security, respectability and a sense of self-definition but for the employer it is also the source of profit and power. In this sense, the social definitions of the objects of experience are always definitions that 'belong' to the ruling class.

If we bring together these two ways of defining ideology – control of 'the means of mental production' and the social origins of experience – we can see how ideology operates. The terrain of experience is not some neutral, open, freely available space, it is always an arena – enclosed and structured by 'the rules of the game'. In this process, control of social institutions such as the education system and the means of communication clearly plays a part. And it is also apparent that the result will be that people's experience of the world is brought into conformity with the demands of the existing organisation of society. The implication of this analysis is that ideology *creates* our experience of the world. The most influential formulation of this argument is to be found in L. Althusser, especially his 1969 paper 'Ideology and Ideological State Apparatuses'.[2]

Ideologies are different in different societies, of course, and may well have different roles within these societies: in *Capital* Marx commented on the different importance of religion in different societies (Marx, 1961, vol. I: 82n). But, says, Althusser, beneath these differences ideology has certain general features which are eternal. Firstly, it has a function: to ensure that people take up places within the existing network of social relationships. Secondly, it has a mode of operation: it creates subjectivity.

The question of the function of ideology is controversial. In the Marxist tradition in general, ideology was held to be necessary only in class-divided societies, since it was there to mask exploitation which would disappear once class divisions were abolished. Althusser is somewhat inconsistent on this point, but ultimately seems to think that ideology will be a feature of all conceivable societies. This conclusion was heavily criticised by fellow Marxists, but Althusser's essay on ideology had the additional strength that it potentially answered another difficult question: what is the relationship between the individual and the social relations within which (s)he functions? Althusser gave a subtle answer: ideology constitutes biological individuals as subjects of social processes, i.e. as entities that are both *subjected to* these processes and perform them, thus constituting themselves as *the subjects of* the processes in question. In so doing, he also solved various other difficulties that had bedevilled more traditional theories. The feature of his argument that lay at the heart of these advances was his formulation of ideology as an 'imaginary relation' between people and their real conditions of existence.

By 'imaginary', Althusser does not mean 'false' or 'unreal': for him ideology is very real because it is incarnated in people's behaviour (and located in state apparatuses: it doubly has material existence). He is using the term 'imaginary' in a sense analogous to the psycho-analytic sense (see above, chapter 4), in which the individual projects an identity on to himself or herself and comes to live the self which is set up in this identity as the principle of coherence of the world. This is done by imposing perceptual patterns upon the world, thereby seeing meaningfulness in everything perceived: it is under these circumstances that the relationship between signifier and signified can be understood as unproblematic.

Although Althusser's sense is not identical to the psycho-analytic one, it retains something of this charge, for the imaginary relationship that he analyses is what gives to the individual his or her sense of place in the world: they intuit themselves as having an identity, says Althusser, on the basis of the place that they see themselves occupying in the network of relations that constitutes the social order. In Althusser's own terminology, 'ideology interpellates [i.e. addresses] individuals as subjects'. As a result, ideology cannot be seen as 'false': the relation that people have with their real conditions of existence is lived in their identity as individuals, and is therefore entirely real. Insofar as there is an element of falsehood about it, this derives from the fact that the real conditions of existence may not be what this lived relationship with them posits them as. Nor is ideology simply ideas: it is the set of practices, or behaviour, that individuals engage in during their lives; these practices are always undertaken within some set of social relationships, and specifically within the 'ideological state apparatuses'.

One major impact of these ideas was in the realm of film theory. We have already seen how developments in post-structuralist theory led to a conception of narrative as a set of places or subject positions, of which the major one was the position of 'imaginary coherence' produced by 'classic realist narrative'. This was the major one because it performed two tasks. Firstly, within narrative it established the set of places that all the other discourses in the text were to occupy – it created a hierarchy of discourses; we shall have occasion to return to this elsewhere. Secondly, by speaking to the 'imaginary coherence' of the subject, it positioned the subject within ideology, since (in Althusser's theory) this is one of things that ideology is: the construction of the subject in the discourses that address the individual as a subjectivity; crudely speaking, post-structuralist theory explains how this process works in Althusser. An example of this is

MacCabe's (1979) essay 'On Discourse'.

In this essay, MacCabe analyses the relationship between the discursive organisation of speech (and by implication narrative) and the field of ideology. In the first part, he demonstrates that formal linguistics is inevitably confronted with elements of language which it is unable to accommodate within purely linguistic models, and argues that only recourse to a theory of the speaking subject and of ideology can solve the problems. The first element of the demonstration is based on the theory of enunciation, as outlined above. Here we learn that all meaning is located at the intersection of the two axes of language – the set of rules or paradigms that constitute it, and the situational logic of utterance. At this intersection is also located the speaking subject, who manifests his or her existence both (a) by application of the rules of language to produce statements that are in conformity with linguistic norms (failure to do so will produce doubts about his or her coherence as a subject), and (b) through an understanding of the situation in which the act of utterance occurs – failure to do so might produce a perfectly formed but entirely inappropriate sentence, as in the example in the film *The Knack*, when the tongue-tied young man, finally alone with the girl of his dreams, desperate to say something, comes up with 'Cardiff's got big docks'. This part of his essay overlaps substantially with ideas we have already seen above.

The second element of his demonstration shows that as soon as one tries to analyse linguistic relationships that cross the boundaries between sentences, it is essential to take into account a layer of meaning that is discursively organised and goes beyond dictionary definitions of words and grammatical rules. For example, relative pronouns inevitably reveal one of two mechanisms, both of which exceed the language system: in the first, the relative pronoun introduces a relationship of equivalence between what it refers to and what it introduces (e.g. 'Moses, who was a prophet and who led the Jews out of Israel and who brought the tablets down from the mountain' or 'Paris, which is a large city which is the capital of France which is built on the banks of the Seine' – three ways of referring to the same thing). In the second, it marks the convergence of two separate discourses around the same point: 'Casals who is self-exiled from Spain stopped performing after the Fascist victory', where it is clear discursively that he stopped performing *because of* the Fascists, but where the grammar does not in itself imply this relationship since the relative pronoun could indicate the relationship of equivalence produced in the first mechanism.

The first mechanism establishes, through a set of alternatives

> the effect of sense and subjectivity and their necessary certainty. Sense does not arrive with each word but is produced across a set of alternatives within a discourse. It is this possibility which produces the effect that 'I' am in control of my discourses, that *I* say what I *say* because I can always go back and offer a set of explanatory alternatives.
>
> (MacCabe, 1979: 293)

The second mechanism produces a binding together of two discourses, here music and politics, in a relation of mutual implication: the sentence about Casals is only comprehensible if we accept that there is a possible interaction between hating Fascism, exile, and refusal to perform; thus the sentence sets up a 'complicity with its reader', which could take the form 'If one was a musician, one would refuse . . .'. And if we reject the complicity we say things like 'He doesn't care about Spain', 'He's just trying to make more money', etc.: 'Another discourse rescues us from an identification we reject' (ibid.: 294).

MacCabe concludes that the isolation of the language system as an autonomous object involves a double separation: the separation from subjectivity and the separation from institutionally defined discourses (here: music and politics); but both these separations, he has demonstrated, are impossible. Discourse demonstrates in its functioning the presence of the speaking subject and the presence of discursive effects (meanings) which always pre-exist the discourse in question, and therefore always pre-exist the discursive activity of the speaking subject. Following Pêcheux (1975), MacCabe refers to this mechanism as 'the pre-constructed', i.e. as that mechanism

> whereby discourse produces within one domain of thought another domain of thought *as if* this other domain had already been introduced. In discourse there is no beginning for the subject who always already finds itself and its discourses in place.
>
> (MacCabe, 1979: 300)

At this point, he shows, discourse becomes part of ideology: the existence of the 'always-already' existing field of discourse (in other writers this is often called the 'discursive formation' or 'interdiscourse') is that entity which addresses subjectivity and in doing so constitutes it as such, the entity which Althusser calls ideology. MacCabe's argument continues with a critique of elements of the positions he has sketched out here, to which we shall return shortly. In the meantime, we should consider the implications of this identification of the field of ideology with the preconditions of the signifying activity of the individual subject.

We saw in our discussion of Marxist theories of ideology that in one formulation of them (we shall see alternatives shortly) *ideology creates the individual's experience of the world*. This notion should be taken literally: there can be no experience outside the field of ideology, everything that constitutes the individual, or subjectivity, or personality (a series of labels for the same thing) derives from this field. The theory of signification that MacCabe advances is largely in accordance with this notion (with one important exception, to be mentioned shortly), for all meaning is constituted at the point where the rules of semiotic systems intersect with discursively established meanings (of objects, words, relationships, institutions, etc); subjectivity *is* this intersection. Here we are in the heartland of a certain moment in post-structuralism; indeed, it is tempting to see in this moment the constitution of post-structuralism considered as a system, were it not for the fact that this set of ideas is subject to a series of restrictions (to be explored).

When these ideas are applied to narrative, they imply that the set of subject positions set up in narrative – by the mechanisms we have already seen – derive from the field of ideology: they are so many forms of experience that the field of ideology makes possible for the individual, and that narrative sets up as sites of experience. The argument that will be pursued here is that this view of narrative is partially correct, partially incorrect. The analysis of how subject positions are set up is unobjectionable, but the analysis of ideology is fatally flawed. That there are subject positions in texts seems incontrovertible; that the field of experience is socially structured and that this is related to a hierarchically organised society equally so; but to argue that all experience is created by and in ideology goes substantially beyond these positions in ways that we shall see are untenable.

6 Hegemony and subject position

A convenient starting place to understand this process is some criticisms of Althusser. The first of these concerns the nature of the subject that is constituted in ideology according to Althusser's arguments.

One of the central purposes of Althusser's theory was to indicate how ideology had a material existence, in the Marxist sense (Marx's definition of materialism, we may recall, is that there is no distinction between matter and mind, that the two entities traditionally distinguished in European philosophy are in fact indissolubly bound together in a series of circuits). One way in which he does this is to invert the traditional philosophical conception of the subject, in which the subject is constitutive of its own activity, in which – to use a frequent modern metaphor – the subject is 'author' of what it does. In Althusser, as we have seen, the subject is *constituted by* the various processes that compose ideology. This is the central burden of Althusser's metaphor of 'hailing' or 'interpellation': the subject is constituted in the act of recognising that what is being addressed by the mechanism of ideology is itself, a subject. Thus the subject is subordinated to processes outside itself, and is not in any way the 'author' of its own activity; this clearly leaves room for a theory of subjectivity in which its constitution is ultimately to be referred back to other social processes, in this instance the economic processes of production and reproduction.

Two criticisms are commonly made. Firstly, it is pointed out by Marxists that if this theory is correct, there can be no source of conflict within capitalist society, since Althusser says all subjects are constituted in the process of the reproduction of capital: there could not be any source of opposition to capital's tactics; ideology would effectively make sure that everyone occupied their allotted spaces and got on with the job. This directly contradicts the Marxist tradition, in which 'The history of all hitherto existing society is the history of class struggle' (Marx) and in which 'Wherever there is oppression there is resistance' (Mao Zhe Dong); moreover, it is subject to considerable empirical disagreement (cf Rancière, 1974; Badiou and Balmès, 1976: 22ff.). It is true that Althusser does refer to class struggle, but this is largely a gesture of good faith in the classics; he also indicates other possible sites of resistance, but they are distinctly peripheral by contrast with the traditional Marxist insistence on the centrality of class struggle; the reasons for this centrality will shortly become clear.

The second criticism suggests that Althusser's conception of subjectivity is inadequate and self-contradictory. Firstly, in Althusser the subject is the bearer of structures that have their origin elsewhere, as we have just seen. By the same token, the subject must not be present in the activity that results in these structures, for if it was, it would be involved in their creation and would therefore not be simply their bearer. Yet, at the same time, it must have the attributes necessary to enable it to be constructed as as subject capable of bearing a structure; but if it has those attributes it already has the essential attributes of subjectivity, and these are precisely the attributes that would enable it to be involved in the creation of what it is supposedly only the bearer of. In short, the attempt to avoid a subject that is constitutive of reality has failed, and the argument is largely circular (J.-A. Miller, 1968; Hirst, 1979: ch. 3; Coward and Ellis, 1977: 20f.).

Secondly, by conceiving of the imaginary as the only mode of functioning of the subject, Althusser has given the subject unity, and a unity which is put in the same place as the unity of consciousness that it was supposedly displacing; but the psycho-analytic tradition has taught us that such unity is illusory (MacCabe, 1979). In psychoanalysis the psyche is irretrievably split between its various levels, and imaginary and symbolic identifications never entirely coincide with each other. From this it can be seen that Althusser's concept of subjectivity is marred by a fundamental oversimplification: it is based on the coherence of the subject, structured entirely as it is by the imaginary identifications proposed in ideology, a subject who is, as a result of this identification, 'the master of both language and desire', whereas psycho-analysis teaches us that we are the master of neither. The consequence of this coherence and mastery is that there is no source in subjectivity for resistance to ideological domination 'for there is nothing which escapes or is left over from the original production of the subject'. Whereas a psycho-analytic account of subjectivity would insist that any identification is constantly threatened by its 'constitutive instability in the field of language and desire' (MacCabe, 1979: 302).

Moreover, sociology shows that the individual is the intersection point of many different processes which only partially overlap – for example, a person's sexual identity has only partial correspondence with the identity that they have in legal processes (e.g. ownership) although both are located in the same biological individual. Furthermore, there are entities that are certainly agents of social processes but which are not reducible to either the individual or the imaginary – for example corporations or law courts (Hirst, 1979: ch. 3).

So far we have seen how Althusser's concern to provide a materialist theory of subjectivity gave rise to certain criticisms. Yet his theory was not intended to provide a theory solely of subjectivity but of other social processes as well, and here too criticisms have been made. One of Althusser's central purposes was to solve a traditional paradox within Marxism: how could everything be determined by the economic base while it was still recognised that political organisation was essential to articulate social change? Althusser's critics argue that it does not go very far in this direction (Hirst, 1979: ch. 3; cf. Laclau, 1977).

For Althusser, the state is nothing more than what is necessary to secure the domination of the ruling class. But this presupposes various things:

(1) Classes exist independently of politics, and are constituted in their entirety in economic processes – but this is the situation Althusser was trying to avoid, since it would make political organisation unnecessary.

(2) Politics and ideology maintain class domination by the creation of subjects; but many of the agents of class domination are not subjects, e.g. corporations.

(3) All ideological apparatuses are the same insofar as they have the same function, but this ignores very real differences in the way they function – e.g. the family operates very differently to the education system – and to identify them on the grounds of a single function is a grotesque oversimplification.

In short, ideologies and political actions can never be reduced to the mere incarnation of pre-existing positions dictated by the economic structure of society. To believe that they can is a classic example of the reductionism Althusser wanted to avoid, and which Mouffe characterises by three features (Mouffe, 1981: 228):

(1)   All subjects are class subjects.
(2)   Social classes have their own ideologies.
(3)   All ideological elements have a necessary class belonging.

That is to say, there is no subjectivity and no ideology which is not anchored in membership of a particular (economic) class, and therefore subjectivity and ideology are always little more than by-products of the economic class formation. Against such an assertion, recent arguments have asserted the possibility of a theory of ideology that is non-reductionist; usually such a theory is called a theory of hegemony, after Gramsci.[1]

For Gramsci, classes are formed in a succession of moments. The first moment he calls the 'primitive economic', in which a professional group is united by their common situation; the second moment he calls the 'political economic', in which such groups unite around features of their situations that transcend narrow professional concerns and provide the basis of a common identity; the third moment he calls the 'hegemonic', and we shall return to the meaning of the term shortly (Mouffe, 1981: 222). What is important for our immediate purposes is to notice that each moment in the formation of a class, according to Gramsci's theory, moves progressively further away from the immediately economic, while never entirely quitting it. By starting here, with the way in which classes are formed, he has avoided the blind alley that easily traps those who start from the notion that classes have a ready-made existence, given by the structure of a mode of production.

We may now move to a direct consideration of hegemony. Starting from the commonplace Marxist notion of a hierarchy of classes based in the economy, Gramsci asks how it is possible for a class to become and remain a ruling class. His answer is that its rule must be consented to by the other classes, for rule by coercion alone is rarely more than temporary. In order to rule, a class certainly must have the state at its disposal, and the state is, of course, coercive; but it is also

> the whole complex of theoretical and practical activities, through which the ruling class not only justifies and maintains its domination, but succeeds in obtaining the active consent of the governed.
> (Quoted Merrington, 1968: 153)

Of course, we should not imagine that this 'success in obtaining consent' is a passive matter, in which a given social group magically manages to incarnate the 'will of the people'. It is something that has to be organised, and part of the modality of its organisation is precisely the use of the coercive force of the state, especially the law which creates norms of behaviour by punishing breaches of them; but crucially, hegemony is not reducible to this.

To gain consent a class must move beyond its narrow corporate self-interest and develop a programme of action which is capable of uniting other social groups behind a common purpose; hence Gramsci refers to hegemony as 'the indissoluble union of political and intellectual and moral leadership' and the 'hegemonic' moment of class formation as one

> in which one becomes aware that one's own corporate interests, in their present and future development, transcend the corporate limits of the purely economic class, and can and must become the interests of other subordinate groups too.
>
> (Quoted Mouffe, 1981: 221f.)

One way to understand this process is to compare it with the notion of an alliance. An alliance consists of two (or more) parties who come to see that they share certain interests, and agree to act in concert; but in doing so each maintains its own identity and in pursuing their common goals they do not create any new, larger unit out of their alliance. But the process of creating a hegemonic class

> involves the creation of a higher synthesis, so that all its elements fuse in a collective will which becomes the new protagonist of new political action . . .
>
> (Mouffe, 1981: 225)

This collective will, Gramsci makes clear, is created through ideology, since its 'very existence depends on the creation of ideological unity which will serve as cement'. The question therefore becomes: 'How can one forge genuine ideological unity between different social groups in such a way as to make them unite into a single political subject?' (Mouffe, 1981: 225). The answer is that it occurs through intellectual and moral leadership, and thus ideological positions are not the by-product of economic processes and of classes constituted there; the subjects of political action arise in the process of struggle for hegemony and therefore they are 'inter-class subjects' (Mouffe, 1981: 227). Yet, at the same time, Gramsci does not lose sight of the traditional Marxist formulation, for he says that only 'fundamental classes' can exercise hegemony, and by fundamental classes he means those that occupy a place defined by the determining layer of a mode of production. Moreover, he argues that there are limits to the action that it is possible for a hegemonic class to undertake, and those limits are imposed by the nature of the mode of production within which it exercises hegemony. What he is arguing is that a mode of production does indeed create places to be filled by agents, which are classes; but that these classes have to be brought into existence by social action, they do not just occur by some spontaneous process. Indeed, it is by exercising hegemony that a class becomes a fundamental class.

These considerations have implications for the theory of the state. In the Marxist tradition, the state is often presented as an 'executive committee for the affairs of the bourgeoisie', but this is not in fact very helpful for it makes the state a by-product of economic processes. Gramsci demonstrates that the process of hegemony may well involve sacrifices on the part of the hegemonic class, for hegemony must be based in genuine concern for the interests of groups over which hegemony is to be exercised, since the state is the terrain on which subordinate groups must be won to the cause of the rulers:

> If hegemony was to be secured without destroying the cohesion of the social formation, and without the continual exercise of naked force, then certain 'costs' might have to be extracted from the dominant ruling class to secure consent to its social and political base. Only the state could, when necessary, impose these political costs on narrower ruling class interests.
>
> (Hall *et al.*, 1978: 204)

Another way to understand this is to see the state as the mechanism in which a fundamental, hegemonic class must appear in order to exercise power (Hall *et al.*, 1978: 196ff.). The state therefore is simultaneously a mechanism for the exercise of class power and yet something that is not just a by-product of the economic power of that class: in order to secure consent for such power it must institute a programme of action that both secures the right conditions for the functioning of the economy and at some level satisfies the demands of subordinate groups. Thus, for example, it is not difficult to see that the rule of law in its current form is in part intended to secure appropriate conditions for a capitalist economy: the law defines and regulates private property; it distinguishes between legitimate and illegitimate ways of acquiring property and enforces the distinction; it enforces contract and establishes employment as a form of contract; etc. Yet, at the same time, the rule of law also benefits subordinate groups, since the law (for example) protects them from the random autocratic exercise of power and protects their property too. The state, that is to say, is always an 'unstable equilibrium' between divergent sets of demands, functioning ultimately to secure the appropriate conditions for the exercise of class rule, conditions which constantly change.

After this long detour through Marxist theories of ideology and hegemony, we are at last in a position to return to the subject of narrative. The last chapter compared two views of narrative: one in which the decisive criterion was truth to the reality of a society, and another where the decisive criterion was truth to a particular experience of the world. By now it is clear that such experience is not something which is independent of the structure of the society in question, but is produced within it, in the form of ideology. We also saw that a large body of commentary on popular fiction was based on the supposition that because it did not present a true understanding of the world around us, it was worthless; the Marxist version of this argument (the Frankfurt School, primarily) saw it as worthless because it did nothing but reproduce ideology, and therefore connived in the subjection of its readers.

However, we have also seen that the theory of ideology itself (certain central features of which are common to Lukács, to the Frankfurt School and to Althusser) was not immune to criticism. Crucially, we saw that ideological positions could not be simply reduced to class positions. In the mechanism of hegemony, ideological positions are always related to securing consent (or to subverting it); hegemony, in short, includes in its mechanism the proposition of subject places, the setting-up of places in an ideological structure which individuals may occupy (or may refuse: no generalisation is possible) and which, if accepted and occupied, would tend to secure the political and economic conditions for the reproduction of class rule. One of the many ways in which subject positions are proposed is through narrative. That is to say, at this point we can see how two areas of concern converge: the analysis of how narrative produces subject positions through its textual operations; and the analysis of how subject positions are produced in other social processes, especially political and economic ones. What is crucial is this: these positions are not simply to be denounced because of their origin, they are to be assessed in terms of where they would lead those who accept them. This is another way of stating a proposition we have already seen, that ideology is a way of securing *in the future* (which always starts now) the conditions necessary for the maintenance of domination.

Now it is central to the theory of hegemony that moral and intellectual leadership by a fundamental class involves a programme of action that is responsive (in some measure) to the demands of subordinated groups, and thus there are always ambiguities in the subject positions that are proposed in it. We shall see repeatedly in the case studies in part II how the subject positions that are offered in popular narrative are simultaneously conducive to accepting domination, accepting an already defined place in the social structure of our society, and at the same time based on a desire for something better; this has often been called the 'utopian moment' of popular narrative. A brief consideration of this theme, based on F. Jameson (1979), will close this chapter.

The commonsense of our culture shows us a boundary between 'high' and 'low' art. 'High' art defines itself as such by refusing the forms of ready comprehensibility and accessibility that characterise 'low' art. At any rate, in capitalist societies 'low' art is usually made available in the form of commodities and produced primarily for profit by the producers. The refusal of easy access and the refusal of commodification go hand in hand in 'high' art, but such art eventually becomes both familiar and commodified anyway. Therefore there is no permanent boundary between 'high' and 'low' art, but a series of ever-shifting, negotiable limits. In fact, the distinction should not be between high and low but between authentic and inauthentic art. Authentic art would be that art which speaks directly to the life activity of some group in the population and which escapes commodification; in practice, in the second half of this century such groups have been peripheral to the major processes and power centres of our society – Jameson mentions black writing and the blues, British 'working-class' rock (Jameson, 1979: 140). Here both modernist 'high' art and mass 'low' art are 'equally dissociated from group praxis'.

Popular fiction (among all the other products of mass culture) manipulates its audience. But manipulation presupposes the existence of wish-fulfilment fantasies on the part of those it manipulates, a desire for something other; popular narrative has the vocation of *managing* this desire, for it

> strategically arouses fantasy content within careful symbolic containment structures which defuse it, gratifying intolerable, unrealisable, properly imperishable desires only to the degree to which they can be laid to rest.

> (Jameson, 1979: 141)

Such works operate by working on real anxieties and hopes about the social order as it exists, and even when dedicated to legitimation of the existing order cannot do their job without deflecting in the latter's service the deepest and most fundamental hopes and fantasies of the collectivity, to which they can therefore, no matter in how distorted a fashion, be found to have given voice.

(ibid.: 144)

Thus manipulation and giving rein to genuine hopes and anxieties are the twin faces of such narratives.

This conception of popular narrative is perhaps easier to understand if rephrased in the terms used earlier. There we saw that the process of hegemony implies that subject positions are produced for people which, if accepted, would in one way or another contribute to the maintenance of a system of domination. These positions do not necessarily correspond directly to the structure of places made available by the economic structure. Thus the economic structure of capitalism (according to Marx) makes available only two positions – exploiter and exploited. These places are in fact occupied by people who are also male or female, speak a language, dream at night, like or dislike football, have consumer tastes and so on. According to the theory of hegemony, the relationships between the places made available in the economic structure and the other places indicated here is not one of simple equivalence or immediate derivation, not even one of necessary correspondence; but the relationships *are* primarily organised around the process of gaining consent for the set of arrangements that provide the basic structure of society, the economic arrangements. Jameson argues that popular narrative in a sense manipulates people: it provides pleasures that are complicit with an order based on domination and exploitation. But at the same time, it can only do so by representing, or referring to, people's real anxieties and hopes, which always derive from some contentious feature or other of the social structure. Such a view of narrative is consistent with the theory of hegemony: narrative produces subject positions, which are manipulative because they tend to slot people into a system of domination; yet they have an element of authenticity because they also defer to people's real emotions about that system (for a similar conclusion based upon a different approach, see Bennett, 1986a; 1986b).

These considerations are abstract, no doubt, and need to be translated into examples. The second half of this book consists of some, others are to be found in these studies: Radway (1981); Gray (1981); Davies (1981); Hall (1986); Bennett (1986b); Bennett and Woollacott (1987). Before we turn to case studies, however, one more concept needs discussion.

7 Genre

'Genre' is the French term commonly used to indicate that texts can be sorted into groups which have common characteristics. For much of this century this notion has been unfashionable in literary criticism, whose overwhelming focus has been the individual text and the reader's response to it. However, in film studies and in the analysis of popular literature it has never been discarded, for here the relevance of membership of a group is obvious: to say that *The Godfather* is a gangster film, or that Agatha Christie writes detective stories, is not a travesty of the texts in question, and it tells us something significant (if obvious) about them. Clearly this is because the commercial structure of film and popular fiction publishing demands a certain level of predictability. This is evident in the commonplace shelf markings in bookshops: 'crime', 'romance', 'war', etc.; also in the use of terms such as 'Western' or 'horror' in film reviewing and advertising.

The concept 'genre' has obvious further uses: if a group of texts has something important in common, then grouping them allows significant generalisations. Especially in the case of the mass media, where individual texts may not be significant except through their cumulative impact as a group, such generalisations are attractive. For example, McQuail, Blumler and Brown (1972) wanted to investigate what gratifications audiences derived from watching different categories of TV shows: quiz shows, domestic and adventure serials. In order to have access to information about audience attitudes, they needed to be sure that the people in question were indeed viewers of such shows. However, specifying individual shows, let alone individual episodes of them, would have made such access more difficult; therefore they investigated viewers who said that their favourite programmes included any in the categories in question. The condition of possibility and the organising presupposition of this investigation is the notion that what each category has in common is more important that what distinguishes the individual shows. The same approach is taken in studies such as *Thrillers* (Palmer, 1978), in which I deduce an ideological stance from common features of all the texts that fit this category. Similar studies abound, for example: Altman (1989), Radway (1984), Wright (1975), Geraghty (1991), or the many psychological and political studies of pornography (e.g. Dworkin, 1981), although some of these studies are based equally on known characteristics of the audience, especially its gender (see chapters 10 and 11). Part II of this book follows a similar path.

The presupposition of such studies is that what the texts have in common is in some measure responsible for the organisation of the reader's or viewer's response to them. McQuail, Blumler and Brown (1972) expressly deny that there is any necessary connection between the nature of the texts and the gratifications found in them, as do other researchers in this tradition; however, it seems unlikely that the meanings attributed by audiences would be utterly unconnected with the immanent nature of the texts. Where a genre has an audience overwhelmingly drawn from one gender (pornography or romance, for example), it is safe to assume some link between the immanent nature of the texts and some feature of the social organisation of gender, one of the forms that ideology takes.

Genre is one dimension of textuality. In what ways can we see genre at work in texts?

Firstly, genre is an element in the 'horizon of expectations' that an audience will have as it follows a story. We have already seen (chapter 1, section 2) that this process operates at various levels in the text; generic identification is one among them. This identification is part of a more general social process whereby members of a society recognise various categories of activity and occasion, and adjust their understanding of what is going on accordingly. For example, if we recognise an event as belonging to the category 'funeral', 'wedding' or 'religious ceremony', we understand others' dress, postures, behaviour, speech, etc., within the framework of this event, and we can understand that different guidelines for conduct exist under these circumstances to what would obtain in an event belonging to the category 'party' or 'entertainment'. This principle can be applied to discursive acts. We recognise the difference between a prayer, a letter, a novel, a news broadcast and so on, and we know that reactions which are appropriate in one instance are not in another: no one says 'amen' at the end of the news, or flees into the countryside during a horror film – though the famous panic induced by Orson Welles' radio version of *War of the Worlds* proves that category confusion *is* possible, if rare (Cantril *et al.*, 1940). Central to correct identification is the label applied to a discursive event by the industry that produces it: film advertisements regularly specify that a story is a 'thriller' or a 'musical', etc. This labelling cues the 'horizon of expectations' the audience brings to the story (Lukow and Ricci, 1984; Neale, 1990). Cantril's study shows that a prime cause of audience panic was tuning in late and missing the label 'Orson Welles' Mercury Theatre'. If we know that a text is a comedy, we are more ready to identify what we see as an invitation to laughter than if we are in doubt about it (on the vexed subject of 'comic cues' see Jefferson, 1979; Handelman and Kapferer, 1972; Palmer, 1987, 21ff.; Palmer, 1991: part 1).

In the first chapter of Elmore Leonard's *Freaky Deaky* (1988), the bomb disposal squad is called in to deal with a booby trap. A known drug dealer has been enticed to sit on a chair whose seat has been fitted with a bomb which will detonate as he stands up. When the squad arrive, they take their time examining the chair and talk about it in a way that suggests something less than urgency – or perhaps it is just laid-back professionalism. They discuss the possibility that the bomb is only a hoax, and that if the man ran very fast as he got up out of the chair, he might just get away with it, but they decide the chances are low to zero. In the meantime, the man in the chair is complaining that he urgently needs to go to the toilet. The cops go out into the yard behind the house, and walk some distance, saying they need to discuss the situation; once out there they talk about something totally different, light-heartedly. After a few moments the bomb explodes, presumably killing the drug dealer; the cops finish their conversation.

Identification of this text as a thriller is likely to lead to a particular interpretation of these events: the cops decided that the man deserved to die, and that they could use him as a guinea pig to see whether the threat of the bomb was genuine or a hoax. The disparity between the situation and the cops' conversation, decodable through commonsense knowledge of the social world, invites this interpretation. But it is likely that prior knowledge of generic conventions will affect the speed with which this process occurs. Firstly, retrospective 'explanations' of unclear events are extremely common in thrillers: at the end of the classic English detective story the detective announces to a stunned audience (and by implication readership) the identity of the murderer, and then describes how he or she came to the correct conclusion. As the thriller tradition lengthened, the explanations became increasingly oblique; in *Freaky Deaky* there is no overt explanation at all, it must be inferred. Secondly, it is generally true in thrillers that anything might turn out to mean something other than what it seems to mean – anything might hide a clue (or be a red herring); any scenery might hide a man with a gun – and therefore the experienced reader is always prepared to reinterpret anything and everything. Thus the implied reader of this sequence, knowledgeable about these conventions, is alert to such indications and follows them up, appreciating the subtlety of what is omitted from the narrative and what it reveals by its absence. While this is only a particular application of the principle of irony, it is one that is dependent upon local narrative conventions – the opacity of events and the 'cool' hero.

A second way in which genre functions is as a norm. In the neo-classical period of literature (the seventeenth and eighteenth centuries), genres were thought to have strict rules, deviation from which would lead to artistic failure. The Romantic interest in individual genius reduced the importance of such concerns, but this traditional use has survived in an attenuated form. For example, Bazin (1955) analyses the Western in terms of a 'classical maturity' of the form exemplified in a few films (e.g. Ford's *Stagecoach*). Such films show what the genre is, and can be used as a measure of other films' success or failure to achieve the same. Schaeffer (1989: 59ff.) shows how such a process was at work in the construction of a canon of literature in the nineteenth century, subsequently fixed in the university syllabus. Genre as a norm is also to be found in readers' judgements. Radway's respondents condemn novels that fail to fit their requirements, and she shows that this condemnation derives from a sense that such novels are failing to conform to a set of ideological norms which are incarnated in the 'good' romances against which they measure the failures (Radway, 1984: 157ff.). At this point, genre considered as a norm is indistinguishable from genre considered as a part of an audience's horizon of expectation.

Thirdly, genre functions as a commercial device. Just as it is used as a labelling device in bookstores, it is available as a guide and a working method to those who create commercial fiction. For example, it is well known that the specialist publishing house Mills & Boon issues a 'form sheet' to prospective authors, indicating to them in outline the rules of the game of romance writing. Similarly, in the heyday of the Hollywood studio system, genre was used as the basis of a division of labour:

Each important studio specialised in two or three genres: Warner Brothers in gangster and war films, Universal in horror, MGM in psychological dramas, 'reverential' biographies and whodunits (a specialty it shared with Fox). Even within these studios, each genre had its particular scenarists, its directors, its sets and sound-stages and its own methods of craftsmanship.

(Vernet, 1978: 13)

These considerations demonstrate that genre, as a level of textuality, has a reality: far from being an artificial device created by critics, it is part of the author's and reader's competence. What remains to be seen is how it functions. The rest of this chapter is devoted to a theoretical outline of an answer; the case studies in part II are all – among other things – further explorations of the same issue.

For reasons to do with the history of literary criticism, there have been many, sometimes incompatible, analyses of the nature of genre (Schaeffer, 1989: *passim*). The most fundamental divergence is between what Todorov has called 'theoretical' and 'historical' genres (1970: 18).

'Theoretical' genres are assigned on the basis of the distribution of some fundamental traits throughout the entire body of all (conceivable) texts. For example, Plato divided all fiction into three categories: the diegetic, where the poet speaks entirely in his own voice; the mimetic, where (s)he speaks only via someone else (i.e. an actor); and the mixed, where both modes obtain (Genette, 1986: 96). Here the fundamental trait in question is the mode of enunciation. In principle, the critic is obliged to assign to this trait the primary responsibility for the nature of the works in question.

A 'historical' genre is any collection of works that can be shown to have some important trait in common, even though the presence or absence of such a trait is not asserted to be a relevant consideration in other areas of fiction. Such genres would be: the Hollywood Western, the Arthurian romance, the Norse saga, the sitcom, the sonnet, etc. Each of these can be defined, but the traits that define them do not derive from some fundamental characteristic of all fiction as is the case in 'theoretical' genres.

It is convenient to start with theoretical genres. On what grounds is it possible to distinguish between them? Broadly speaking, there have traditionally been two types of grounds: firstly, the enunciative situation, as in Plato; secondly, the subject matter of the texts. (This distinction reproduces the linguistic distinction between 'utterance' and 'statement' – see chapter 4).

Distinctions based on the enunciative situation distinguish between theoretical genres insofar as enunciative situations are universal and finite in number: that is to say, a question is always a question, a narration is always a narration, a prayer is always a prayer; a promise, a threat, etc., likewise. These are held to be universal features of all conceivable verbal communication situations (Schaeffer, 1989: 82ff., 157f.). Thus to take again the example of Plato's classification of fiction: at any given moment, the author must either speak in his own voice or use the voice of another, namely one of his or her characters. This distinction is universal, true of all verbal texts; therefore there are three theoretical genres derived from permutating and combining these two possibilities. Aristotle takes up Plato's distinction but modifies its terms: he discards the possibility of pure diegesis (the poet speaking entirely in his own voice), probably because Plato's example (the dithyramb) had already disappeared from Greek fiction by Aristotle's time; when he discusses diegesis his examples are always epic poetry, especially Homer, where the poet both speaks in his own voice and uses the voice of characters, thus mixing diegetic and mimetic modes. For Aristotle, therefore, there are only two genres based upon enunciation (the mimetic and the mixed) despite the fact that *in theory* the diegetic must exist in order for the mixed to exist (Genette, 1986: 95ff.).

Schaeffer develops the possibilities of the enunciative situation further, distinguishing also, for example, between texts spoken by real, fictitious or faked narrators: in the case of the real narrator we would have a text in which the actual author appears directly – a signed letter, for example; an instance of a fictitious narrator would be Scheherazade in the *Arabian Nights* or any first-person narration by a character, as in Chandler's Philip Marlowe novels; a faked narrator would be a real historical character appearing in fictitious guise, as for instance when words are put into such a person's mouth by a subsequent writer. Schaeffer also distinguishes between fiction and non-fiction as a basic enunciative modality, which does not coincide with the first distinction, since real, fictitious and faked narrators may appear in varying dosages in both fiction and non-fiction. He develops a further set of distinctions based upon the addressee of the text: is it addressed to someone in particular (a letter, a panegyric, a prayer) or to anyone who happens to receive it (the public who buy copies of a book)? As is well known in the history of English literature, Wordsworth bases his revolution in style partly upon the fact that he is writing for an 'absent public', i.e. one who reads poems in print, rather than listening to them recited, as was still the norm earlier in the eighteenth century. These distinctions also enable us to define such genres as the epistolary novel or the news.

Certainly this process can be taken even further. We may distinguish not only between oral and written delivery, but also between other media too. Chatman has analysed how the differences between film and printed prose as media affect the narration of the 'same' story, using Renoir's adaptation of a Maupassant short story as an example (*Une Partie de Campagne*). Maupassant writes, of the heroine on a swing,

> She was a pretty girl of about eighteen; one of those women who suddenly excite your desire when you meet them in the street . . .

It is impossible to translate 'pretty' into film, since it is the narrator's evaluation, and also sufficiently vague to allow flexibility of interpretation by the reader; in the film we simply see an actress whom the director thinks corresponds to this ideal (in 1936). Similarly, the generalisation about such women in Maupassant tells us something about the narrator (urban, cynical, randy); in the film, we see the girl from the point of view of the young men who will later seduce her and her mother – they are shown as voyeurs (Chatman, 1980: 126ff.). In short, the transition from one enunciative modality to another has resulted in a shift in narrative structure.

A well-known point about soap opera refers to a similar distinction. In soap, non-regular viewers of a series may simply fail to see pertinent features of an incident because they do not have enough knowledge of the relationships between the characters to understand what is going on. As one recent writer has put it, the 'implied reader' of soap opera is more likely to be a middle-aged housewife than a male semiotician (Allen, 1983: 103). In other words, the serial features of soap opera make it enunciatively and narratively distinct from otherwise similar texts such as romance and melodrama (see below, chapters 10 and 11).

It is tempting to think that in these two examples it is the medium that is responsible for the differences noted. But strictly speaking this is not so, since both print and film have various different enunciative possibilities – we have seen examples in print; in film, documentary is clearly different from fiction. Where the TV example is concerned, the medium does not in itself create the serial format, though it certainly favours it, since the serial format was invented on radio, and anyway there is much TV that is not serial. Moreover, it is possible to rethink the concept of 'medium' in enunciative terms. Plato's distinction between diegesis and mimesis does not work for film because the camera bears the narrative and is neither the poet's own voice nor the voice of a character. However, we could also say that film has a different dosage of diegesis and mimesis to both theatre and novel as well as a different set of technical means of production.

We may none the less doubt whether enunciative situations are as universal as Schaeffer indicates. While it is apparently true that a question is always a question, the ambiguity of the 'rhetorical question' (question or assertion?) somewhat erodes the clarity of the distinction, as does the old joke 'Is that a threat or a promise?': both indicate that variations in the relationships between the partners to the dialogue may change the nature of the speech actt. More importantly, it is clear that there are enunciative situations which are culture specific, not reproduced outside of particular sociological boundaries. For example, in Japanese and Korean, social status is grammaticalised and the personal pronouns used in ordinary direct speech vary according to the ranks of the participants in dialogue (Lyons, 1977: 641). The 'royal we' of the old regimes in Europe is similar: this is an enunciative situation defined by the social role 'royal public speech', which is not reproducible elsewhere. In traditional Winnebago society, there are two completely different categories of story which are told, one when the snakes are above ground, one when they are below; again this is an enunciative situation not produced elsewhere, defined in a set of 'religious' beliefs. In Britain, the Christmas pantomime traditionally includes roles played by large men in female costume; because of the enunciative situation, it is known that the 'travesty' is comic, not sexual. These examples demonstrate that it is not always possible – perhaps never possible – to separate enunciative situations from elements of the social structure, ultimately institutionally defined. This implies that attempts to list a set of 'universal' enunciative positions may be vain.

The second basis for distinguishing between theoretical genres is the subject matter of texts.

In Aristotle, genres are distinguished on the same enunciative grounds as in Plato. However, these grounds are doubled by a set of new distinctions based on subject matter: here the basis of the distinction is the level of the people and actions represented, which must be either above, below or equal to us – in terms which are either moral or social or both. Clearly all conceivable actions must come into one or other of these categories, and therefore the genre distinction is still a theoretical one (Genette, 1986: 97–100). Aristotle's classification of genres is representable as a diagram:

| | | *Mode* | |
		Imitation	Narrative
Actions represented	Above	Tragedy	Epic
	Below	Comedy	Parody

As Genette shows, it is this mixed way of distinguishing genres that was inherited by Renaissance and post-Renaissance critics. It was modified by the Romantics in a historicist manner: genres were shown to correspond to different types of social order, and were organised in an evolutionary scale. Both Genette and Schaeffer show that such theories are marked by a high level of inconsistency.

In recent criticism, distinctions based on subject matter have usually been oriented towards historical genres rather than theoretical. Consideration of part of Northrop Frye's schema will demonstrate why (Frye, 1971: 33ff.). Here Frye divides fiction into five modes where the hero is either (a) superior in principle to the reader and the laws of nature (myth); (b) superior in degree to reader and nature (legend and fairy story); (c) superior in degree to the reader but not to the laws of nature (high mimetic); (d) equal to both reader and laws of nature (low mimetic); (e) inferior to the reader (irony). This set of distinctions can easily be read as an analysis of theoretical genres, where the fundamental trait is the hierarchical relationship between a single fictional entity (the hero) and the world outside the text in the form of the implied reader and a conception of the order of nature. This is how Todorov reads Frye (1970: 13–17).

However, if we are strict about using these distinctions as the basis of a set of *theoretical* genres, we must recognise that there are several possible combinations of the entities in question which Frye does not mention. For example, in theory (which is what we are talking about) there ought to be a genre in which the hero is superior in kind to the reader, but not to the laws of nature, and another in which (s)he is superior (or inferior) in both kind and degree to the reader but not to nature; the first instance might fit some examples of science fiction, with a human-ish hero from a 'superior' civilisation (a

Spock-like figure, perhaps), and in the second category one might put some of Tolkien's characters. In a sense it is stupid to blame Frye for not including genres that do not exist, but the point about theoretical genres is that the matrix of possibilities that derives from permutating and combining the traits out of which they are made up allows one to predict future texts that do not exist yet, just as the grammar of a language allows one to make up sentences that have never been spoken before. If we remember this, we can see that in fact Frye's schema is really a list of historical genres, inductively based, and the claims that both he and Todorov make for its status as theory are exaggerated (Brooke-Rose, 1981: 55ff.).

Despite appearances, this is not a criticism of Frye: it is intended to demonstrate only that distinctions based upon subject matter are rarely, if ever, as universal as earlier centuries imagined. Specifically, it seems to be impossible to construct any schema based upon subject matter in which every text fits unequivocally into one category or another; as Frye remarks about his own classifications, all texts fit into various parts of it, and the purpose of the schema is much less some watertight system than an attempt to alert readers to various features of texts which are 'intertextual': 'Much of our sense of the subtlety of great literature comes from this modal counterpoint' (Frye, 1971: 50f.). Thus it seems impossible to use subject matter as the basis for distinguishing theoretical genres, and such attempts are in fact delineations of historical genres.

On what grounds is it possible to distinguish historical genres? Many attempts to create such classification systems have been made, elements of which will be summarised in the case studies in part II. Briefly, they may be based upon enunciative elements or upon contents; defining soap opera in terms of seriality and in terms of definitions of action deriving from modern social gender roles clearly involves both types of definition. Defining sitcom in terms of plot elements, the nature of comic enunciation and TV seriality also refers to both forms of classification. Probably the majority of such attempts have been based more upon contents than upon enunciative modality: Wright's analysis of the Western is a good example (see above, chapter 2).

More importantly, analyses of historical genres have tended to fall into two broad categories: studies in which what is sought is a tight, exclusive definition, where the boundaries between belonging and not belonging to a genre are clear; and studies where a loose definition is sought, where genre is not a precisely ordered group of texts, but an approximation, a horizon of expectations for the readership, a series of imprecise 'echoes' between texts, one regime among others of the organisation of intertextuality and in no way privileged above the others.

An example of the second way of analysing genre is to be found in Bennett and Woollacott's *Bond and Beyond* (1987). Here the authors demonstrate that the novels and films about James Bond cannot be understood by referring to a single fictional framework (nor indeed to a single sociological one): the stories have the impact that they have, on particular reading publics, within a variety of frameworks. Thus, for instance, when the novels first appeared in Britain in the 1950s they were seen primarily (the evidence of reviews suggests) as new examples of an older British form, the 'imperialist spy thriller' as practised by authors such as John Buchan. This genre, as Denning (1987: 18ff.) has shown, appealed to a wide variety of readers, from all classes, and was characterised by the portrayal of violent action in the service of nationhood, usually at the expense of 'unsavoury foreigners'.

Clearly there are elements in the early Bond novels which relate them directly to this tradition, and readers who were already familiar with it would no doubt have readily assimilated the Bond novels to their earlier fictional experiences. However, this genre had virtually no currency outside Britain (and perhaps the Commonwealth countries), and the Bond novels – especially after the success of the early films – were internationally successful. The evidence of reviews in the USA suggests that the Bond stories were first seen as examples of the hard-boiled detective tradition, and were readily compared to Mickey Spillane's immensely successful Mike Hammer stories, especially as Hammer was as often pitted against Soviet agents as against Mafiosi and assorted American thugs. Indeed there are elements in the Bond novels which more easily fit with the American tradition than the British one, especially the portrayal of sexuality, central to the American novels and to Bond, distinctly peripheral if not entirely absent from the British tradition. There is some evidence (Worpole, 1983: 31ff.) that British working-class readers were more interested in the American hard-boiled tradition than the British spy-thriller.

The success of the films in the early 1960s, and the novels written subsequently, leads one to seek yet a different kind of explanation of the stories. As Bennett and Woollacott point out, the Bond films were received in the 1960s as part of a generalised cultural anti-conservatism which 'in some respects' squares badly with the genre-based readings, especially that which asserts the primacy of the traditional British imperialist spy-thriller. Here the authors lay stress on the new way in which women's sexuality was represented in the Bond stories. Whereas in British film, and to a lesser extent American, women's sexuality had been presented primarily in the context of marriage, the family and domesticity, and attempts to break out of that order had tended to be portrayed negatively, in the Bond films women were portrayed as sexually 'free' in the sense that their sexuality was no longer tied to the family in the same way. Of course, as the women's movement has often pointed out since (e.g. Haskell, 1974), this freedom in no way challenged the status of men as dominant in the social order, since the Bond girls have always functioned as objects of male desire rather than subjects of female desire; none the less, this new freedom from domesticated sexuality was welcomed by women as much as by men, and may explain – Bennett and Woollacott hypothesise – the success of the Bond films with a female audience too. Certainly in the films many of the traditional spy-thriller elements are the subject of mild parody, whereas Bond's sexuality becomes increasingly the focus of the stories and often the main skill which is responsible for his success against his enemies as he recruits their female allies to his bed and his cause.

Such an interpretation of the Bond stories pulls against any notion of genre which is fixed and stable, where there is a single coherent way of organising material which is constant across a body of texts:

> there is no place – no cultural space – in which the individual texts of Bond can be stabilised as objects to be investigated 'in themselves', except by abstracting them from the shifting relations of inter-textuality through which their consumption has been regulated.
>
> (Bennett and Woollacott, 1987: 90)

At the other end of this scale is to be found a series of studies such as Wright (1975) and Radway (1984), which demonstrates the existence of a single matrix of fictional procedures underlying a large body of texts. Both Wright and Radway are summarised elsewhere in this book, and the example chosen here is my *Thrillers* (Palmer, 1978). The argument pursued in this text is that a large corpus of fiction, often known under various titles such as 'detective stories', 'hard-boiled detective stories', 'shockers', 'spy stories', 'crime fiction', etc., is in fact unified by a common procedure: the investigation of a criminal mystery by a hero. This procedure is not only common to all such texts, but more importantly it dominates the internal composition of each of them, in this way: firstly, the hero is the main focalisation device, the person whose point of view dominates the flow of each text, both because all other characters are contrasted unfavourably with him and because our information about the course of events is largely dependent upon his investigations; secondly, the criminal mystery dominates each text to the extent that all the events in the narrative contribute to the enigma and its solution by the hero. Thus the combination of these two elements into a dominant procedure produces the specific qualities associated with such texts, and at the same time shows how they are capable of producing meaning. Genre is therefore seen here not just as a series of features that texts share, but as a feature which is directly responsible for the place that all the other elements in these texts occupy, elements which may be very varied but which are always pulled into the space assigned them by this dominant procedure.

A second stage of this argument shows how this procedure itself derives from the field of ideology, and therefore has an existence independent of the texts in question; this existence is the way in which such texts are rooted in ideology. This material consists of a vision of the relationship between the (male) individual and the social order. The central character, the hero, is alone capable of dissipating the threat to the social order that is posed by an act of criminal violence: it is he who reveals the culprit's identity and apprehends or eliminates him or her. At the same time, the hero always responds to prior aggression: at the beginning of the story (or, perhaps, immediately before its beginning) order rules, but is then disrupted by criminal action; the hero acts ultimately to restore order on society's behalf. In doing so he defines himself as admirable because more adept at restoring order than others. He is thus able to assert himself in a totally untrammelled manner, just as the villains do, but with entire justification, since he is acting on behalf of others, in order to restore a disrupted order. The actions that the villain and the hero undertake may be similar in many respects, but they are always morally distinct because of the justification of response to prior aggression and the criminal attempt to undermine the social order. Thus the central thematic material of the thriller presents a definition of individualism and a definition of the social order: the social order is naturally good, all evil in it implicitly derives from criminal conspiracy; the individual is defined by the capacity for self-assertion over others.[1]

Without trying to assess which of these two approaches to historical genres is correct, we may say that the examples chosen represent polar opposites to their analysis. In one version, genre is a loose assemblage of themes and readings, a horizon of expectations infinitely renegotiable by various reading publics; in the other it is a definite (if infinitely extendable) list of texts unified by a common procedure which is responsible for the internal organisation of each constituent text.

It is interesting to note that in the most influential single text on genre theory produced during recent years, both these tendencies are present. Neale (1981a) argues that cinematic genres cannot in fact be differentiated from each other on the basis of a set of formal properties as if these properties were in some way the essence of a genre, rather a genre should be seen as a system of orientations circulating between audience, industry and text. But he also argues, apropos particular genres, that they can be distinguished from each other by particular combinations of discourses. Thus, for example, if narrative is always initiated by disequilibrium, the discursive source of disequilibrium is different in different genres; in the Western, the detective story and the gangster film, it is violence; in the musical and melodrama, sexual desire; in horror, the transgression of human/natural boundary. These link with 'more specific generic elements and . . . codes that are specific to cinema'. Genres differ in the articulation of shared discourses to each other, and to these other elements:

> Generic specificity is a question not of particular and exclusive elements . . . but of exclusive and particular combinations and articulations of elements, of the exclusive and particular weight given in any one genre to elements which it in fact shares with other genres.
>
> (Neale, 1981a: 9)

We have seen a series of conflicting, incompatible ways of analysing the theory of genre; is there any way of choosing between these various approaches?

Schaeffer (1989: 156ff.) suggests a partial way beyond some of the impasses we have noted. He points to an asymmetry between genre distinctions based on enunciative modalities and genre distinctions based upon content. Where the distinction is enunciative, it establishes nothing more than membership or non-membership of a class, and tells us nothing about the contents of any of the texts in question. Common membership of such a class in no way implies any other sort of equivalence between texts: the fact that *No Sex Please, We're British* and Sophocles' *Oedipus the King* are both plays tells us nothing more than that. Such distinctions are relatively easy to establish conclusively – it is not difficult to distinguish a play from a letter from a prayer from a novel – and membership of a class so established is exclusive: a text is assigned in its totality to one or other. Genre distinctions based on content, on the other hand, are never exclusive, because it is empirically verifiable that there are no texts which share 'supra-sentential textual segments' of sufficient importance to assign the texts as a whole to membership of the same class. Therefore genre classifications based on content are always one system of intertextuality among others which traverse a given text: Schaeffer's arguments here are no different from Frye's or Bennett and Woollacott's.

What we learn from this is that one category of genre classification can be accepted unproblematically, but that such classification may tell us nothing interesting about the texts in question. However, despite Schaeffer's unwillingness to contemplate systematic links between enunciative modality and content (1989: 169f.), enunciative mode may well in fact be significant at the level of content too, as the recent debates about the difference between TV and film as media show (see e.g. Kaplan, 1983; Newcomb, 1988; Paterson, 1980). This indicates that the distinction between the two forms of classification of genres is probably not as watertight as first sight suggests. Moreover, Schaeffer's assertion that at the level of content, texts never have sufficiently important procedures in common to warrant including texts 'as a whole' in any single genre classification, must be assessed in the light of the numerous studies – many quoted in this volume – which show such procedures at work. What is crucial in this debate is the question of aesthetic domination: for Schaeffer, what texts have in common is never arranged hierarchically, the various elements that are common are simply arranged side by side, in passive contiguity. But in the studies quoted here (Neale, 1981a; Palmer, 1978; Radway, 1984; Wright, 1975; Todorov, 1970) the procedures which determine membership of a genre are always procedures which are responsible for the placing of all the other elements used in the texts. Here genre is always a matter of 'aesthetic domination' or of a 'hierarchy of discourses'.

It would seem, from the evidence of the arguments followed here, that if there is to be a resolution to the question of different ways of analysing genre, it may be that the hierarchy of discourses is it, in this sense: where it is possible to show that a given group of texts in fact does have a dominating procedure in common, then we are in the presence of a genre; where no dominating procedure is involved, then the mere fact of some common elements should not be taken to indicate genre – or at least it should be recognised that the word genre is being used in two different senses, where one sense is much stronger than the other, which may be regarded either as heuristic convenience, or as an indication of some form of 'horizon of expectations' on the part of the audience. Where genre is used in the strong sense, it is probably the case that many texts will not belong to any genre at all; where it is used in the weaker sense of a horizon of expectations, it is likely that all texts will be traversed by some level of genre-based expectations, but the dosage will vary greatly. In general it seems likely that the strong sense will be more readily applicable in the mass media and popular literature than it will in canonical literature of the modern period.

One final point needs to be made. The conceptions of genre which have been discussed so far tend to be essentially static, or synchronic: genre is defined as such-and-such, and the definition is thought to obtain in a certain number of cases *whose distribution through time is non-relevant*. In this conception, genres do not change: they either exist or they do not; modifications to them are always seen simply as ways of working through implications that were latent in earlier stages. However, there are exceptions. For example, Lukow and Ricci (1984) read the succession of gangster films between 1932 and 1939 in an explicitly diachronic manner. Here genre is one of the 'relays' that link a film to its audience, others being advertisements, fanzines, titles and star identities, etc. But genre is a dynamic construct (ibid.: 30), and they show how the development of the gangster tradition involved placing the spectator differently in relation to that tradition as the sequence of films unfolded. For example, in *The Roaring Twenties*, a series of devices addresses the spectator directly, without being incorporated in the narrative (i.e. these are 'extra-diegetic'): a written 'Foreword', an introductory pseudo-newsreel, an off-screen narrator, montage transitions between events that constantly interrupt the story, superimposed dates, etc. These devices invite

> the audience to remember the genre and to place it historically within a larger framework. They contain some extraordinary structures of historical figuration which sew the film into the genre's history while at the same time *distancing* it from that genre.
>
> (Lukow and Ricci, 1984: 34)

In the case of Bennett and Woollacott (1987), modification is built into the definition of genre, since it is no more than an approximate assemblage of expectations and themes, constantly subject to change as reading publics change. There seems little doubt that future work on genre must start from non-static definitions (Neale, 1990).

Part II
Case studies

8 Crime fiction: the genre dimension

What does it mean to speak of *crime* fiction? Many stories include criminal activity in their material: *Oedipus the King*, *Crime and Punishment*, *Little Dorrit* and *Scarlet and Black* are just a few; yet none of them would normally be called 'crime fiction'. A story is usually labelled a crime story when it is clear that the portrayal of criminal activity is absolutely central to the nature of the story. As we have seen in the previous chapter, one of the ways of understanding genre is in terms of some 'dominant procedure' that is responsible for the way in which the text as a whole unfolds. A clear example of this is the classic English detective story, where the entire story is concerned with the elucidation of a criminal mystery: whodunit? Once the identity of the murderer is known the story finishes. In my *Thrillers* (1978) (summarised in chapter 7) I argued that this procedure (somewhat extended) could be used as the basis of an account of crime fiction in general.

However, it is evident that there are in fact problems with this account. As D. Bennett (1979) shows, the classic English detective novel is characterised by a double narrative: the narrative of the investigation and the narrative of the murder. Sequentially the narrative follows the investigation, which gradually restores fragments of the 'lost' narrative of the murder. The puzzle-like quality gives the reader the illusion that (s)he has as much chance as the detective of solving the mystery, although in reality (a) the author weights all the chances in the detective's favour; and (b) the narrator, whether first person or third, may be unreliable – the classic instance is *The Murder of Roger Ackroyd* (Christie, 1967). The two narratives are kept in balance – neither is more important than the other, since the narrative of the investigation is entirely oriented towards producing the narrative of the murder, even though the former dominates the sequence of the novel.

In the hard-boiled thriller, the narrative of the investigation is likely to be more important than that of the murder, since revelation of criminal identity is far from the most important thing in the text. There is no pretence of 'fair play' between author and reader: the latter knows perfectly well that only the detective can solve the puzzle, whose skills include skills of violence and the capacity to judge the reliability of others in non-logical ways. Such fundamental differences may make it fruitless to think of these novels as 'the same as' classic English detective stories. The 'hard-boiled school' could be argued to have at least as much in common with stories about gentleman adventurers (such as John Buchan's novels) as with detective stories like Agatha Christie's (Glover, 1989); certainly the two types of story had different reading publics (Worpole, 1983: 30ff.; Denning, 1987: 24f.). Moreover, my discussion of the thriller hero largely ignored the relationship of gender to the types of action held up to our admiration, a clear omission (Glover, 1989). Furthermore, there are many crime stories where either there is no mystery at all or where it is relatively unimportant (such as many of the James Bond novels and especially films), and where the hero may be less than admirable in some way or other: in gangster stories (e.g. Burnett's *Little Caesar* (1929) and the subsequent best-selling film) he may be as evil as he is admirable. In novels such as Cornell Woolrich's, and the many films made from them (*Rear Window*, *The Bride Wore Black*, *Phantom Lady*, *The Night Has a Thousand Eyes* to name a few, the hero may be too weak to cope with the situation; in novels about people on the run he may simply be concerned to save his own skin and only partially capable of doing so (e.g. Goodis, 1956). In all of these instances, mystery is a minimal component of the narrative.

This lists a series of texts and narrative themes that are in one way or another anomalous with respect to my earlier theory of thrillers. One solution to such anomalies is to divide the corpus of crime fiction into subgenres. In an early text on *film noir*, Borde and Chaumeton (1955: 7) distinguish between crime fiction from the point of view of law and order, and crime fiction from the point of view of the criminal; this distinction seems to make obvious sense, since the gangster story is different from the detective story in precisely this way. As Shadoian (1977: 3) argues, the gangster becomes a metaphor for opposition to the social order in general; and in the films that he analyses, the gangster is presented as a sympathetic figure, at least partially. There are also more complex subdivisions, involving categories such as the 'caper story', the 'police procedural', etc. Such attempts are never exhaustive, and tend to obscure more than they reveal (see Cawelti,

1976; cf. Denning, 1987: 7f.). The dubious nature of such an enterprise is easily shown: until the Second World War, Erle Stanley Gardner's Perry Mason stories counted as 'hard-boiled' and were published in *Black Mask*, the classic private eye magazine; since the Second World War they have usually been regarded as closer to the classic English detective story. Similarly, in film history, the iconography of the gangster film was easily transferred to stories about hard-boiled private eyes when Hollywood censorship effectively eliminated the gangster film in its earliest form (Clarens, 1980: 116–39).

Such classification systems are primarily an attempt to handle generic innovation, and it is always questionable whether there is some deeper layer of meaning below the level of the obvious surface identifications, which is also common to all crime fiction. A prime candidate is clearly the universality and centrality of the portrayal of crime in crime fiction: what is the significance of the fact that crime fiction is about crime? We can only answer this question by considering the nature of crime as a discursive construct, or at least those aspects of it which are relevant here.

Crime, at least in modern societies, is always a challenge to the legitimacy of a supposedly universal social and moral order (see Palmer (1976) for a discussion of differences in the pre-industrial period). Crime therefore represents one of the frontiers of society: to step into crime involves stepping beyond the bounds of a particular moral universe. Of course, it is true that in the real world, different sections of the population evaluate participation in different criminal activities in a variety of ways; but the most widely accepted morality of our societies, the one that is backed by the force of institutions such as the education system, the criminal law, and the informal judgement system of 'respectability', indeed asserts just this. In a real sense, the commission of crime sets one beyond a particular boundary, at least until others are convinced that reform is sincere and permanent. As a result, crime is among other things always potentially exciting – 'daemonic', as Auden calls it in a discussion of the detective story (Auden, 1948): stepping across the moral boundary is inherently risky and involves a certain level of self-commitment. Investigation of crime is therefore always an attempt to reinforce moral boundaries and to suppress the activity of someone who has chosen to live beyond the margins of what is permissible; it is usually also an activity fraught with risk.

These considerations apply with increased force where violence, and especially murder, is concerned. The person who commits murder has taken one of the few virtually irrevocable steps beyond the boundaries of our moral universe and has therefore enacted a self-commitment of the highest order. The level of potential excitement is increased by so much. To choose to act violently is to choose a course of action from which there is no turning back, in the sense that if we accept to escalate any confrontation to the level at which it takes the form of physical force, there is no instance of judgement which lies beyond it and to which we can refer the discord in question in an attempt to return to a status quo ante: to step down under these circumstances is always to admit defeat. In this sense we can say that violence is the *ultima ratio* of our society, the 'reason' which obtains when all other forms of reason fail.

This discursive construction of violence is seen with particular clarity in traditional philosophical debates about the role of violence as the foundation of the social order. The problem which is addressed is this: how does the state of civilisation, the fact of living in an organised community, emerge from the state which precedes it, the state of nature, as Hobbes calls it? The common answer refers to the necessity of force in this process, since in the state of nature, men's desires are ruled by nothing other than the possibilities of satisfying them, and therefore any situation in which the satisfaction of individual desires is to be subject to the common good must be characterised by some mechanism for subduing recalcitrant individuals. This – in an oversimplified form – is the answer given by Hobbes. In Hegel the answer takes a somewhat different form, since Hegel's starting-point is not the relationship of men to natural resources, but the relationship of men to each other, and he postulates that all relationships are necessarily characterised by domination and subordination. In Rousseau, the 'social contract' is intended to avoid the postulation of violence as the basis of sociality, but he is unable to answer the awkward question as to how the willingness to submit to the law, which is a product of the law, can also serve as its foundation.

As has often been observed of these thinkers, basic to their thought is the notion that men in the state of nature are the same as men in the state of society, and therefore the mechanisms of the state of civilisation are simply those that nature demands to make men civilised; it follows from this that anything postulated about the transition from the state of nature to the state of civilisation must also apply to the state of civilisation itself. Violence is intrinsic to this latter situation too, for it is only through the use of force – actual or potential – that any community can guarantee its existence both in terms of its relationship to other communities, and in terms of its internal structure. Its external relationships are founded on violence in the sense that there is no other ultimate arbiter of independence than the capacity for self-defence, and its internal structure is founded on violence in the sense that whatever set of relationships may compose that structure, their continuance can ultimately only be assured by the use of force to prevent their replacement by something else; an obvious example is contract, where enforcement must be possible if one party reneges.

However, there is a flaw in this argument. Central to the premisses of each of the arguments about the role of violence in the foundation of the social order is the assumption that the world is fundamentally composed of entities which are identical, separate and independent, and whose fundamental characteristic is to be in competition with each other in one form or another – for scarce resources or for domination. In short, it is basic to these arguments that the world is fundamentally composed of individuals, and that the fundamental characteristic of individuality is competition.[1] But we should not think that the demonstration of logical flaws in the classical argument about violence and its application to vicarious individual violence lessens its applicability here. Quite the contrary, it demonstrates all the more clearly how and why it is applicable; for the fundamental postulate of such arguments, we have seen, is the nature and position of the individual within the social order. Thus this representation of the individual in his (the role of gender will be analysed later) commitment to violence is one more version of the ideology of individualism, making a particular contribution to the definition of individualism as primarily competitive. Indeed, the positioning of the spectator/reader in relationship to the hero's skills of violence – the aesthetic of admiration – is the modality in which texts of this variety make their distinctive contribution to ideology.

What this argument about the nature of crime and violence demonstrates is that the ubiquitous presence of crime in crime fiction is not without effects on its aesthetic structure. We can turn to a further example to see how far it is possible to pursue this argument.

In crime fiction the hermeneutic code is constructed in a particular relationship between story-time and narrative-time. Drummond (1976) demonstrates how this process works in the pre-credit sequence of an episode of the British TV police series *The Sweeney*. As is usual in detective fiction, the narrative opens with an act of disruption or disequilibrium initiated by a criminal act, performed by someone other than the hero, which is usually mysterious to the audience as well as to the hero (Palmer, 1978: 23). In the pre-credit sequence in question a series of shots shows 'life as normal' in a police station. Suddenly a large number of alarm bells start to ring, leaving the police dumbfounded with helpless amazement since the scale of the disruption visibly exceeds any response possible to them. The source of the disruption is only partially explained: the film cuts to a man on a roof who is clearly involved in some activity that is responsible, but whose nature is entirely unclear. In the sequence of shots portraying the police station, the space is fragmented by a series of close-ups in a staccato rhythm, which indicates the uncertainty the police feel: thus a vacuum is created, the vacuum of these policemen's incapacity to deal with a situation; into this vacuum step the recurrent central characters of the series. Through the programme as a whole this enigma is further elucidated, and ultimately resolved, by the actions of the central characters.

What we see here is how some events in story are represented extensively in narrative (the events inside the police-station) while others (involving the villains) are only shown in enigmatic excerpt. In other words, the hermeneutic code – that general procedure whereby narrative enigmas are set up, creating the desire for closure and resolution on the part of the reader – is commonly constructed on a particular narratological basis in much crime fiction. (More exactly, this is part of the hermeneutic code, since another important part is the question: will the hero succeed in solving this mystery?) In the texts analysed here this code, constructed on the basis of discrepancies between story- and narrative-time or space, controls much of the flow of the subsequent narrative: to this extent my earlier assertion (Palmer, 1978: 22f., 86f.) that mystery is an essential component of thrillers can be rephrased in narratological terms. But we have already seen that there are many crime stories in which mystery plays either no part or a distinctly subordinate one. Can we replace the notion of mystery with the more precise narratological concepts of hermeneutic code and the relationship between story and narrative, and find some more widespread common ground in crime fiction?

F. Iles' *Malice Aforethought* (1979) is an example of a crime novel in which there is no mystery in the usual sense: we know at the beginning that Dr Bickleigh is going to murder his wife; the interest of the story derives from why and how, and from suspense about whether he will be discovered. Specifically, the novel opens with a sentence in which the doctor's intentions are made clear:

It was not until several weeks after he had decided to murder his wife that Dr Bickleigh took any active steps in the matter.

(Iles, 1979: 7)

In narration these two events (decision, action) occupy a different place to the ones they occupy in story. In story-time, everything begins with Bickleigh's childhood, education and marriage (narrated very briefly in chapter 2); the events in story that are accorded more detail in narration begin with a tennis party given by the Bickleighs, at the end of which the doctor wishes his wife were dead. Four chapters later, in narration, he effectively decides to kill her, and starts the process in the following chapter. Once the narration of the tennis party has begun, story-sequence and narrative-sequence do not diverge very much. That is to say, the opening sentence of the book encapsulates events in story-time that occur long after the next event that is narrated, namely the tennis party. The effect of this transposition in sequence is to change the meaning of everything that follows. Much of what follows in the first half of the novel is a 'comedy of manners' (see Grella, 1970, for a discussion of the relationship between the classic English detective story and the 'novel of manners'): we watch a series of minor social conflicts, deceptions and misunderstandings, all narrated in an ironical manner to make it clear that Bickleigh has a limited understanding of other people's opinions of him. However, these events are all narrated in the context of the reader's knowledge that Bickleigh is going to murder his wife, and therefore we are constantly led to ask ourselves what relationship there is between this prediction and what we are witnessing at such-and-such a moment in the narrative. In narratological terms, the first sentence sets up a hermeneutic enigma: how, when and why will Bickleigh kill his wife? Will he be caught? Each event in the proairetic sequence that follows (tennis match, amorous rendezvous, etc.) occupies some place or other in the hermeneutic code as well, that is, its meaning is changed by being placed after the narration of the doctor's intention.

Two things may be learnt from this narratological rephrasing of commonsense analysis of the text. Firstly, all narratives have both a hermeneutic and a proairetic code; what is distinctive about *Malice Aforethought* and thrillers in general is that what links the two codes is a criminal action, murder. It is axiomatic among critics and practitioners of the classic English detective story that everything in the story should have a direct link to the solution of the murder mystery (e.g. Haycraft, 1941: 225f.). In narratological terms, this means that every element that figures in the proairetic code should also figure in the hermeneutic code too, whence the high degree of unity often displayed by such texts.

As we have already seen, the portrayal of violence logically implies the portrayal of a certain level of personal commitment and a certain conception of the individual, and therefore the link of the two codes in the act of murder gives a very particular meaning to all the events that are subsumed into them. That is to say, to open a novel by announcing the intention to murder changes the meaning of what follows in a different way to opening it with a different intention: the same narratological procedure has a very different meaning depending upon the wider cultural meaning of what is announced. This is because the cultural concept in question occupies a particular place in the ideological field as well. Here it is clear how the analysis of a narratological structure leads us directly into the field of ideology, since it is the nature of the concept (the signified) 'murder' that brings together the set of narrative codes in the particular constellation that we can see in *Malice Aforethought*. A brief contrast will illustrate this: the narratological procedure used at the beginning of *Malice Aforethought* is also used at the beginning of *Daniel Deronda* (Eliot, 1876), in the out-of-sequence statement of Gwendolen's gambling and family bankruptcy; but it has a very different meaning to what it has in Iles' novel because of the ideological difference between being a murderer and being bankrupt.[2]

Moreover, there are similarities between this narratological structure and that analysed earlier as the basis of the notion of mystery in mystery stories. We saw in a series of examples that some narratological device or other – usually an omission – is used to hide some feature of story in narrative. This occlusion constitutes the mystery, the criminal mystery, which is a central part of the form that the hermeneutic enigma takes in these texts; at the same time, it is this criminal mystery in the form of the hermeneutic enigma that gives meaning to the events that constitute the proairetic code of the texts. Thus, in mystery stories in the traditional sense, a 'gap' in narrative sets up the hermeneutic code, a gap which conceals some feature of a criminal act, usually the identity of a murderer. In a story without a mystery, such as *Malice Aforethought*, a sequential inversion in narrative produces a hermeneutic enigma based on a criminal act. Despite the differences already stressed, the similarities are striking: a hermeneutic enigma based on criminality structuring the meaning of actions in the proairetic code.

What we have seen in this narratological convergence between two plots which are apparently based on very different principles of construction (hiding versus revealing to the reader) is a small hierarchy of discourses, a two-level hierarchy, in which the superordinate level is the cultural concept 'crime' and the subordinate level is various proairetic sequences of everyday actions and the order in which they appear. That is to say, the nature of 'crime' as a social category is such that it not only institutes a particular version of the hermeneutic code in these narratives, but is also responsible for the way in which the proairetic code is related to it. In a sense, all that is being said here is that these are all crime stories; but the advantage of narratological analysis is that it reveals in some detail *how* they are crime stories, by showing how the category 'crime' is responsible for various organisations of meaning in the texts.

Our next example is focalisation techniques (see chapter 4). In narratological theory, these are usually presented as a distinct level of narrative, and as elements in a grammar of narrative (Rimmon-Kenan, 1983: 85; Chatman, 1978: 22ff.). That is to say, they appear as something like a 'vocabulary' arranged in paradigm sets according to structuralist linguistics. However, more detailed consideration of some examples will reveal that this paradigm-like appearance is in fact questionable, and that they are subordinate to a hierarchy of discourses.

In Elmore Leonard's novels we see a range of devices used to move flexibly between different forms of focalisation. Within the corpus of crime fiction, Leonard is remarkable for the large number of different focalisations that his texts encompass, and yet we shall see that this is perfectly compatible with a clear hierarchisation of discourses.

In *Swag* (Leonard, 1984: 70) we read this description of elements of a hold-up being carried out by the two central characters. The scene is set in the conventional third person, past tense mode: 'The bar was . . .'; 'When they went in at 1.30 a.m. . . .'; but it rapidly starts to include fragments whose enunciative features make it clear that at these moments at least, the focalisation is internal, the narrator is seeing things through the eyes of the characters: 'the tables were empty now'. The use of 'now' conflates two time-scales – the past of the narration, the present of the events to the consciousness of the characters. The following sentence reads 'Once they pulled their guns, Stick would cover the people at the bar . . . while Frank concentrated on the bartender'. Here the use of 'would' indicates that the narrator knows the future in relationship to the events, because 'he' knows the

character's intentions – the 'would' is 'will' in indirect reported speech.
Here the conflation of three time-scales – the past of the narrative,
the present of the character's statement ('I'll cover the people at
the bar'), the future of their intentions – produces a high level of
integration between the narrator and the characters' point of view
(perhaps helped by the extreme condensation). The narrator seems
exceptionally omniscient, and therefore the focalisation seems closer
to internal than would normally be the case in external focalisation.
A similar example is to be found on p. 87: 'He wondered if she had
seen him, the glow from his cigarette'; the omission of a link between
'him' and 'the glow' is true to a 'stream of consciousness' and creates
a slippage between internal and external focalisation; this promotes
identity between narrator and character despite the lack of first-person
narration.

A similar device is to be found at points where focalisation is
non-problematic. In *Swag*, Stick knows Mona is a prostitute but has
been trying to talk her into bed as if she were an 'ordinary' woman.
Eventually the conversation goes thus:

> 'It was on television. I think the Monday night movie . . .'
> 'I guess I was out.'
>   Stick hesitated. 'Working?'
> 'Could've been.'
> 'How much you charge?'
> 'Fifty', Mona said, 'How's that sound?'

(Leonard, 1984: 90)

Then there is a gap of two lines on the page indicating an unstated
passage of time, and the narrative cuts to them in bed. This passage
is noteworthy because of the obvious implied omission of relevant
material from story in the flow of narrative: the clear implication
is that Mona knows that Stick knows she is a prostitute, that
she sees through his conversational tactics, that Stick eventually
realises that she knows and changes his tactics accordingly. The
omission of the unstated passage of time underlines how direct the
relationship is between acceptance of a commercial contract and its
implementation, thus underlining that Stick has indeed been forced
to change tack.

Here we see a process that is essentially similar to the processes used
in the focalisation procedures described above. There we saw how
changes in the relationship between story and narrative (conflation
of time-scales) produced a particular form of integration between
narrator and character; here we see how deliberate omission of

elements of story shows the narrator (and as a result the implied reader) as someone who understands these social processes so well that exhaustive description of them is unnecessary – an example of the often-commented 'street-wise' quality of Leonard's writing. In other words, here the narrator and the characters seem to have the same 'take on life', and thus the characters' point of view seems to inhere in the flow of the narrative as a whole.

What can we learn from these examples? Essentially we have learnt that focalisation techniques are not separable from the relationship between story and narrative, for it is the selection of story elements that constitutes focalisation procedures. As a result, it is clear that even if such procedures are in some measure elements in a paradigm, if there is in a sense a 'grammar' of them, none the less they take their place in a sequence whose order is also decided on the basis of something external to the grammar in question: the hierarchy of discourses that constitutes the text or constitutes some intertextual entity such as genre that traverses the text. In these two examples it is the 'exceptional' nature of the sorts of activities that are associated with crime. We may note also the separation of focalisation from the 'point of view of the hero', which I earlier maintained was typical of the thriller (Palmer, 1978: 59ff.); clearly crime fiction presents a wider variety of uses of focalisation than I suggested.

These various procedures also set up subject positions for the reader. We have seen how the linguistic mechanism of enunciation necessarily sets up positions for speaking and listening (reading, viewing) subjects to occupy (we also know that they may be refused or modified). We have seen how enunciative features of texts – for example, the implied time-scales of adverbs and verbs in Elmore Leonard – interact with other focalisation techniques and the relationship between story and narrative. In these focalisation techniques and in these relationships between story and narrative are created the places, or the identifications, that are made available to the reader or spectator. That is to say, these devices in narrative set up subject positions in a way directly analogous to the subject positions created in linguistic enunciation.

In other words, it becomes clear that writing about crime in the framework of popular genre fiction implies subordinating other meanings to the connotations produced by the category crime. More exactly, it is clear that the sheer act of writing fiction containing crime does not imply anything of the sort: texts as various as Dickens' *Little Dorrit*, Dostoevsky's *Crime and Punishment* or Antonioni's *Blow Up* indicate that descriptions of crime can be incorporated into quite different fictional textures. What constitutes crime fiction as such is that the presentation of crime comes to dominate the fictional structure by taking a particular place in the hierarchy of discourses that constitute the texts.

9 Crime fiction: *film noir* and gender

The preceding pages have been focused around two interrelated questions: firstly, is crime fiction a genre; and secondly – much more important – is there some common meaning to be found in all crime fiction, deriving from a common thematic concern with crime? If such a principle is to be found, it will derive from the more general principle of the 'hierarchy of discourses' already discussed (see chapter 4). Indeed, it is just this principle which has been seen at work in the two examples that closed the previous chapter: focalisation procedures and the relationship between the hermeneutic and proairetic codes in crime fiction. This principle suggests that while the discourses which compose the myriad crime narratives might in fact be very different from one text (or 'subgenre') to another, what is responsible for subordinating certain of them to certain others might none the less be omnipresent. In this chapter we consider two particularly ambiguous examples: *film noir* and gender.

The French term '*film noir*' originally meant simply 'crime film' and was primarily applied to Hollywood (Borde and Chaumeton, 1955; Guérif, 1979); when reapplied by English-speaking critics to American film it acquired a more limited sense, but one which is none the less difficult to pin down. This is because (it is commonly argued) *film noir* is not a genre, in the sense that genre is defined by common plot elements (e.g. crime): it is rather a mood, a tonality, a set of visual motifs and associated themes, elements of which are to be found in 'almost every Hollywood dramatic film between 1941–53' (Schrader, 1972; but see Hirsch, 1981, p. 72 for an argument to the contrary).

The recurrent visual motifs have been analysed in detail by Place and Peterson (1974). In *film noir*, scenes were lit differently to the normal Hollywood practice. Screen lighting was traditionally based on three types of light: key light, which is a hard direct overhead light that casts high-definition shadows; fill light, a soft diffused light which fills in shadows; and back light, from behind the actors, which adds highlights to their outline and differentiates them from the background. In the early 1940s, the dominant lighting practice was 'high-key', in which the ratio of key light to fill light was such that the fill light killed most of the shadows, giving an even light over most of the frame and portraying faces with no 'unnatural' areas of darkness. But in *film noir*, 'low-key' lighting was used, a greater ratio of key to fill, which created areas of high contrast and shadow; at the same time, lighting was positioned low on the floor, to give an even eerier effect. Even leading actresses were shot in this way, against the normal practice of filming them in diffused light to show them 'at their best', i.e. most feminine. The hard, *noir* lighting gave leading ladies, such as Barbara Stanwyck,

> a hard statuesque surface beauty that seems more seductive but less attainable, at once alluring and impenetrable.
>
> (Place and Peterson, 1974: 31)

Scenes taking place at night were traditionally shot by day, using filters to make it look like night ('day for night'). In *film noir*, night-time scenes tended to be shot at night ('night for night'), which gives a more authentic effect but is more expensive; even cheap 'B' *noir* films tended to be shot in this way. The emphasis on night is linked to the predilection for the play of light and shadow: shadows in pre-war Hollywood composition were used to emphasise the hero, but in *noir* they are equally likely to obliterate him. Traditional norms of *mise-en-scène* were violated in the interests of greater dramatic impact: editing would place an extreme high-angle long shot – 'an oppressive and fatalistic angle that looks down on its helpless victim' (ibid.: 32) – next to a 'choker close-up' (where the face fills the screen) 'to create jarring juxtapositions'. Composition would stress oblique and vertical lines in the frame rather than horizontal, thus making the screen 'inherently unstable'. Compositional tension was preferred to violent action when conflict was to be expressed, for violent action would favour the tough hero (as in the pre-war gangster films such as *Little Caesar*) whereas compositional tension reduced his influence (Schrader, 1972; Schrader's own film *American Gigolo* demonstrates these principles).

These visual motifs delineate a set of themes: a tough, lonely, cynical hero, who frequently loses at the end; the world without innocence of the nocturnal urban decor; a sexuality which is simultaneously exciting and threatening; a world which is so corrupt that it is not worth fighting for, and where there is no link between morality and success (see also Farber, 1974). They delineate these themes partly through the visual connotations, partly through the narratives of which these motifs are part, for they create a 'visually unstable environment in which no character has a firm moral base' (Place and Peterson, 1974: 32).

It is clear that not all of any *film noir* is likely to conform to all the visual patterns outlined here. In *The Big Heat*, for example, the hero's home is always filmed high-key: domestic space is filled with a diffused, even but bright and soft light; this is the space in which his wife always appears, conforming to a definition of femininity which is synonymous with domesticity. In sequences where he meets a 'gangster's moll' in a hotel bedroom, everything follows the *noir* visual patterns: a version of femininity and potential sexual encounter defined by the absence of domesticity. The famous jump cuts from high-angle long shots to choker close-ups are most commonly used to film someone on the run. This implies that the visual motifs associated with *film noir* are in fact a way of portraying certain categories of event, action or character, which are particularly plentiful in these films.

It is likely that in *noir* the scenes which are most typical of this style (full of shadow and compositional tension, moving rapidly from long-shot to extreme close-up, etc.) are also scenes which are especially central to the typical *noir* themes of anguish, loneliness, trying to cope with a threatening world. This could be demonstrated by showing that such scenes are accorded a 'disproportionate' amount of time in narrative, i.e. either: (a) more time than their duration in story; or (b) a duration much closer to story duration than that accorded other, less important story events. But what is crucial here is a second form of emphasis, which we could call 'spatialisation' (as opposed to the 'temporalisation' of the previous example). In film, choice of story-time is also choice of story-space, by definition; this space is then defined by the placing of the camera and the lighting among other things (for reasons of simplicity, the most important will be our focus here). *Noir* lighting schemes are a way of creating a spatialisation which has a particular emotional impact through things like the play of light and shadow.

A survey of *film noir* would reveal whether such scenes, which are both typically *noir* in style and accorded exceptional importance in duration, are also ones which are thematically related to the typical concerns of crime fiction, especially the hard-boiled thriller: fear of violence, betrayal of trust, etc. (cf. Palmer, 1978: 40–53). We may take the film version of Woolrich's *Phantom Lady* (1983) as an example. This is atypical of the thriller tradition in that the 'hero' spends most of the story in jail, condemned to death for a murder he did not commit, while his secretary and a friend attempt to find the evidence that will save him. As so often in *film noir*, the adequacy of the protagonist to deal with the situation is questionable, and is the main source of suspense. At the beginning of the film the hero goes to a bar to forget a row with his wife and there meets a woman who is particularly uncommunicative but who agrees to go to the theatre with him. These scenes are shot in a lighting scheme which is less high-key than some subsequent scenes, but which does not stress *noir* elements such as deep shadow masking the human form, large threatening shadows looming over figures, distorted composition in the frame, etc. Subsequently he returns home to find the police in his flat and his wife murdered. At this point, *noir* lighting starts to obtrude: the subsequent scenes are shot partially in a very harsh light that flattens characters' faces and casts looming shadows on the walls, or in a deep chiaroscuro that makes it difficult to see human outlines. It is at this point that the threatening nature of his situation becomes clear, since visibly the police suspect him of the killing. The film then cuts to his office; his secretary – who will organise the hunt for evidence in his favour – finds out about his plight. This scene is lit in a traditional high-key manner, to show her 'at her best'; as soon as she plunges into the 'underworld' where she needs to find clues, the lighting of her face changes and she sits in deep pools of shadow.

In *Phantom Lady* the most typically *noir* filmic elements are used at points in the narrative where thriller themes emerge: the 'descent' into a world which is unknown and may well contain (the threat of) criminal violence. Such filmic techniques are well suited to these points in narrative because they were devised as the visual analogue of anguish. *Phantom Lady* was directed by Robert Siodmak, whose first films had been made in Germany: the *noir* lighting schemes were imported from the German expressionist cinema (Eisner, 1973). Did such technical elements have the same meaning in the pre-war German cinema as they came to have in Hollywood crime films? Certainly they were widely used in Germany in non-crime contexts (for example, Murnau's *The Last Laugh*) as well as in crime ones (e.g. Lang's *M*). What seems to be the case is that there they referred to emotional themes similar to *noir* ones: isolation, fear, inadequacy, etc. While it is clear that they can be used in other contexts as well (such as a melodrama like *Gilda*, in which crime only plays a peripheral role) there is clearly an elective affinity between them and the themes typical of crime fiction.

The final dimension of crime fiction to be considered is gender. In *Thrillers* (Palmer, 1978), the question of gender is virtually reduced to the incidence of erotic encounter (esp. 29–39). Clearly this is inadequate (Glover, 1989: 70). The question should be displaced, towards the relationship between the narrative form of the thriller and gender as a social construct. We can start by asking whether crime fiction is a male genre in the sense that it appeals to a male readership, and whether it is possible for a thriller to have a female hero.

In general, crime novels seem to appeal to a predominantly male readership, with the exception of the classic English detective story, a form of fiction written in a significant measure by women for women (Glover, 1989: 71f.). And yet it is also evident that many women have attended all sorts of thriller films – Bennett and Woollacott have debated at length the reasons for the popularity of the James Bond stories for a female audience in the 1960s (1987: 211–30). Figures for female viewership of TV crime and police series are probably not reliable because of the influence that male 'heads of household' have on family viewing (Morley, 1986).

Turning our attention to the second question, many classic English detective stories have female heroes (Agatha Christie's Miss Marple is the most famous) as do occasional tough thrillers such as *Coma* and *An Unsuitable Job for a Woman*; some recent women crime writers have deliberately used the thriller format as a way of foregrounding questions of gender (e.g. Wilson, 1984 and 1987; Paretsky, 1982). Yet, in general, a woman hero is relatively rare, and when she appears the possession of attributes commonly held to be feminine is problematic. The heroine of *Coma* is constantly hampered by her gender and in the end has to be rescued by her boyfriend. Women who are 'out of place' (i.e., not in place within the family) are represented as easily deviant (Kaplan, 1986).

Cowie (1979; 1980) considers the position of a woman hero in *Coma* in just these terms. Does this film, she asks, subvert stereotypes by presenting a woman in what is traditionally a man's role, namely the fearless investigating hero who eventually cracks the case? She answers the question by examining how the narrative constructs her as a character and how it therefore offers the spectator a subject position *vis-à-vis* her: the film offers a definition of what it means to be a strong woman with a sense of a wrong to be righted and invites us to respond to her in these terms. Susan Wheeler, the protagonist, is a junior doctor in a large hospital where a number of patients admitted for routine operations mysteriously go into irreversible coma, including her best friend. She sets out to find a medical explanation and eventually unearths a criminal conspiracy, to which she nearly falls victim, and has to be rescued by her boyfriend, another doctor who has doubted the rationality of her investigations.

In the thriller the centrality of the hero derives from the fact that (s)he is 'the place of knowledge', the focus of our interest and desire for a resolution to the mystery. In *Coma*, Susan only appears to be in this place, for she is 'consistently displaced from [it]' (Cowie, 1979: 72) because attention in the film is constantly deflected from Susan's task as detective to a second, 'false' mystery: are Susan's suspicions in fact justified, or is she just another paranoid, 'difficult' woman? This displacement is only possible because the central character is a woman, for in the conventional thriller, with a male detective, such doubts on the part of the other characters would never contaminate the audience's estimation of the detective's rationality and ability. It is through this second false conspiracy that the suspense of the film is created, that emotion is set up by delaying the desired resolution of whatever obstacles there are, while at the same time amplifying the partial knowledge the audience has of the threats to resolution that stand in the protagonist's way. In *Coma* these threats are more visible to the audience than to Susan, who appears to be relatively helpless before them: she is 'the victim of the narrative, acting blindly in comparison with the audience's knowledge' (Cowie, 1980: 61). In short, although Susan is indeed the detective and does many things that a traditional detective would do – including fighting off a hired assassin – she does so in a way which never reassures the audience that she is competent to deal with the various situations with which she is confronted.

There are therefore two 'strategies of identification' or two types of subject-position in the film for the spectator to adopt: firstly, one in which Susan acts as the traditional detective, given more knowledge than the spectator, determining the action, a strategy where we see things from her point of view; secondly, one in which the opposite is true, where Susan tends to be acted upon, to have less knowledge than the spectator. In the first narrative strategy, Cowie argues (1980: 62f.), Susan's admirability is not premised upon her femininity, but upon her characteristics as a narrative agent: it is 'the effect of the narrative action and filmic narration

. . . gender per se is not determining' (ibid.: 63); on the other hand

> the protagonist is a woman and to that extent the image or form of identification and reading the film encourages at this point is atypical in combining this mode of narration and gender designation.

> (ibid.: 63)

In the second strategy we identify with Susan as someone who is a (potential) victim but also think she may be unjustified in her suspicions. Such identifications are the product of the narrative structure, especially of *mise-en-scène* and editing rhythms, not of character traits attributed to characters (ibid.: 66). Thus the issue of Susan's femininity, the issue of a female hero, is dismissed as a very secondary consideration since: (a) the character traits that characterise the hero are non-gender specific and (b) character traits are of secondary importance anyway.

Clearly, Cowie's analysis is inconclusive, but it has the merit of pointing to the elements of thriller structure that make central female roles within this genre difficult to sustain. Where a male hero's difficulty in convincing others that his suspicions were justified would probably not lead the audience to question his competence or his sanity, here they do, and the mechanism of suspense multiplies the audience's uncertainty. However, it is not difficult to find examples of thrillers where the (male) hero's inadequacy is used as an element of suspense. For example, in *Bellman and True* the central character is a computer and electronics specialist who is forced by a criminal gang to help them in a robbery. It is a relatively conventional heist/caper movie, except that he is a weak man: alcoholic, easily manipulated by women, indecisive, incapable of fighting back. One of the keys to the gang's hold over him is the threat to harm his stepson, who is the one firm point in his life. Eventually he decides to fight back against the gang, because he finds out that the woman with whom he has struck up an erotic relationship is betraying him. He originally approaches her because he can't stop his hands shaking, and she seduces him, very directly, in a way that seems charitable. She betrays him in several ways: she is using sex to get at the money he will eventually have from the robbery; she is in fact gay; and she inadvertently lets the boy know that she is after the money and manipulating him, and that his mother didn't want him. The point at which the father turns against the gang is when the boy reveals what has happened. That is to say, the worm turns when gender identity is totally threatened, it is his sense of being entirely revealed to be less than a man that leads him to reassert himself: he kills the gang, steals the money himself and sets out for a new life with his son.

While this film is in no way favourable to women (who are entirely cast as castrating bitches), it is clear that an identification point for the audience based upon male weakness is indeed possible. Certainly it is the case that ultimately a more traditional form of masculinity is reasserted. But everything that in *Coma* undermined the heroine's place as the film's 'place of knowledge' in *Bellman* undermines the adequacy of a male protagonist and yet still allows the same mixture of desire for narrative resolution and suspenseful fear that is to be found in *Coma*. The implication is that the character traits of the protagonist are by no means as easily separable from the point-of-view structure as Cowie argues, and the stereotypical allocation of character traits to gender is part of the process of identification. The protagonist of *Bellman* is in effect castrated through much of the film: incapable of effective action, abandoned, manipulated by women; through violent action he regains his 'manhood'. Susan in *Coma* is given attributes that are stereotypically associated with both genders. In both cases the mixing of gender stereotypes results in certain characteristic narrative tensions, which are manifested narratologically, in *mise-en-scène* and editing.

What is logically implied here is the relationship between focalisation devices and features of the discursive organisation of our society; in fact, we have returned to the terrain of the hierarchy of discourses. Elements of a description of the relationship between social gender and thriller narative are to be found in Glover (1989), who argues that in the inter-war period, crime fiction was 'remasculinised' by the return of violence to the centre of the agenda, whereas in the classic English detective story the violence was largely off-stage (cf. Worpole, 1983: 39ff.). Where the latter was written in considerable measure for a female readership (since many of the 'little libraries' that were set up after the First World War and that stocked such books were largely patronised by women), the 'tough thriller' was read largely by men. Remasculinisation consisted of introducing the gentleman adventurer of *Boy's Own* fiction into the world structured by criminal mystery, but a criminal mystery premissed upon 'an ecology of male power' (Glover, 1989: 74). The result is the separation of popular fiction into male genres and female genres, where male genres celebrate masculinity in terms of toughness and decisive action.[1]

It remains to demonstrate in somewhat greater detail how these processes occur, using the example of R. B. Parker's *Looking for Rachel Wallace* (1980).

Parker's series hero Spenser – who has all the usual macho credentials – is regularly presented as a modern Galahad/Gawain by other characters in the novels, notably his regular girlfriend, but a knight-errant who is moving in a culture highly influenced by feminism. Parker's novels self-consciously try to come to terms with what masculinity means in this context. In *Looking for Rachel Wallace*, Spenser is hired as bodyguard for a lesbian radical feminist writer who has received death threats. In the opening chapters the contradictions of this situation are explored, ultimately to Spenser's disadvantage. When she is evicted from a meeting by force he rescues her – also by force – and she sacks him: it is made clear that he rescued her because his pride was offended by an attack on a woman he was defending. He has failed to understand that by rescuing her he has publicly undermined everything she stood for, and has ruined the political effect of her being evicted by men from a meeting with other women. Subsequently she is kidnapped, and Spenser finds her, killing the kidnappers on the way. On this occasion she does not object to being rescued. In a final statment she says she still disapproves of everything he stands for, but is very grateful for what he has done, gives him a kiss and says she will 'in a way always love you for those moments' (ibid.: 216) when he rescued her, and they both cry. It is clear that his tears are caused by the realisation that his misjudgement when he first 'rescued' her is what allowed the kidnappers to get at her so easily.

Evidently the situation which structures the plot has been chosen in order to give an opportunity to confront, as directly as the genre allows, various issues connected with the challenge that feminism represents to traditional conceptions of maleness. Whether it even attempts to confront the issue of male power seems more problematic, for in the end it is inevitable that Spenser will be needed because the kidnappers can only be met with force and the police are not sufficiently competent. In the relationship between story and narrative, the fundamental focus of the text is established through the decision about what events and perceptions to prioritise; thus the overall shape of the narrative creates a situation in which skills which are traditionally male are foregrounded. The hierarchy of discourses which constitutes the genre, which establishes a contract with the reader, also settles which categories of action are to be presented as the most worthwhile, and we have seen that associating them across the traditional divide between the genders creates tensions in the narrative framework.[2]

In summary, we can see that making crime and/or its investigation the dominant procedure of a text is responsible for other features of textuality. We have seen across a range of examples how the category 'crime' is responsible for articulations of the hermeneutic and proairetic codes, and of focalisation techniques (since they are constituted in the relationship between story and narrative). That is to say, taking the social category 'crime' as the central element in narrative structure creates a particular hierarchy of discourses – this is especially clear in the instance of gender – and this sets up a series of subject positions for the reader or viewer; of course, as we already know, such positions may well be refused, or negotiated into a modified meaning, but we should remember that such meanings are always established in a dialogue with a text which has a structure, they are not established by fiat by the audience, in the absence of any dialogue. Unfortunately, little is known about crime audiences beyond their gender and size.

At various points references have been made to ideology: in what ways does crime fiction, as discussed here, refer us to this field? Certainly gender is one way: insofar as gender is a social construct, any fiction that secures specific subject positions for genders makes some contribution to the constant shifting balance of power that constitutes hegemony. Clearly not all crime fiction defines gender in the same way; but in general it proposes that stereotypically masculine qualities are superior to feminine ones, and it offers a particular definition of what masculinity is (at the same time offering a definition of what the individual is, and tending to conflate the two); in doing this it necessarily favours a space in the social structure defined in these terms.

A second way is in terms of definitions of what constitutes a valid contribution to nationhood (Denning, 1987: 37ff.; cf. Bromley, 1986). Bulldog Drummond, for example, is a character who is replete with all the middle-class prejudices of the inter-war years – anti-Semitism, xenophobia, hatred of the organised working class and 'profiteers'. These beliefs combine with the narrative structure of the thriller to produce a hero who excites the reader by eliminating these entities. This produces what Denning calls 'the Janus face of populism and nationalism' (Denning, 1987: 56): on the one hand a representation of the desire for a nation free of all sources of evil and freed by the activities of someone who refuses to bow to any authority he does not recognise; on the other a respect for naked power exercised directly through physical force.

At another level, the way in which crime and its investigation are represented is not neutral with respect to central institutions in our society: notably the police (Drummond, 1976; Hurd, 1981). At yet another level, the way in which we are invited to enjoy the exercise of the skills of violence, or to identify with its potential victim, constitutes an argument in favour of an atomistic definition of individualism, as we have already seen. Before we see this in an entirely negative light, however, it should be stressed that this is also a utopian vision: here the individual is presented as someone capable of working out his or her own destiny freed from trammels of any kind, able to assert fully both individuality and sociality together. That this utopianism overlooks everything that is important about modern societies – including gender interdependence – does not reduce its attractiveness to an appreciative audience, indeed it may increase it.

Thus, in all these ways, crime fiction opens out onto the field of ideology and hegemony; if this chapter has concentrated on narratological structures, this is primarily because much of what has been written about crime fiction has tended to concentrate on ideological matters, and it is equally important to demonstrate *how* it is able to make a contribution to the incessant shifting of subject positions, and the incessant attempt to secure them to some strategy or other for the composition of the social order.

10 Soap opera, romance and femininity

In this chapter we turn to a body of popular narrative whose common feature is its audience: both soap opera and romance are created primarily for women – romance entirely, soap largely though no longer exclusively. We saw in part I that, in the case of broadcast fiction, the target audience is an essential part of the definition, and therefore understanding, of the fiction itself. Here, applying the principle to print as well, a specialist publishing firm such as Harlequin/Mills & Boon, concentrating on romantic fiction, targets an entirely gender-specific audience. Recent literary criticism takes the implied reader, thought of as a feature of the text, as a focal point for analysis, and recent TV criticism has stressed the extent to which TV is a 'dialogic' form, where the audience actively participates in the construction of meaning (Cassidy, 1989). In the case of soap and romance, the clearly identified audience is in fact the main reason for recent critical attention, even when it is not the chief methodological principle (Brunsdon, 1981: 32; Baym, 1978: 11, 13ff.). Thus this chapter is concerned primarily with the extent to which focusing on the audience is capable of providing an explanation of such fiction.

A body of fiction especially for women emerged gradually during the history of printed literature, largely in the form of the novel (see Showalter, 1978; Baym, 1978; Moers, 1976). In this literature, woman's place in the social order, especially as it is mediated through her relationship with men, is the central concern. Specifically, even if this literature is not self-consciously feminist, as some of it was in the late nineteenth century (Showalter, 1978: 24–32), it is concerned with women's strategies for coping with a life defined on the basis of male power: in George Eliot's words, it was a question of where 'the duty of obedience ends and the duty of resistance begins' (quoted Showalter, 1978: 24). It is this agenda, derived from the eighteenth- and nineteenth-century novel, that Modleski (1982) shows dominates the women's genres of the twentieth century.

There is unanimity among historians of popular narrative that soap opera was originally aimed deliberately and exclusively at women in its earliest days on American radio. The stories were carefully calculated to appeal to women listeners, as the types of situations and characters were largely derived from the domestic novel (Cantor and Pingree, 1983: 20ff.). Its foundations, according to a 1930s advertising executive, were 'simple characterisation, understandable predicaments, the centrality of female characters and . . . philosophical relevance' (quoted Wober, 1984: 65). The slow pace of the stories and the frequent repetitions of material were calculated to be comprehensible to women listeners who were simultaneously engaged in attention-demanding household tasks, a feature which has remained true of television soaps (Cantor and Pingree, 1983: 23; Hobson, 1982: 111ff.).

Over the years the audience composition has changed significantly. Originally exclusively female and adult, soaps now have an audience with a sizeable male and young female component. Many recent soaps have deliberately sought a younger audience to attract advertisers. (Cantor and Pingree, 1983: 114–22; Cassata and Skill, 1983: ch. 11; Buckingham, 1987: 16ff.).

Discussion of soap narrative must start with its fundamental defining feature: the serial format that is typical of broadcast fiction. Tulloch and Alvarado distinguish four types:

(1) The continuous serial, consisting of an indeterminate number of episodes, with a large number of interweaving narrative strands, most of which are continuous between episodes.

(2) The episodic serial (often also called the mini-series): here we find similar narrative continuity, but over a limited and specified number of episodes.

(3) The sequential series: each episode is a 'complete narrative structure' but has an enigma at the end which links it to the subsequent episode – e.g. *Dallas*.

(4) The episodic series, where each episode is connected to the next only by the cast of main characters: police series and sitcoms are very typical of this form (Tulloch and Alvarado, 1983; cf. Geraghty, 1981).

Today these forms are predominantly associated with the broadcast media, but they clearly have their origins in nineteenth-century publishing practices: novels were published in instalments from the 1830s onwards (Dickens and Sue are the most famous instances), which approximates to the episodic serial. Subsequently, magazines published series of short stories with the same leading characters, a format which Conan Doyle claimed to have invented with the Sherlock Holmes stories in *The Strand* magazine (Skovmand, 1989: 130); this is consistent with Tulloch and Alvarado's definition of the episodic series. Soap opera clearly fits their definition of the continuous serial.

While none of these formats has an exclusively female audience today, the continuous serial is linked to it by its origins in radio soap in the inter-war years in the USA. In recent debates, attention has been focused on the possibility that there is an elective affinity between the female audience and the continuous serial form. The feature of continuous serials that is the focus of this debate is the impossibility of narrative closure in this format: because the serial will always continue, potentially indefinitely, no story can ever be finished in the sense that the audience can never be sure whether there is in fact something more to be said on the subject. By the same token, because the same leading characters are ever-present, anything that happens may have continuing relevance to their lives. Indeed, even a series that is cancelled can never resolve the enormous multiplicity of story-lines that have been generated within it. The longest-running soap – *The Guiding Light* – has been on the air five days a week since 1937.

Soap operas, in the sense in which they have been discussed here, are primarily associated with daytime television – indeed, some historians of popular culture insist that similar series on primetime TV are not soap opera at all. According to Cantor and Pingree (1983: 26f.), primetime series differ from daytime soaps in three main ways:

(1) The budgets are very different – primetime series have much higher per episode costs – and editorial control is exercised in a different way.

(2) The number of episodes in primetime series is limited (typically, to 22 per season) whereas daytime soaps usually have five episodes per week – but this is not true on UK television, where two episodes per week is more normal.

(3) The content is different: the setting of daytime soaps is largely domestic, whereas primetime series have many other settings, and the number of events per episode is much higher in primetime series.

Lastly, in daytime serials it is normal for narratives to be completely continuous across episodes, but it is normal in primetime serials, even where the structure is basically continuous, for at least some narrative strands to be resolved in each episode. When *Hill Street Blues* was first aired in the USA, the amount of narrative non-resolution was a source of contention between the production company and the network; when its producer, Steve Bochco, went on to produce *LA Law*, it was a condition of the broadcasting agreement with the network that there should be a substantial amount of narrative resolution in each episode (Feuer *et al.*, 1984: 25f.).

It is clear that decisions about narrative structure are not ultimately separable from decisions about the target audience. In general, serial fiction, and especially soap operas, are subject to a number of calculations that are not commonly found in other narrative forms, and which derive from their broadcast format. Because they are intended to last for a long time, they represent a considerable investment; although they are cheap to run (and immensely profitable for commercial broadcasting organisations), they are expensive to launch as they involve large casts and a large number of episodes need to be shot in advance. On the other hand, once the initial costs have been met, continued existence is cheap; and soap series can be allowed to play to small audiences for a longer time than would be the case with primetime series in order to build an audience (Cantor and Pingree, 1983: ch. 4). Buckingham (1987: Introduction and ch. 1) demonstrates that *EastEnders* must be understood in the context of the BBC's desire to restore its place in the ratings in the mid-1980s. BBC management were looking for a programme that they could use to start building a channel audience from the early evening onwards, using it on alternating days with an already established chat show. The decision to use a cast including many young characters was part of an attempt to catch a wider audience than the usual (elderly) soap audience in the UK, as was the decision to adopt a setting and themes that allowed consistent focus on 'contemporary reality'.

These brief case histories demonstrate the usefulness of knowledge about a target audience in assessing the nature of popular narrative. We shall see in a later chapter how this may be used in conjunction with other information about broadcasting institutions to provide a large element of a coherent account of narrative structure. In the meantime, it is clear that our account of soap opera and romance must take the fact of a female audience as its focus.

The implications of this focus can be approached by a consideration of the changing 'mode of address' of US soaps over the period of their existence (Allen, 1985: 152–74). Allen argues that soap must be understood in the light of changes in definitions of women's roles in the USA during the twentieth century, and especially changes in 'domestic ideology' (ibid: 146). Around the time of the First World

War, domestic ideology came to be defined predominantly in terms of restricting women's influence to the home, abandoning previous attempts to influence men in their public conduct. At the same time, running a home and being a mother was redefined as a demanding expertise, and women were encouraged to see themselves as romantic partners after marriage as well as before. Women, in short, were offered a subject position in which they would influence the world by being homemakers.

Soap opera in its radio days was characterised among other things by a narrator who clearly embodied a perspective in terms of which the behaviour of all the characters was to be evaluated. This perspective was one which fitted clearly with the framework of domestic ideology, and the narrator was also the announcer who spoke the advertisements, making a link between the nature of the product and the story that had just been told; advertising is intrinsic to the ideology of domesticity since it identifies homemaking tasks and proposes ways of fulfilling them. In general, the narrator inhabited both the world of the story and the real world: he (since it usually was a male) thus opened up the boundaries of the narrative space to make links between it and the world of the listener and of advertised commodities. Also, by addressing the actual listener directly, the narrator attempted to fix her in the role of the implied listener whose space was constructed in the narrative (ibid.: 160–4).

This narrational structure disappears with the advent of TV: Allen demonstrates through an analysis of *The Guiding Light* – briefly produced on both media – that the narrational material is excised from an otherwise unchanged script. This is due to the availability of the video channel to provide information that might otherwise have to be verbally narrated, and also because the norm of realist film-making (as we have already seen) is that the camera delineates a sharp and clear distinction between the space and time of the story and the space and time of reality: confusion between the two must be avoided. Thus the clear hierarchy of discourses established by the narrator is replaced by a more flexible arrangement, where the plot encourages the audience to adopt a particular point of view. This is reinforced by the 'tent-pole' character – so-called because she is the mainstay of the series: a dominant elderly matriarch who comments on everybody's actions and who, in early TV soaps, directly gave advice on household matters. But it is evident that these arrangements are less clearly oriented towards the unequivocal establishment of a hierarchy of discourses than the narrational structure normal on radio. At the same time, soaps expanded from a normal 15 minutes per day to 30 in the mid-1950s, and to 60 in the 1970s: this led to a vastly increased cast of characters. Thus the well-defined hierarchy of values and clear link to the world of the actual listener established by the narrator is dispersed in TV soap, whose advent coincides with the post-war world and the new multiplicity of role definitions available to women (ibid.: 168–73).

In Allen's analysis we can see three clear implications. Firstly, that soap opera and its audience are by no means static entities: different modes of address inscribe different implied audiences, and this correlates with sociological changes in the actual audience (this is perhaps the least developed area of investigation of popular narrative, as we have already seen). Secondly, Allen points to the centrality of the relationship between the mode of address of soap and the nature of the audience. Thirdly, he indicates that the referential concerns of soap stories – domestic activities – are also related to the nature of the audience. It is the second and third of these implications that now become the focus of our attention.

All analyses of soap agree that the real-life activities that are the referents of soap narratives come largely within the arena of the domestic: empirical content analysis, more traditional literary analytic methods and structuralist analysis all concur. Thus Cantor and Pingree (1983: ch. 5) show that the content of soaps is overwhelmingly 'personal relations'; all soaps exaggerate the percentage of women who are full-time housewives, and underrepresent the percentage of people who are unemployed, in comparison with real-life statistics derived from the census (ibid.: 87ff.). Although soaps give increasing representation to women working outside the home – in line with increased female participation in the real-world labour force – it is relatively rare in soap to see people actually doing their job, and women are seen working only half as often as men (ibid.: 89). Analysis of the portrayal of mothers in soaps reveals that 'evil' characters behave overwhelmingly in non-traditional ways for women, whereas good characters behave according to traditional stereotypes of women's roles: mothers are overwhelmingly portrayed as benevolent and knowledgeable about personal and domestic matters; non-mothers as far less knowledgeable, and equally likely to be non-benevolent as benevolent. When conversations are analysed, women talk to women mostly about family and personal matters, men talk to men about professional matters, and women and men talk to each other about romantic matters; women dominate conversations about domestic matters, men dominate conversations about professional matters.

These conclusions are based on a 1974 study; updated figures suggest a less clear division of labour between the sexes in more recent soaps. We have already seen the difficulties that easily arise in the conduct of such analysis, which must lead us to question the reliability of conclusions based on them. However, since all studies, whatever their methods, come to compatible conclusions where the referential concerns of soap are concerned, there seems to be little reason to reject these arguments, whatever doubts we may have about their methods. Similar analyses are to be found in Cassata and Skill (1983: chs 2 and 10).

G. Swanson (1981) uses a method based upon Lévi-Strauss' analysis of the Oedipus myth (summarised Culler, 1975: 41ff.), namely a structuralist method. Her example is *Dallas*, a primetime series rather than a 'true' soap; critics usually argue that primetime series are less concerned with domesticity than daytime ones, but Swanson shows that this is not true of *Dallas*. She observes that any event in the series is given meaning by its place in a matrix of meaning defined by two oppositions: the event either benefits or threatens the family (cf. Feuer, 1986: 106); and it is either functional or dysfunctional in relation to the role that the character(s) involved incarnates, where role is understood as whatever is stereotypically held to be true of that sort of person in our society. Thus the basic structure of the text of *Dallas* consists of forces that place any event in relation to family and to stereotypical role, and Swanson demonstrates that actions that reinforce role – i.e. actions where a character acts in accordance with their stereotyped role – generally tend to benefit the family:

> this correlation shows a definite stance; that one has to cede to stereotypes in order that the family line be perpetuated and safe from invasion.
>
> (Swanson, 1981: 81)

E. Seiter shows through analysis of the story-lines involving two characters for one year of the US soap *General Hospital*, that all the narrative elements involved are directly linked to women's domestic concerns, with an 'essentially Victorian' conception of sexuality: unsatisfied men are not responsible for their actions, villainesses disrupt family life through sexual competition with their friends, etc. (Seiter, 1982: 151–6, 160). Although the men in the serial may have positions of greater authority than the women, in the sense that in the real world the jobs that they have would give them greater authority than the jobs that the women have, none the less the serial valorises women's human knowledge and interpersonal skills more than the occupational skills of the men. As C. Brunsdon says: the representation of work is overwhelmingly in terms of the interpersonal concerns involved, and thus soap 'colonises the public masculine sphere, representing it from the point of view of the personal' (Brunsdon, 1981: 34).

So it is that different methods of analysis lead to a (hardly controversial) conclusion: soap is about domestic concerns. Recent debates, however, have focused more on the relationship between the narrative form of soap and femininity than on referential concerns. This may be because establishing referential concerns in fact tells one less about soaps than first sight suggests. For example, it is clear from the above examples that soaps are about families; but it is also clear that most of these families are in a near-permanent state of disarray: quarrels, misunderstandings, divergent desires between partners, infidelity and divorce – the entire catalogue of everything that can break families up is amply represented on the screen (see e.g. Seiter, 1982: 160; Feuer, 1984: 14f.). Should this be taken to indicate a pro- or anti-family stance?

A further point is that, although villainesses may behave in ways that contradict traditional women's roles and disrupt families through sexual competitiveness, it is clear that they are among the characters whom soap viewers most like (Cassata and Skill, 1983: 34f.; Modleski, 1979: 16). But it should be said that Cassata and Skill check audience fascination with villainesses against audience attitudes towards them: aggressive, powerful women are seen by the audience as 'manipulative and self-indulgent . . . jealous and insecure . . . perhaps as a punishment', which clearly implies a negative judgement as the corollary of the fascination, and leads the authors to the conclusion that soap audiences' definitions of femininity are traditional.

Empirical content analysis is often riddled with fundamental ambiguities. For example, Cassata and Skill (1983: ch. 2) show that there are systematic correlations in soap between the categories of competition and co-operation, on the one hand, and various demographic groups on the other: co-operation is associated with a pro-family orientation, especially among women characters, whereas competition is associated with non-marriage, career and status-orientation, especially among male characters; but such an analysis says nothing about whether these forms of behaviour are offered for approval or disapproval by the narrative, or whether they are in fact approved or disapproved by the audience.

Certain of these ambiguities may be resolved by reference to narrative structure, and feminist critics have, in general, based their interpretations on various features of it. The feature of narrative structure which is at the centre of these debates is the well-known lack of closure, or narrative resolution: because the serial never ends, there is no end to the stories told. Soap may have a beginning, but thereafter it is entirely composed of an indefinitely expandable middle. The notion of closure is central to traditional aesthetics because it is only through the story ending that is possible to say what is the meaning of the events portrayed: until the ending they may change their meaning, and it is for that reason that the chorus at the end of Sophocles' *Oedipus the King* says

> none can be called happy until that day when he carries/His happiness down to the grave in peace.
>
> (Sophocles, 1947: 68)

This is not because happiness is impossible in life, but because things can always change and therefore no definitive account of the meaning of any sequence of events is possible until they are over. Thus closure is the place where the meaning of events becomes fixed: no closure, no fixing of meaning. The experience of a realist text is based on the desire for final resolution: we read in anticipation of the finality of resolution. This is a basic postulate in traditional theories of narrative (for a summary, see Torgovnick, 1981: 3–19).

Its particular relevance to a female readership is demonstrated in Radway, where women readers' strategies for reading are analysed (1984: ch. 2). Centrally, this includes finding time for reading, and selecting books according to the time available: they distinguish between 'quick reads' and 'fat books' that take longer. The importance of the distinction is that it is based around the question of how to find time for uninterrupted reading, which in turn is a product of their desire for the emotional gratification of getting to the end, in other words of finding the resolution of the narrative. Indeed, even in a book they do not like – usually because of excessive violence against the heroine – they feel obliged to read to the end in order not to become 'stuck in the heroine's nightmare' (ibid.: 59, 70f.).[1] But in soap there is no end, and therefore, as Seiter says

> The violation of conventional principles of organic unity [especially the lack of narrative closure] prevents the production of any single meaning in the narrative.
>
> (Seiter, 1982: 159)

Thus soap breaks radically with traditional aesthetic norms, and we shall see shortly that this has led to further debates. In the meantime, lack of closure is linked to feminine identity in various ways. Seiter contrasts the narrative complexity and irresolution of soap with the high degree of resolution typical of male genres (Seiter, 1982: 158; cf. Modleski, 1979: 20). Lovell argues that seriality and non-closure favour independence on the part of the characters, since closure usually involves the implication of permanent relationships and therefore the return to a patriarchal order (Lovell, 1981: 50ff.). Lack of closure derives partly from the never-ending nature of serial fiction, but also from its many story-lines (multiple diegesis), which interact with each other in multiple and unpredictable ways producing a 'polyphonic' narrative where it is inevitable that viewers will interpret the interactions in divergent ways (Cassidy, 1989). This in turn relates to feminine identity in various ways.

Firstly, the multiple story-lines and the large casts allow many different possible identification points for the spectator, rather than the single identification point usual in male genres. Modleski (1979: 12–15) argues that this implies that the focus of the stories is less individual characters than the 'underlying moral process of the world', and that this constitutes the spectator as an 'ideal mother', someone who is wise enough to encompass the conflicting interests of the whole 'family' of characters, and who can therefore place them in the context of an overall moral perspective. Thus soaps assert the primacy of the family, not through the portrayal of some ideal version – as we already know, they conventionally portray it in turmoil – but 'by appealing to the spectator to be understanding and tolerant of the many evils which go on within the family'.[2]

Multiple diegesis also results in another often-commented feature of soap: the spectator knows far more about what is happening than any single character, and is thus able to see that characters are regularly hiding things from each other, lying, and otherwise obfuscating (Geraghty, 1981: 24f.; Ang, 1985: 73). Concomitantly, it is regularly the case that any individual action is commented upon repeatedly by different characters in different combinations, as they assess its (potential) impact upon different people. A recurrent narrative device is the reaction shot used for this specific purpose: A tells B about something that C has done, but without knowing that B has very particular reasons for being interested in this action; the camera then cuts to B's face to allow the audience to observe the effect this information is having unbeknown to the speaker (Allen, 1985: 70). Of course, dramatic irony such as this is a staple of earlier narrative forms, but in soap the multiple diegesis allows its deployment on a massive scale.

In part, the interminable multiple commentary on single actions is a structural necessity for an audience whose viewing is commonly interrupted by household tasks, and who may only be able to watch occasional episodes – specialist magazines keep the occasional viewer up to date with story-lines, and in the US FM radio broadcasts the soundtrack of soaps to enable factory workers to keep abreast of developments (Hobson, 1982: 26, ch. 6; Cantor and Pingree, 1983: 24; Brunsdon, 1981: 33). This form of dramatic irony is thus structurally related to the fact of a female audience, and can be interpreted in relationship to traditional female interpersonal skills; for example, the constant use of close-ups enables the audience to read characters' non-verbal communication against what is actually said, and

> those who are in powerless social positions must be particularly skilful at interpreting non-verbal information in their interactions with others. Soap operas are a means for women to rehearse this ability.
>
> (Seiter, 1982: 157)

Brunsdon (1981: 34–6) argues that multiple diegesis foregrounds emotional and moral dilemmas as the main subject matter of soap, and that it is this foregrounding that provides the continuity of any given series rather than traditional 'linear narrativity', i.e. a sequence of events in which one event leads to another in a causal chain. It invites the viewer to rehearse various possible outcomes – any or all of which may occur – and the real story is not about 'what will happen next?' but about 'what kind of a person is this?'. Soap series thus demand a specific cultural competence on the part of the viewer – interpersonal skills and a relevant moral framework – which is traditionally a female attribute.

In these arguments what we see is the assertion of a structured relationship between the female audience for soap and the narrative structure that is typical of it. We have already seen that this structure is more typical of the daytime soap than of primetime series, and it is in the daytime that the concentrated female audience is to be found. Put at its clearest and most condensed, the argument runs that this narrative structure has various features that appeal to the frame of mind and the cultural competence of women rather than to those aspects of masculinity. However, various factors make this identification less clear than the arguments here suggest.

11 Reading as a Woman

I. Ang argues that the satisfaction sought by the spectators of *Dallas* with whom she corresponded was based on an 'emotional realism' articulated through melodrama (Ang, 1985: 87). That is to say, at one level the viewers know that *Dallas* is a fantasy: they see the flow of events as unreal and the glamour as deriving from the fantasy world of advertising (ibid.: 42, 48, 78); but they perceive as real the 'flux of emotion' aroused by events, and their letters show an intense desire to believe in the characters (ibid.: 30f., 42). Ang calls this 'the tragic structure of feeling'. (A similarly ambiguous attitude towards the relationship between fantasy and reality is revealed in Radway (1984: 186f., 202f.).) To respond to the text in this way is to respond to the elements in it which derive from the melodrama tradition, namely:

(1) the conflicts are between people who are supposedly closest to each other (not between enemies as, for example, in the thriller); this encourages intensified emotional confrontations, and favours the arena of the family and the personal (Ang, 1985: 69f., 76);

(2) The events are very exaggerated – everything becomes a crisis. The exaggeration allows the events to stand as metaphors for 'life's torments in our culture'; for example, alcoholism stands as a metaphor for self-destructiveness. These metaphors are highly unoriginal and it is their lack of originality which gives them their power, through 'direct comprehensibility and recognisability' (ibid.: 62–4);

(3) Soap slows life down. (This is literally true, in that reaction shots show in sequence two things that in 'real time' are happening simultaneously, and they are constantly used; we have already seen (in chapter 3) that 'stretching time' is a technique for emphasising what is to be considered most

important in narrative.) It is brought about by the attribution of great significance to apparently trivial things. Indeed, all events in the drama are very clearly imbued with meaning – nothing is insignificant, the most trivial incident becomes charged with emotional weight. This process is very reassuring because it reveals that there is a close relationship between morality and daily life; it compensates for the 'vague sense of loss' typical of modern life (ibid.: 79ff.).

These elements of melodrama derive from a long tradition of popular writing (see Gledhill, 1987: 14–28 for a brief history and 350ff. for a bibliography). In the nineteenth century this was based on a more or less standardised repertoire of situations, characters and plots – for example, the persecuted virgin and her villainous upper-class seducer – which by the early twentieth century had become such clichés that they were readily parodied. Since then, this repertoire has largely disappeared, but the more basic features of melodrama have arguably subsisted (Gledhill, 1987: 29–37).

Brooks (1976: chs 1–3) argues that melodrama as a form is a response to modernism, it deals with the experience of modern society; it is based on the assumption that any means chosen to represent the modern world will always be radically in deficit in relation to certain key features of experience: there will always (at least, within modern society) be the unrepresentable. This is what melodrama aims to tap into, not by representing it, but by engaging with the emotions that unrepresentability can arouse. Melodrama is part of modernism because modern society is a 'post-sacred' society. In such a society there can be no transcendent value system, belief in which would guarantee a sense of meaningfulness in the everyday life of the individual; such a society needs a means of investing individual everyday lives with significance and justification, organised on a secular basis. Because this is a secular society, such a replacement for the sacred must be conceivable in personal terms: all the values involved will be values that will be translatable into the terms of personal activities and attributes. Melodrama attempts this when it uncovers the domain of operative spiritual values which is both indicated within and masked by the surface of reality: for example, the signs of virtue which are masked by calumny and persecution, but which ultimately always proclaim their effectiveness through their recognition and the usually consequent happy ending. By doing so, melodrama reassures us that the universe is in fact morally legible, that it possesses an ethical identity and significance.

At the same time, our modern society is overwhelmingly oriented towards what Freud calls the 'reality principle', in other words a way of living in which we learn at a very early age to subordinate our innermost desires to the accommodations for them that our world makes available. This process is a process of repression; and what is repressed is never obliterated, it is hidden in the subconscious, but constantly erupts into conscious life. Melodrama plays on this repression: the spectacle, moral polarisation and dramatic reversals for which melodrama is so often criticised serve the purpose of clarification, identification and palpable demonstration of repressed ethical and psychic forces. What is from one point of view a cheap appeal to the shallowest of emotions – a commonplace criticism of melodrama – may better be seen as a testament to forces, desires and fears which, though no longer granted metaphysical reality, nevertheless appear to operate in human life independently of rational explanation. It is the process of repression that makes it impossible for these ethical and psychic forces to be directly representable, and hence creates the space in which melodrama can operate.

In the nineteenth century this appeal could be well-nigh universal: it was central to Victorian morality that sentiment was the visible demonstration of virtue, and therefore the extremes of emotion were perfectly acceptable displays. However, this realm was also the realm in which women were, so to speak, granted pre-eminence, and thus men were put in a somewhat contradictory situation: the demands of sentiment and virtue were also the marks of femininity. Towards the end of the century Victorian culture was 'remasculinised' – men no longer wept in public, for example – and art forms based upon such appeals to sentiment started to be thought of as essentially and exclusively feminine. At the same time, the critical divide between 'high' and 'low' culture is located between realism and tragedy, on the one hand, and melodrama on the other; thus high culture is based upon masculine genres, and feminine ones are relegated to low culture (Drotner, 1989).

Modern melodrama, including soap opera, retains certain basic features from this tradition. In melodrama, personal identity is seen overwhelmingly in terms of position within the structure of the family (Nowell-Smith, 1987: 72f.). Identity, according to Freud, necessitates resolution of the Oedipus complex and must thus take place in an inter-generational setting (we have already seen that such a resolution is in fact impossible, and that therefore identity, for the Freudian tradition, is never fixed and secure). Typically, in modern melodrama, both men and women experience great difficulty in finding a satisfactory place in the family structure, and great difficulty in fulfilling their desires, for the places made available to them by the family structure rarely coincide with what they want – hence the family in permanent disarray that we have seen to be central to soap. The task is already difficult for men, but '"masculinity", although rarely attainable, is at least known as an ideal. "Femininity" . . . is not only unknown but unknowable' since in the world of melodrama women are by and large condemned to passivity and suffering, and are therefore unable to do anything in their attempts to find identity (Nowell-Smith, 1987: 72). The exception to this rule is the villainess, who is the obverse of female passivity. Drawing on a tradition established in the Victorian sensation novel, and especially *Lady Audley's Secret*, the villainess is the woman who refuses to accept the restrictions on her desires that would be imposed by acceptance of woman's lot in the traditional sense; indeed, she turns the traditional forms of women's weakness into strength – passivity and dependence upon men are turned into devious manipulation, and thus become strength (Showalter, 1978: 165ff.; Modleski, 1979: 16).

We have already seen that melodrama typically does not represent the conflicts that underlie its subject matter, but presents their results in a heightened emotional manner; here it is the heightened emotion that is the mark of the underlying, unspeakable, non-representable, repressed desire. Commonly, this takes the form of elements of *mise-en-scène*, which come to stand in for the underlying pressures, just as the hysterical bodily symptom stands in for the underlying psychic pressures that take its form (Nowell-Smith, 1987). Elsaesser (1972) analyses in detail how this process works. If we compare the family melodrama with the Hollywood action film, we often find similar overt themes in the story-line, but whereas the action-based films (such as thrillers and Westerns) take place in an 'open' world where the 'central conflicts' can be 'externalised and projected into direct action', melodrama takes place in a world which is visually closed, where

> the social pressures are such, the frame of respectability so sharply defined that the range of 'strong' actions is limited. The tellingly impotent gesture, the social gaffe, the hysterical outburst replaces any . . . cathartic violence.
>
> (Elsaesser, 1972: 56)

Another form of contemporary melodrama for women is the

romantic novel, which has been much discussed by feminist critics. In general, such comments have been largely negative, concluding – in outline – that this literature presents women 'as some men would like to see them – illogical, innocent, magnetized by male sexuality' (Douglas, 1980: 28; cf. Modleski, 1980; Snitow, 1979). Thus, for example, Modleski (1982: 42–8) stresses how common it is for women characters in Harlequin romances to feel anger at male distance and the 'belittlement' it implies, but the reader familiar with the conventions of the genre knows that the man's unpleasantness is in fact a sign of a love he is as yet unaware of. The story will end with this love recognised, thus ending the unpleasantness and the anger, but at the price of the ultimate belittlement of the woman: subservience to male power in love and marriage. This view has been criticised by Radway (1984), who argues that for women the act of reading the romantic novel is more complex than earlier studies had allowed. (We have already seen the method she used, and its implications, in chapter 1.) Whereas the feminists quoted above saw the romance as primarily a celebration of women's subordination, the readers interviewed by Radway see it both as a celebration of women's independence and as an encouragement to realise that independence in their own lives (Radway, 1984: 77f., 101f.). What readers appreciate is an

> intelligent and able heroine who finds a man who recognizes her special qualities and is capable of loving and caring for her as she wants to be loved.
>
> (ibid.: 54)

This relationship must be portrayed as a gradually developing court-ship, in which the woman tries to deal with the emotions and attentions of a man who wants her but does not understand either her or his own feelings (Radway, 1984: 64f.; cf. Modleski's 1982 argument cited above). At the end, however, she will have created a situation in which these obstacles will have been lifted:

> such an ending [says] that independence and marriage are compat-ible rather than mutually exclusive . . . a utopian vision in which female individuality and a sense of self are shown to be compatible with nurturance and care by another.
>
> (Radway, 1984: 55)

The act of reading stories with this fundamental structure has a meaning for the woman reader: it is an exit from a world grounded in commitments which are based on her subordination to the needs of others – primarily husband and children. In a sense this is escapism, but it is an escape into a fantasy that is structured by what it is an escape from: the 'utopian vision' is based in a 'nurturant' sexual relationship, in which it is the woman's emotional needs that are paramount, needs which (Radway says) are not fulfilled in daily life because of the conditions imposed upon women by the patriarchal structure of society (ibid.: 112ff.). Specifically, the patriarchal family produces in women, through their upbringing,

> an ongoing need for nurturance and attachment . . . that continuously demands the balance and completion provided by other individuals . . . (usually through) a relationship with an adult male.
>
> (ibid.: 135–7)

This conclusion is based on an analysis of what the actual readers Radway interviewed found to be most satisfying about the books that they regarded as the best romances; it is confirmed by an analysis of what readers dislike in romances they regard as failures. In failed romances, the hero's inability to understand the heroine's needs brings about an exaggerated version of the behaviour to which this lack of understanding gives rise in all romances: 'independence, taciturnity, cruelty and violence' (Radway, 1984: 158). That is to say, the basis of the narrative and of the main characters is not fundamentally different in failed and ideal romances, but the emphasis on 'unacceptable' features of the hero's masculinity is far greater in the failed version:

> It seems entirely plausible, then, that these particular stories of a man's transformation from enemy into lover might be less convincing and enjoyable than the ideal version of the transformation because, unlike that version, they do not so effectively set to rest the anger and fear his early behaviors evoke in the reader. Instead of quashing the reader's fear that such is the inevitable character of the male personality, this reading experience might exacerbate that concern.
>
> (Radway, 1984: 158)

Other possible causes of failure are lack of clear narrative focus on the relationship between one man and one woman, and a fear of the validation of female promiscuity: the majority of the readers interviewed say that 'bed-hopping' by the heroine is an unacceptable feature of romance, despite the acceptability of explicit sexual description under other circumstances. Radway hypothesises that portraying a heroine who is neither harmed nor disturbed by her ability to have sex with several men . . . is classified as 'bad' because it makes explicit the threatening implications of an unleashed feminine sexuality capable of satisfying itself outside the structures of patriarchal domination that are still perpetuated most effectively through marriage.

(ibid.: 74; cf. 169ff.)

In short, both failed and successful romances mobilise various features of male and female gender roles, playing on women's fears and aspirations about men. Successful romances produce for their readers what Radway calls 'the promise of patriarchy', in other words they offer (vicariously) the satisfaction of female desire in a way that is plausibly in accordance with the organisation of a patriarchal order; failed romances try to do this, but are organised in such a way that the promised they hold out is not plausible.

At the beginning of the last chapter the audience for soap and romance was singled out as the focus for analysis: to what extent has it been possible to use the fact of a largely (but not exclusively) female audience as the basis of an explanation of these forms?

We have seen that in recent debates various features of these narrative forms have been related to female concerns. It is not difficult to demonstrate that the sorts of events that are portrayed in soap and romance have a close relationship to activities and interests that are traditionally and stereotypically thought of as female: in soap opera, all activities are portrayed from the point of view of domesticity and personal relationships; in romance, relationships are seen from a point of view that coincides with the concerns that women have in a patriarchal society. However, once we try to go beyond positing a simple reflection of women's concerns in this way, it is difficult to find any unequivocal relationship between femininity and narrative form. For example, Radway criticises earlier feminist commentaries on romance for ignoring the way in which the act of reading such fiction corresponds to women's perceived needs; earlier feminists saw this fiction as fixing its readers in a version of femininity that was compatible with patriarchy, and therefore in some sense contrary to female needs. Similarly, many feminist critics have seen a relationship between the narrative form of soap opera – especially its lack of closure and lack of clear focalisation – and valuable features of womanhood. Yet Radway demonstrates that the women she interviewed value narrative resolution very highly. It is clear that what femininity or womanhood means in these contexts is open to debate, since it is apparently compatible with very divergent phenomena.

There are various possible resolutions to these paradoxes. One would be to point to the different demographics of various soap audiences and to show that they see different things in these narratives. Cassata and Skill (1983: 26–31) show how different demographic groups in the audience see different qualities in their favourite characters. The demographic groups were: (a) 12–17 years old; (b) 18–24 single, educated and working; (c) 18–24 homemakers of low educational achievement; (d) 25–39 single, educated and working; (e) 25–39 homemakers of low educational achievement. There were few responses from women over 40. In general the responses showed that different groups of women did indeed see different qualities in their favourite characters:

> The teenage respondents seem to be more cynical about their favorite characters, seeing them as less believable and more 'good' than the other respondents . . . . The 18–24 year old women were less concerned with their characters' family involvements. The [highly educated] group preferred career-oriented, powerful women, whereas the [less-educated] group interpreted their characters as being rather jealous and insecure people. The 25–39 age group offered almost reversed interpretations of the 18–24 year olds. The [highly-educated] group were least interested in the career-orientation of their characters, and most interested in the family commitment. The [less-educated] group gave the least critical appraisal of their favorite character. They tended to give a consistent middle-of-the-road evaluation.
>
> (Cassata and Skill, 1983: 31)

A second approach is taken by Ang (1985: 120–30). She demonstrates that *Dallas* – in this respect typical of soap – allows a multiplicity of subject positions for viewers. For example, it is clear that some viewers are only interested in some characters, and simply pay no attention to what others are doing (ibid.: 46). Indeed, it has been hypothesised that one of the crucial differences between soap and traditional narratives is that the latter are 'goal-driven' – i.e. the sequence is related to the overall tensions and route towards resolution – whereas soap is 'menu-driven': the audience selects which bits of narrative are relevant to its own concerns (Altman, 1986). If this is true, then Ang is no doubt right to insist on the multiplicity of possible readings of any single soap.

Specifically, soap (this is true of romance too) is primarily about tensions within gender relations and the family, presented entirely in personal terms. In soap no overall solutions are offered to these tensions, since the stories never end; in romance, as we have seen, a 'utopian' solution is offered, in which the hero always changes in accordance with stereotypical feminine desires. In either case, different readings are possible, depending upon the value orientation of the audience: feminists may see such narratives as a denunciation of patriarchy or as an encouragement to accommodation with it; traditional women may see them as no more than a moving reflection of the emotional problems they themselves experience, or as an encouragement to take control of their own relationships (Radway, 1984: 78).

In fact what 'reading like a woman' means has been the subject of considerable debate over the last decade. According to Culler (1983: 43–64), there are different feminist positions on this subject. At the first level of feminist criticism

> the concept of a woman reader leads to the assertion of continuity between women's experience of social and familial structures and their experience as readers.

However, it is clear that 'feminist readings are not produced by recording what happens in the mental life of a female reader' since women can and do read in a way no different from men. Although the examples that Culler gives are somewhat different, it is clear that these two points correspond approximately to the attitudes to soap opera and romance that we have already seen: to validate these forms on the grounds of a correspondence between them and female experience and/or expressed needs is to give authority to any reading produced by someone who is female on the grounds that the experience of being female is sufficient basis for such authority. On the other hand, it is clear that not all readings by women are feminist; as Radway points out (1984: 78), what the readers she interviewed mean by 'independence' is not the same as what feminists mean by it. One way beyond this dilemma is to argue that 'reading as a woman' is in fact a theoretical construct, the adoption of a particular stance towards texts. Showalter (quoted Culler, 1983: 50) argues that feminist readings derive from the *hypothesis* of a female reader and the way this alerts us to meanings in the text that would otherwise be lost. This formulation demonstrates the ambiguity of the notion of experience: the experience of being a woman is something that not only precedes and causes the reading, that gives the reading authority, but also has to be produced and achieved in the reading:

> In this sort of analysis, feminist criticism does not rely on the experience of the woman reader as it does at the first level, but employs the hypothesis of a woman reader to provide leverage for displacing the dominant male critical vision and revealing its misprisions . . . an appeal to the potential experience of a woman reader (which would escape the limitations of male readings) and then the attempt to make such an experience possible by developing questions and perspectives that would enable a woman to read as a woman – that is, not 'as a man'.
>
> (Culler, 1983: 57f.)

Culler concludes: the appeal to experience is inevitable

> but 'experience' always has this divided duplicitous character: it has always already occurred and yet is still to be produced – an indispensable point of reference, yet never simply there.
>
> (ibid.: 63)

Culler's stress on the ambiguity of the relationship between the experience of womanhood and the act of reading is also to be found in Toril Moi's *Sexual/Textual Politics* (1985). She demonstrates, through critiques of Anglo-American feminist criticism, that the ambiguity of women's experience is responsible for a series of inconsistencies in arguments based on it. For example, Showalter distinguishes criticism of male authors which must be 'suspicious', from 'gynocritics' (women's analysis of women's writing) which is to be based on 'sympathetic, identity-seeking approaches' (Moi, 1985: 75ff.). Confronted with a male text, the feminist critic must look for absences and hidden contradictions; but in women's texts will look only for evidence of the (presumably authentic) experience it seeks to communicate. Showalter rejects literary theory as male, seeking to replace it with 'the close and extensive knowlege of women's texts which constitutes our essential subject'. Why, Moi asks, should the (female) critic adopt two such divergent attitudes towards texts? The feminist critic here is as much the servant of her mistress as the traditional (usually male) critic is at the service of the canonical text: the text is the authoritative incarnation of experience, the critic the attentive listener. Confronted with a woman's text, the female critic must adopt an essentially male attitude towards it. We might add that Showalter's recommendations would probably preclude critical readings of women's texts such as those produced by

Radway, structured as her argument is around symptomatic silences in the texts.

These issues are arguably even more important in the understanding of filmic images of women than in the case of literature, for in film the gap between sign and referent is arguably smaller than in verbal media, and this works to 'naturalise' images of women, to bring them closer to the lived experience of being a woman, in other words closer to ideology. At the same time, the nature of patriarchal society makes the experience of femininity for a woman narcissistic, since to be a woman is to exist in order to be seen, to be the object of desire. Images of women in the cinema are thus necessarily closer to personal experience than other forms of representation, and Hollywood practice anyway has tended to make women into 'objects of gaze' rather than active protagonists in narrative (Doane, Mellencamp and Williams, 1984; Gledhill, 1984).

Moi pursues the argument concerning the ambiguity of women's experience further in a series of commentaries on feminist applications of psycho-analysis. All of these applications have in common the attempt to abandon any relationship between biological and social gender, i.e. to define 'being a woman' (if it is possible to *be* a woman, since this implies a form of identity that they reject) not in terms of some essential femininity that derives from being biologically female, but in terms of ways of experiencing and acting in the world that break with the dominant patriarchal order. The reason for this strategy is that if one asserts that anything is quintessentially female, that implies that there is indeed some female essence, which is (in principle) accessible to knowledge and is the basis of social gender differences. Being a woman is not therefore *being* anything, it is a way of not-being male, of defining oneself in relationship to a set of power relations. However, this produces a political problem: if womanhood is denied as a form of identity, how is it possible to speak with an authority derived from the experience of being a woman? What is the source of the authority they wish to claim as opponents of patriarchy?

To conclude, what we may derive from this debate is a sense of the restrictions imposed upon explanations based upon target audiences. To be sure, the knowledge that soap and romance are 'aimed at' women is an indispensable starting-point for their analysis. But what we need to know is how they address women: in other words, in what position do they set out to place their audience, who is the subject they seek to address? Ultimately, the reason why we need to ask these questions is because the subject that they are addressing is in fact intensely ambiguous: her biological gender tells us less about her than we need to know, and the margin involved consists of the strategies for being female that the texts propose (masculine gender is similarly problematic, of course). On the other hand, it is equally clear that the textual strategies in question do not constitute the audience: their womanhood is also – and primarily – constituted in the social relations that define men and women. These relations are not static, as we have already seen: women's changing position in the labour market and the changing structure of the family both act to redefine femininity and masculinity. It is only through an investigation of the interactions of these various forces that a full understanding of the functioning of texts such as soap and romance can be achieved.

12 Sitcom: commercial imperatives and humour

Situation comedy (sitcom is the usual abbreviation) is a form whose initial definition derives from its dependence upon broadcast media. It is broadcast comedy in serial form: that is to say, a comic episode is broadcast at regular intervals (usually once a week), involving the same principal characters in situations whose main features are recurrent because they depend upon the relationship between the characters in question; this is known as the 'premise' of the series. Clearly this definition leaves much that is central to sitcom untouched, but it is none the less an important element in understanding it: the nature of broadcast series makes the humorous element of sitcom much less comprehensible to an occasional viewer than to a regular one. A viewer who is unaware of the recurrent relationship between the characters may simply fail to recognise what is provoking gales of laughter from the regular viewer in the next armchair; this indicates how deeply the enunciative situation typical of a genre (see chapter 7) may penetrate into the text–audience relationship.

Traditionally, the sitcom format demanded that the situation should be the same at the beginning of each episode: whatever happened during an episode, we could be sure that its effects would be erased during the following week. However, recent UK sitcoms, especially those written by Carla Lane, have somewhat eroded this principle. For one critic (Grote, 1983), this feature of sitcom is its most fundamental, defining characteristic, and we shall see that his theory of the form is largely based upon it. Of course, this is not a necessary feature of broadcast media, since other serial formats are possible, as we have already seen.

Sitcom readily lends itself to several different forms of explanation. Firstly, since its enunciative situation derives from broadcast media, it can be understood partly in terms of the histories of the institutional imperatives of these media. Secondly, its organisation around humour ensures that some reference must be made to a cultural element found in many forms other than the narratives in question. Thirdly, sitcom most frequently gains its comic effects by reference to readily recognisable features of the everyday social world, and it is legitimate to compare it with the social reality it refers to.

It is convenient to begin with the question of institutional imperatives. The most studied relationship between institutional imperatives and the development of sitcom is the 'new generation' of US sitcoms in the early 1970s, the most cited of which are *All in the Family*, *M*A*S*H* and *The Mary Tyler Moore Show* (see Newcomb, 1974; Feuer *et al.*, 1984; Mintz, 1985; Horowitz, 1984; Zynda, 1988). All of these shows were widely praised for their originality and for their capacity to handle socially controversial material.

There is a consensus about the history of US television which sees these shows (together with drama series made by the same production companies, such as *Hill Street Blues*) as rescuing US television from the stifling mediocrity of the 1950s and 1960s. This was achieved by being more directly oriented towards real issues, more like drama than earlier sitcom, and by using more complex, less 'single-trait' stereotypical characters thereby evoking muted laughter based on recognition of the characters' humanity (Zynda, 1988: 126–34). Specifically, these shows changed sitcom. Earlier US sitcoms were basically simple narrative vehicles designed to deliver the maximum number of jokes, usually 'one-liner' quips; there was little interest in 'character', and narrative tended to be little more than the traditional music hall or vaudeville sketch. The new generation of sitcoms was based on the interactions of an ensemble of characters, where the emphasis on character is all-important.

Thus, to take the example of *Cheers*: the basic premise of the later series is that superstud Sam Malone has had to sell the bar and been forced to accept his subordination to a very beautiful woman manager, who refuses all his advances. Typically, the jokes are inseparable from a trait basic to one or other of the characters, such as the centrality of successful seductions to Sam's self-identity or the centrality of independence and business success to Rebecca's. In a typical episode, Rebecca's estranged sister comes to the bar to try to patch up their relationship. Sam immediately concludes that if he can engineer a reconciliation between them, they may well be sufficiently grateful to both go to bed with him. The reconciliation is a total flop, but on the way he finds out that they are blindly jealous of each other's sexual relationships, and constantly try to steal each other's men. He then pretends to each of them that the other wants to go out with him, and makes dates with them a couple of hours apart. Unfortunately, they both turn up at the same time, and in a fit of jealous rage Rebecca pulls out a gun and shoots her sister, demanding that Sam help her to get rid of the body. As he rushes around in a panic, it becomes clear that the killing was faked and the whole thing had been pre-arranged between the sisters, with the connivance of all the other characters; the joke is well and truly on Sam. However, dealing with Sam's ludicrous advances has really reconciled the sisters and they say – no doubt with a measure of irony – that they are genuinely grateful: '*How* grateful?', asks Sam in the pay-off line.

Here the entire narrative is premised upon the character traits of the protagonists, and each of the jokes is related to the overall narrative drive. In the final joke, for instance, the humour derives from the incongruity of someone being so obsessive that even in this extreme situation he is unable to give up hope of sexual success. This obsessiveness is central to Sam's character, and it is the exaggeration typical of the joke form that reveals it: comedy and character are intertwined.

According to Feuer and Kerr (Feuer *et al.*, 1984: chs 1 and 3), the development of this style of comedy (ensemble playing, the importance of character) is inseparable from the institutional development of US television, and especially its changing economics, at the turn of the decade (1969–71). In the 1950s, the dominant form of television financing had been through sponsorship, where a programme is financed by a commercial organisation, who use the airtime during which it is broadcast to advertise their own product. As the result of some scandalous abuses, and of changes in federal law, from around 1960 television was increasingly financed by 'spot advertising', in which ad agencies buy selected moments of airtime to advertise any product for which they think that moment is suitable; thus programmes were no longer financed by individual commercial organisations, but by advertising revenue from a range of sources. This arrangement had various effects: it led to an increase in editorial control of programme material, since no single outside source had overall control over financing; it led to a search for increasingly detailed knowledge about the identities of audiences, since advertisers now wanted to find the most favourable audience for the product they were promoting, and would hunt for the appropriate spots in airtime.

Also during the 1960s, US television was increasingly abandoned by the youth audience, which sought alternative sources of entertainment. At the end of the decade, the main TV networks were engaged in fierce struggles for audiences, and at the same time it became clear that a small audience with a high disposable income was at least as desirable as a large one with a low disposable income: the affluent youth audience, the one that had abandoned TV, became the most desirable one. At the same time, changes in federal monopoly legislation forced the networks to buy more product from independent producers. The stage therefore was set for independent production companies to devise programmes that would recapture this young affluent audience, and despite initial difficulties, this occurred. Feuer and Kerr characterise this process as 'quality television producing a quality audience'.

What is the explanatory value of these considerations? Kerr puts very clearly what is at stake in taking this approach (Feuer *et al.* 1984: 87f.): the economics of television are largely responsible for the structure of TV production companies; at the same time, the production company in question – MTM TV – has a recognisable house style: quality TV. It ought therefore to be possible to give a systematic account of the relationship between the two elements or, as Feuer puts it, to theorise 'the relationship between commodity production and textual production' (Feuer *et al.*, 1984: 34).

Even if there is no causal relationship between marketing considerations and textual production, the analysis of TV economics summarised in outline above provides a framework within which it is possible to assign different responsibilities to different personnel. The vague notion of a collective author is thus given a more precise profile, in the sense that different roles are distinguished within the production process, roles filled by different individuals, each of which is responsible for different parts of the production process (see also Introduction). In order to go beyond this rather nebulous presentation, it is necessary to take particular examples and see how the various roles apply in actual situations.

Feuer *et al.* demonstrate that there are direct thematic links between the target audience of MTM and what appears on screen. For example, the female characters in MTM shows directly mirror the birth of the 'new woman' for the female baby-boomers who were a large part of their target audience (Feuer *et al.*, 1984: 36), and at the same time the stories are all set in a surrogate family in the workplace, a response to the breakdown of the nuclear family in the real world (ibid.: 57; cf. Zynda, 1988: 132). They show that much of the comedy in *The Mary Tyler Moore Show* derives from the wry recognition that family relationships are not superior to other forms of sociality, but that female friendships are; this is linked to the feminist slogan 'Sisterhood is powerful'. The case is clear: the demography of the target audience is linked to the content of the shows. However, while this certainly supports the claim that institutional imperatives have explanatory power, we must ask how far this principle can be extended. A comparison between the production techniques of *All in the Family* and *M*A*S*H* is suitable ground for testing it.

Both are among the list of shows which are conventionally credited with the renewal of US TV referred to here, and even if the processes internal to the different production companies involved do not quite coincide with the processes in MTM TV described by Feuer *et al.*, it is clear that they did in fact appeal to essentially the same audience, since *All in the Family*, *The Mary Tyler Moore Show* and *M*A*S*H* were programmed in a block on Saturday nights in the early 1970s, on the grounds that each would reinforce the audience for the others (Feuer *et al.*, 1984: 7).

All of these shows have clearly distinct identities: the comedies that Norman Lear produced, such as *All in the Family*, were abrasive treatments of contemporary issues, based around an outrageous caricature 'who gives voice to socially ostracised thoughts in a way that excites us without implicating us' (Sklar, 1980: 6). MTM's shows were based upon character rather than upon issues and depended upon an ensemble of more evenly weighted characters. *M*A*S*H* was only partly comedy – indeed, many people involved in its production denied it was a sitcom at all – and depended very largely upon ensemble playing and upon the mixture of comedy and drama. Thus each production company is producing something that has a clearly separate identity, within the confines of what is acceptable to its target audience.

This process can be pursued into the heart of the production methods (Barker, 1984). *All in the Family* was filmed always within a space defined in the same way as theatrical space: separated from the audience by a line that the camera never crosses – in the theatre this line is the proscenium arch, and this type of filming is called 'in proscenium'. Therefore the TV audience always sees the characters and the events in question from the outside, since the camera never goes into the space the characters occupy to show events from their point of view. Clearly this production method is linked to the basis of the show: the gross caricature that is at its heart, for a gross caricature demands to be seen from the outside. The decision was also taken to shoot the series in real playing time, using three cameras; that is to say, the duration of the pro-filmic event and the duration of filming were the same, and all editing was done during production, by switching from one camera to another. Using this technique involves very precise timing by the actors: the pauses between words and the physical movements within stage space must be exactly co-ordinated with camera movements. By contrast, M*A*S*H was shot with a single camera and not in proscenium: the camera moves among the characters in a very fluid way, constantly shifting points of view as the interactions between the characters shift their basis. Since a single camera was used, all editing had to be done post-production, and thus precise timing by actors was unnecessary.

First sight suggests that such features of these shows cannot be explained on the basis of the principle that Feuer *et al.* advance: the shows were targeted at essentially the same audience, and it is this targeting that is said to be responsible for the nature of the shows; yet the shows are clearly very distinctive in their presentation. However, we should note that Feuer *et al.*'s principle still provides us with a framework within which we can start to understand the processes described here, for the analysis of MTM TV and its relationship to the networks shows us how decisions about audience and budget create the framework for editorial decisions: the structure of a studio settles who will take the various decisions in question, and within what constraints. Thus, while it is clear that marketing decisions in no way determine, in the causal sense, what appears on the screen, none the less they do define the outline of a strategy: they set the goals to be aimed for, and it is in the context of aiming for these goals that editorial decisions are taken. To this extent one can say that institutional imperatives have a high explanatory value.

However, another historical comparison points elsewhere. British television had developed an essentially similar style of sitcom at a much earlier stage of television history – indeed, as is well known, Norman Lear's *All in the Family* was directly based on the BBC's *Till Death Us Do Part*, broadcast from 1965 onwards. This style of comedy – based upon character – had been developed in earlier BBC series, for instance those starring Tony Hancock: the radio series *Hancock's Half Hour* and the subsequent television version called *Hancock*. Although extended analysis would be necessary to prove this point in detail, it is clear in general that Hancock's form of comedy depended upon the same relationship between incident and character as MTM-style comedy such as *Cheers*. Hancock plays a character who is consistent across episodes: punctilious but inaccurate about social correctness, obsessed with self-improvement, easily victim to one-sided understanding of situations, and at the same time convinced that he is the centre of the known universe; the humour in each episode stems from the interaction between such a character and a series of situations in which his version of what the world is like is severely tested. In one of the most famous episodes, *The Blood Donor*, much of the humour derives from the fact that he is convinced that being a blood donor makes him someone rather special, who deserves public consideration, including, for instance, the right to say who his blood will be given to. It is then the incongruous contradiction between voluntary public service and the obsessive sense of personal entitlement that is the source of much of the humour. Just as *The Mary Tyler Moore Show* caught humorous ambiguities surrounding the birth of the 'new woman', so Hancock encapsulated the contradictions between the ideals of respectability and collectivity so sharply focused by the war-time experience, and the abrasive new individualism of the post-war period.

How does this example affect our assessment of the explanatory power of institutional imperatives? The core of Feuer *et al.*'s argument is that 'quality TV' was produced in the hunt for 'quality demographics': in other words the decision to make character the basis of comedy was produced in the search for a limited, sociologically specific audience. But it seems unlikely that the BBC was motivated in quite the same way. Although it is certainly true that the advent of commercial TV in the 1950s, ending the BBC's monopoly, led to attempts at audience maximisation, this is very different from the US situation at the end of the 1960s, where audience maximisation was what was being discarded in favour of 'quality demographics'. In short, the example of BBC sitcom (other examples could be cited: for instance, *Steptoe and Son*) suggests that 'quality TV' – specifically, character comedy – can certainly be sought on the basis of other types of programming decisions.

This should not be thought to imply that institutional imperatives have a low explanatory value – clearly this form of study of fictional texts has very high explanatory power, as we have seen – but there are limits to what it is capable of telling us.

One of the features of sitcom that it does not explain is the mechanism of humour: the funniness of sitcom largely disappears in this account. Another is the historical relationship of sitcom to earlier forms of humour and comedy. Both of these subjects may be approached through a consideration of D. Grote's *The End of Comedy* (1983).

Grote's thesis is that although sitcom uses many of the same techniques for the arousal for mirth as traditional comedy, none the less it is a fundamentally different form, and the differences lie in its narrative shape. There is some consensus among literary historians and theorists that the mainstream Western comic tradition – that starts with Athenian Old Comedy, passes through the Roman theatre to the Renaissance and continues in literary comedy at least through the nineteenth century – has a common narrative form and that this form has an intrinsic meaning. In this analysis, comedy is about the realisation of desire against opposition: typically, comedy is about young lovers whose happiness faces obstacles in the form of some absurd refusal of their union, usually from the older generation; in order to overcome it, they have to turn to various subterfuges, often helped by an ingenious servant. Thus this comedy is the assertion of life-giving forces against the forces of death and decay, and comedy always recommends some form or other of social change (cf. Frye, 1971; Langer, 1953: 326–48; Palmer, 1987: 25–9).

We should note immediately that this theory reduces the importance of funniness and promotes the importance of narrative shape; indeed, Suzanne Langer's influential theory asserts that humour is not a necessary feature of comedy at all (1953: 336). Sitcom is very different, Grote argues. Seriality imposes a particular narrative form: at the beginning of each episode the situation must be the same as at the beginning of all the others, and therefore the narrative of sitcom is always circular: at the beginning of each episode something happens to disrupt the normal state of affairs; by the end of the story the status quo has returned (see Mintz, 1985: 118 for summaries of similar arguments by other critics). This status quo is always implicitly the set of relationships that construct a family, since the characters of sitcom always compose pseudo- or real families, in the sense that they are bound together for the duration of the series in a set of highly charged, interminably reproduced relationships (cf. Zynda, 1988: 134f.; Bathrick, 1984: 100ff.). The contrast with earlier forms of comedy is clear: where the latter all validate change, sitcom returns to stasis, the stasis of the family-like group; thus, the conclusion runs, sitcom is a deeply conservative form.

Grote's argument, reduced to its simplest form, is this: sitcom borrows comic techniques from previous comedy – its form of funniness is no different – but it ties humour to a different narrative shape, and is therefore fundamentally different. One of the central implications of this argument is that humorous techniques are subordinate to narrative, that narrative shape produces meaning independently of the humorous techniques that arouse pleasure during the narrative. Undoubtedly this opens up a further debate, about the relationship between humour and narrative. Perhaps what the viewer seeks when tuning in to sitcom is humour, not narrative – indeed, the narratives of sitcom are minimal. Yet, as Newcomb argues, 'the more fundamental appeal of the sitcom is the fact that everything always comes out all right' (1974: 40), and this is a product of narrative shape. We must ask therefore: is humour the form of pleasure that the sitcom viewer seeks when tuning in? Or is the narrative shape in question actually the basis of its attraction? Which of these two, or what combination of them, is the root of the implied contract with the audience that the genre proposes (see chapter 7)? In order to answer this question we need to make a brief detour through the theory of humour.

It is a commonplace among recent theories of humour that it arises from incongruity (Palmer, 1987: 19–74). The definition of incongruity which applies here is that what we observe does and does not make sense simultaneously; in other words, if we look at it from one point of view it appears to be nonsense, but from another point of view it does make sense. To take a brief example: Bob Hope, asked on a chat show if he had known Doris Day for a long time, replied 'Oh sure! I knew Doris Day before she was a virgin!'. From one point of view this statement is nonsense: there is no such thing as pre-virginity, by definition. However, from another point of view it does make sense: if ever an actress adopted a public screen persona in which virginity was integral, it was Doris Day, and in that sense she 'became' a virgin. Bob Hope's crack plays (incongruously) on these two ways of understanding the situation. What is significant for our purposes about such a definition of humour is that it shows that humour clearly has its own structure. If humour, as it operates in real life in the form of jokes, laughter at various situations, etc., is an entity that has its own rules, then its operations are independent of individual narratives: any narrative that wishes to be funny must follow the rules of humour-creation. Indeed, this is implicitly recognised in arguments such as Grote's, where narrative has its own shape and simply 'imports' humour as and when necessary. But the question which must be answered – and very rarely is – is this: in what way can narrative and humour be combined? Does importing humour into a narrative have any effect upon that narrative?

We can see from this example that the basis of humour is a relationship of logical implication between propositions, arranged in a sequence. This principle is the basis of how jokes interact with the larger-scale narrative which constitutes a sitcom episode, and which is the object of Grote's analysis. This is best understood on the basis of some examples.

The British sitcom series *Porridge*, starring the well-known co-median Ronnie Barker as Fletch, is set in a jail, where he is doing time ('porridge' is prison slang for time served), and where his witty manipulation of his fellow inmates and of the prison staff ensures him a pleasant life. In an episode entitled, 'Men Without Women' Fletch uses his fellow-inmates' fears about potentially unfaithful spouses for his own purposes. He charges them for writing letters to their wives accusing them of infidelity, thus getting all the women to come and visit them. However, his wife doesn't visit; the presumption is that she is being unfaithful, and he is given compassionate leave to go home and sort things out. In practice, the final scene of the episode reveals there is nothing wrong at home, and he has engineered the whole event so that he could get a weekend off. During the episode the prison officer McKay, who is proud of his decades of military service as a drill sergeant, mocks Fletch for being the prison 'agony aunt' and boasts about the superiority of service wives to prisoners' wives. McKay is especially proud of the military orderliness of his own domestic arrangements, but Fletch uses this to undermine his authority:

> Do everything by numbers, did you? (in mock parade-ground tone of voice) I am going to make passionate love to you . . . . Stand by your bed! One, two . . . Wait for it, wait for it! Two, three . . . . Knickers down!

Clearly the humour of this moment derives from the incongruity analysed above: the incompatibility of military hierarchy and sexual passion. The conjunction of the two is brought about by earlier strands in the narrative: McKay mocking Fletch and boasting about his domestic life. And while it does not directly bring about any subsequent events – in that sense it is a dead end, an 'interruption' of the narrative – it none the less fits very clearly with the sequence of events portrayed here: it shows yet again Fletch's capacity to manipulate events and people; it is a miniature version of his overall project to subvert the prison system for his own purposes; and it is directly related to the topic of the whole episode, since it is caused by McKay mocking the matrimonial advice role that Fletch has temporarily adopted.

The episode of *Cheers* referred to earlier provides a similar instance. The pay-off line from Sam ('*How* grateful?') derives its meaning, which is the source of its comic impact, from what has gone before – not just from our general knowledge of Sam's character, important though this is in the comic impact, but from the narrative of the episode, the sequence of his attempts to manipulate the situation to his own advantage. Indeed, this line only reveals Sam's obsessiveness because of its relationship to the narrative of the episode as a whole: spoken at an earlier stage of this sequence of events, it would not have the same meaning.

Thus we can see that individual jokes in a sitcom narrative are inseparable from the narrative within which they function: each joke is prepared in earlier stages of the narrative as a whole. What this reveals is that, ultimately, it is not possible to separate narrative shape from the structure of humour in the case of comic narrative. This, in its turn, is heavy with implications for the Grote thesis about sitcom, and for our understanding of the form of sitcom in general (see Palmer, 1987: 115–41).

A second way of analysing the relationship between narrative and the mechanism of humour points in the same direction. In much comedy – the most traditional as well as sitcom – the entire story is no more than an extended joke. For example, in Boccaccio's *Decameron* (I.iv), a novice monk smuggles a girl into his cell; the abbot sees her, finds her pretty, and makes love to her as well, but the novice sees the event. When the abbot threatens to expel him, the novice replies that he was unaware of the rules, but now that he has the abbot's example before him he will always conform to it. The abbot realises the implication and between them they smuggle the girl out of the monastery. The whole point of the story is the witty inversion/subversion that terminates it. Much sitcom follows the same pattern, for example the 'Men Without Women' episode of *Porridge*. Fletch's witty subversion terminates the episode by revealing that the events we have been watching had a very different meaning to the one we assumed.

In each case the witty ending conforms to the model of incongruity. In the Boccaccio story, the novice's words to the abbot have a double meaning: the discrepancy between the two meanings is very great, and the thought has to be formulated with verbal precision in order to fit both meanings. One of the forms of incongruity is surely ambiguity, especially where the meanings in question are so diametrically opposed to each other; indeed the difference between the two meanings is also the difference between hypocrisy and virtue. In the case of *Porridge*, it is incongruous that the apparent meaning of events should be so diametrically opposed to the real meaning. Thus in each case, the ending of the story follows the pattern of humour creation: each story is, in a sense, an extended joke. At the same time, the fact that these events constitute the ending of the story is important. In order for a story to end satisfactorily, it is usually argued, the audience must feel that all the tensions aroused during the story have been resolved, that there are no loose ends lying around. In these stories this is achieved by the wit of the endings: the gust of laughter is what convinces us that the story is over, that everything is resolved. (This is not to say that everyone would in fact be convinced: feminists might well be rather unamused by the Boccaccio story.) If we are convinced by the ending, this is because in it the previous meanings are so totally reversed: in other words, the structure of the humour and the structure of the narrative are one and the same in this instance.

There are divergent opinions about the relationship between narrative and humour. At one extreme is Mintz's judgement, that humour in sitcom is the servant of narrative rather than its master (Mintz, 1985: 117); at the other is Eaton's claim that, in comedy, narrative is merely the vehicle for 'those excesses – gags, verbal wit, performance skills – which momentarily suspend the narrative' (Eaton, 1981: 22); intermediary positions will be found in Neale (1981b) and Lovell (1982). It is only when the structural relationship between humour and narrative is analysed in particular instances that it is possible to go beyond generalisations and assertions of this nature.

An example of this is to be found in Mellencamp (1986), an analysis of *The Burns and Allen Show* and *I Love Lucy*. Mellencamp demonstrates that in these two shows the narrative acts to contain the threat posed to a male order by two 'crazy' women: Gracie Allen 'unmakes decorum' (ibid.: 84), but George Burns' privileged access to the camera – nods and winks to the audience, benevolent explanations of Gracie's absurdities – counterbalances this undermining of order. Similarly with Lucy: her dissatisfaction at domesticity leads her to a series of activities that undermine male dominance, yet at the end of the narrative she is always returned to her place; but the spectator's pleasure is premised not upon this return but upon the chaos she creates on the way, due to her inspired clowning. In both cases, narrative equals containment, it 'embodies a political determinism in which women find a subordinate place' (ibid.: 91); but in sitcom it is not narrative but comic performance that dominates, thus the impact upon gender construction in the real world depends upon how audiences react to the structure of humour.

At this point we may return to Grote's thesis: that the circularity of sitcom narrative makes it a conservative form. Two considerations point in the opposite direction. Firstly, Mellencamp's argument about the subversion of narrative. Secondly, this circularity is a comic circularity, because narrative and humour are inseparable; thus we may evaluate it differently. Certainly we know that at the beginning of any episode the set of relationships that constitute the premise will be in place, and it seems largely true that these relationships are family-like; at least in many sitcoms the level of emotional investment in them in combination with their recurrent nature gives them a significant resemblance to family structure.

However, two things restrict the impact of these observations. Firstly, at the end of each episode it is frequently the case that the situation is significantly different from what it was at the beginning. At the end of the two sisters' episode of *Cheers*, Sam is publicly humiliated; at the end of the 'Men without Women' episode of *Porridge*, Fletch has succeeded in subverting the prison system, albeit temporarily. Perhaps we might say that these changes are unimportant because we know that by the beginning of the next episode things will have returned to normal. Yet – secondly – this in itself could mean something else: Rebecca humiliates Sam to teach him a lesson about his attitude towards sexuality and herself, but we know that he will learn nothing from it and she will have to fight him off again and again, which will be one of the main sources of humour in subsequent episodes; Fletch subverts the prison system, but this subversion is very limited, and he will be back inside again, his future attempted subversions another source of humour. In each instance what we are looking at is a form of comic frustration: it is ridiculous that Fletch should be repressed by men he can constantly get the better of; it is ridiculous that it should be Rebecca and Sam who are forced into each other's company. Again and again in sitcom series the basis of the humorous situation is ultimately the absurdity of people who need each other like a hole in the head but cannot break away from each other; this derives from the nature of humour and of serial fiction.

In a televised *South Bank Show* lecture on the future of British TV, Colin MacCabe compared the best of sitcom to Samuel Beckett's plays: in each case we see people trapped in the mesh of a language that they want to master, but which ultimately masters them. While this is no doubt true of some series characters (Hancock and the son in *Steptoe and Son*, for instance), I would prefer to compare sitcom to Kafka. We know from Max Brod's *Diaries* that when Kafka read his works aloud to his friends in Prague, they were frequently shaken with helpless laughter, which I suspect derived from a sense of ridiculous impotence and frustration. All allowances made for obvious differences, I suspect that the basis of much sitcom is similar, and that while it is no doubt true that in much sitcom (e.g. *Mork and Mindy*) the circularity of the form goes hand in hand with the type of happy integration that Adorno hated in it (Adorno, 1975: 603f), in many instances the circularity is an index of comic frustration. The best example is probably the BBC series *Fawlty Towers*, where the central character's enforced co-habitation with those he regards as his inferiors is a calvary of ridiculous frustration (see Palmer, 1987: 115–40 for a fuller account). What the principle observed here suggests is that the level of integration that Grote detects is not a product of the form itself but of a particular application of it.

13 Sitcom and social reality

It has been a commonplace of recent British debates about film and TV comedy that there are largely two forms of comedy: a form where humorous technique achieves the disruption of the mechanisms whereby meaning is achieved (the Marx Brothers, for instance) and a form where humorous technique is used to portray various forms of social disruption in a fundamentally realistic manner – most sitcom falls into this category (Ellis, 1975; Eaton, 1981: 22; Cook, 1982). I have shown elsewhere (Palmer, 1987: 143ff.) that the distinction between the two forms of humour is not fundamentally valid, in that the semiotic mechanism is the same in both instances. However, there certainly are different degrees of social realism in different forms of comedy: the new generation of American sitcoms is clearly directly concerned with social issues in a way that Laurel and Hardy or Jerry Lewis, for example, are equally clearly not. While it is impossible to summarise everything that has been said on the subject, we may at least indicate what methods have been used, with what effect, in this analysis.

Oakley (1982) uses traditional critical methods to denounce the implicit conservatism of the very popular British series *Yes Minister*, in which the protagonists are a Minister (Secretary of State) and his senior civil servant. The entire subject matter of the series is the conduct of national politics, and since its first broadcast (in 1980) it has been widely hailed as a 'radical' series, largely because of its high degree of cynicism about political and administrative processes. Oakley demonstrates that the political cynicism involved is of a particularly Thatcherite (or Reaganite) variety: it amounts to the conviction that the national bureaucracy is only there to obstruct efficiency, to feather its own nest, to ensure that administration remains the preserve of a small, self-serving elite. Specifically, he shows that this view is written into the structure of the series' humour: each of the cynical jokes he quotes invites us to laugh at the machiavellian tactics of the senior administrator, who thus implicates – by metonymy – the bureaucracy as a whole. Oakley concludes:

> Very real public anxieties about the remoteness of political power and the influence of civil servants are touched on only to be largely effaced by the structure of the programmes . . . reinforcing 'common sense' concepts, particularly ideas about 'bureaucracy', 'politics' and 'politicians'. The way this is done is conservative in the important sense that socially interventionist political action is presented as implicitly pointless and doomed to failure.
>
> (Oakley, 1982: 76, 67)

In this study the overt butt of jibes is shown to be, consistently, a particular element in the social structure: it is perhaps as much this as the premise of the series that provides its identity. Specifically, Oakley argues that it is these jokes *in the context of Thatcherite attacks upon the welfare state* that have this meaning. However, we may legitimately ask whether the jokes would mean the same thing to a left-wing opponent of Mrs Thatcher as they would to one of her supporters. Although there is no study of such variations in meaning for this series, there is a study of a similar phenomenon.

Vidmar and Rokeach (1974) analyse 'selective perception' of the bigotry of Archie Bunker, the central character of *All in the Family*, a series that was modelled directly on an English predecessor (Alf Garnett and *Till Death Us Do Part*). The context in which the study was undertaken is the evidence that came to light in the early 1970s of a dual response to this programme both in the USA and the UK. In England the programme was attacked by conservative moral entrepreneurs such as Mrs Whitehouse for being left-wing propaganda disguised as comedy; but it was also clear that many people in the audience laughed with Garnett rather than at him (Whitehouse, 1971: 78f.; Speight, 1973). In the United States, *AITF* was awarded the 1972 Image Award by the NAACP for its contribution to race relations, but it became clear that much of the show's fan mail was applauding Archie Bunker's bigoted tirades (Vidmar and Rokeach, 1974: 37).

How is such 'selective perception' possible? Vidmar and Rokeach's answer, in brief, is that people viewed the show through the filter of their own prejudices, each seeing in the show what they already saw in the world around them. As well as revealing widespread liking for the programme, and a very low level of distaste for its possible offensiveness, viewer responses to questionnaires showed that a majority (between 60 and 65 per cent) admired Archie (the equivalent to Alf Garnett) more than his liberal son-in-law, that around 40 per cent thought that Archie usually 'won at the end' of the programme, and that only a minority (in one sample 10 per cent, in another 32 per cent) thought that Archie was most often the butt of the humour (1974: 40). The respondents were also asked questions designed to separate 'prejudiced' from 'non-prejudiced' viewers (i.e. racists from non-racists, more generally conservatives from liberals). When the responses outlined above were split according to the social attitudes of the respondents, it became clear – according to Vidmar and Rokeach – that those who liked Bunker were in general those who were most prejudiced. As well as generalised liking, high prejudice is significantly correlated with other judgements about Archie. High-prejudice viewers are more likely than are low-prejudice ones to think that:

(1) Archie wins;
(2) other characters are made fun of rather than Archie;
(3) Archie makes better sense;
(4) Archie's ethnic slurs are not wrong.

In general, Vidmar and Rokeach's theory seems well supported by this evidence. However, there are various anomalies in their argument which need exploring. Firstly, it is not made clear whether the people who disliked Archie because he was a bigot, etc., were also low in prejudice. Although such an inference is plausible, the statistical tables reveal that a significant minority of high-prejudice viewers preferred Mike to Archie, and that a majority of low-prejudice viewers prefer Archie to Mike. Secondly, virtually all viewers agree that Archie makes less sense than Mike – a maximum of 10 per cent think Archie makes more sense. Thirdly, when respondents are asked who is most often the butt of the humour, there is a very great discrepancy between the two samples of respondents: in the US adolescent sample, differences between low-and high-prejudice viewers dwindle to insignificance, whereas in the adult sample there is a considerable difference.

What do these anomalies suggest? Firstly, we should recall the inferential process involved here. In general, such studies argue that if x is more likely than y to do q, then some feature of x is causally related to q. Under these circumstances, given the nature of the inferences, there will always be processes revealed in the statistics that suggest the adoption of subject positions that are opposed to those cited in conclusion. For example, some high-prejudice viewers prefer Mike to Archie, and many low-prejudice ones prefer Archie to Mike. The authors argue that high-prejudice viewers are consistently more likely to prefer Archie, which is true, but the argument based on probability necessarily refuses to recognise any inferences that might be based upon the opposite identification. I would prefer to ask the following questions. What mechanism makes it possible for each of these anomalous processes to occur – for some people to like Archie but think he makes less sense than someone they like less? For some people to dislike what Archie stands for but still prefer him to someone who (*ex hypothesi*) stands for the same as they do? For some people to stand for the opposite of Archie but still think it is the others who are the butt of the humour?

In each case the answer is essentially the same: the ambiguity which is intrinsic to humour (Palmer, 1987: 179ff.). A brief example will demonstrate this mechanism. During the Second World War this joke circulated in occupied Eastern Europe:

> A rumour goes round that the Nazis are going to kill all the Jews and all the barbers. One evening, in a bar, a group of citizens are pondering this rumour. Eventually one says 'Of all the nonsense. Why the barbers?'
>
> (Quoted in Skvorecky, 1986: 252)

Is this an anti-semitic joke? It is easy to interpret it this way: the speaker (in the joke, not the person who tells the joke) has simply assumed that the first part of the rumour is utterly unimportant (or so obviously true that it is not worth mentioning), and it would be easy to laugh at the implied insult to the Jews derived from the incongruous reasoning process he has followed. But it is equally easy to see it as a joke aimed at anti-semitism: seen in this light we would laugh at the exaggerated nastiness and stupidity of the speaker's reasoning process, and in wry recognition of its frequency in less exaggerated form. In either case the source of the humour is the incongruous reasoning process, and it will probably be some feature of the circumstances under which the joke is told that is responsible for its political dimension: its meaning could diverge fundamentally depending on the identity of the joker, for instance whether (s)he was Jewish or not.

Although this principle does not apply universally (see Palmer, 1990), it easily applies to many of the jokes in *All in the Family* and *Till Death Us Do Part*: much of the humour, especially in the US version, consisted of insults often expressed in the form of absurd reasoning on Archie's/Alf's part. For example: an argument between Alf and his wife and daughter about why his underpants are so filthy turns into a deliberately aggressive tirade on women's subordinate status:

> God – *He* – *He* put woman here just for man, didn't He? . . . . Yer Garden of Eden – all God done there was made man – Adam. But God, in his infinite wisdom, realised that he couldn't expect man to run the Garden of Eden on his own. So He, God, He took a rib an' made Eve . . . so she could clean . . . an' wash up . . . an' look after Adam's house for him. So, you see, if it hadn't been for man, and man's need for a home help, woman wouldn't have got born at all, in the first place.
>
> (Speight, 1973: 108)

Here, Alf's rhetoric creates a situation in which it is possible either to laugh with him, because of the ingenuity of the put-down of his wife and daughter, or to laugh at him, because of the prejudiced stupidity of the argument; the argument's origin in Alf's personal habits only strengthens each of these processes. Such a conclusion is, of course, not inconsistent with Vidmar and Rokeach's analysis. However, what is significant is that in both these instances, the audience could still be expected to laugh; and it is easy to imagine audience members laughing at the stupidity of the argument and yet still liking Alf because he makes them laugh, or because of the sheer energy of his commitment to prejudice. Moreover, as you watch a show like this, it is not easy to be sure whether you are laughing at Alf because of his stupidity, or with Alf at the family members he is insulting, or just laughing at the fact of a well-expressed insult. Perhaps it is in mechanisms like this that ambiguities such as the ones revealed in Vidmar and Rokeach's findings have their roots.

If this analysis is correct, it has implications for the final way in which sitcom is often said to refer to the social world: the commonplace argument that sitcom deals in stereotypes.

The uses and limitations of the concept of stereotype are usefully summarised by Neale (1979). A stereotype is a form of character construction – 'a stable and repetitive structure of character traits' (ibid.: 33) – and thus it is only one part of any given text, that element of the text which links it with other texts with similar characters; of necessity therefore a discussion of the stereotypes in a text (or group of texts) must omit other ways in which texts function. Thus, such a discussion of sitcom would inevitably omit considerations such as Grote's.

Stereotypes are usually evaluated according to two strategies: by comparing them to the real or to some ideal. In the first instance, a stereotype may be compared with a commonsense summary of lived experience – for example, a romantic novel might be dismissed as an inadequate presentation of what love is 'really like'. Or a presentation of a particular social group might be seen as untrue because it is too limited – such would be the implications of the charge that TV drama portrays women predominantly in the 'sexually eligible age group' (Gerbner and Gross: 1976). In the second instance, a stereotype is measured against some sense of what a person or a social group is capable of being: typically, the analysis of a stereotype is used as the basis of a demand for a more 'positive image' of the group in question. Frequently, of course, both arguments are pursued: programme x, (or genre x, or author x, etc.) misrepresents such-and-such a group, who demand a more positive image. Such claims have a cutting edge in USA, since federal legislation enjoins fairness towards all sections of the population.

The measurement of stereotypes derived from Gerbner's 'cultural indicators' programme conforms to Neale's description of the second strategy of comparison (see ch.1). Neale concludes that the concept 'stereotype' is only useful if it is used in conjunction with an analysis of how texts produce meanings that are associated with particular characters or character types, since otherwise stereotypes will be taken to be empirical entities which are always already present in a culture and simply repeated in any given text; the reality is that they are produced and reproduced in individual texts (and other discourses) through describable discursive strategies.

In these chapters sitcom has been analysed in several different ways. These were:

(1) the institutional imperatives of broadcasting organisations;
(2) the relationship between humour and narrative;
(3) the mode of portrayal of real-life entities in various sitcoms, especially the question of stereotyping;
(4) the supposition that sitcom is in some sense a genre (although this has not been the subject of explicit comment until now).

Institutional explanations

We have already seen that this form of explanation is by no means a complete one. However, it has very considerable strengths. Specifically, where popular narrative is concerned, it has the great advantage that it provides a precise replacement for the concept of the author. We saw in the introduction that the concept of the author holds a privileged place in critical understanding of canonical literature: it is the place where vision and cohesion reside. Popular narrative, on the other hand, is neither visionary (or only rarely) nor cohesive: it is traversed by all the forces that were analysed in part I: enunciative mechanisms, genre, ideology, etc. The disadvantage of generalisations such as these is that, in any given instance, the configuration of these forces will not be predictable on the basis of this generalisation: for example, in a well-defined genre such as the crime novel, it is difficult to distinguish genre from commercial pressure – since commercial pressure primarily takes the form of conformity to the 'rules of the game' – and what is clearest to *aficionados* is the difference between authors. Explanations such as Feuer *et al.* (1984) provide the precise configuration: in a situation of economic change, producer x and programmer y sought a new type of programme; they found a star, they found scriptwriters, they obtained a budget, etc. The rather vague notion of a 'collective *auteur*' is given flesh and blood, each individual series is shown to have an identity which is related to the institutional imperatives within which it was born (cf. Buckingham, 1987).

Humour and narrative

Clearly, no explanation of sitcom can avoid reference to humour, and it is evident by surveying writings on the subject that the relationship between humour and narrative is not easy to analyse; it is equally evident that it is essential to do so. The explanation of the relationship that has been used here is based on post-structuralist principles, in various ways. Firstly, there is the textual process which brings humour and narrative together. We have seen that humour necessarily involves chains of reasoning; these chains of reasoning are what hold the humorous narrative together, they are what bind the sequential elements of the narrative into a chain. Secondly, there arises the question of subject positions in the text. In general, sitcom follows the rules of realist film-making, in which we 'trust' the camera to reveal the truth (whereas the characters may lie, or not know enough, the narrative is always ultimately adequate: here it is the camera-based narrative that is the superordinate discourse in a hierarchy of discourses). But within this overall narrative framework, the mechanisms of humour invite particular identifications: at any given point the invitation to laugh implicates the audience as people who are prepared to laugh at whatever is proposed as the subject of laughter. To use again the example of *Cheers*: if we laugh at Sam's discomfiture after the fake death of Rebecca's sister, it is because we think it is right to mock sexual obsession, or at any rate this sexual obsession.

Social references

Here it is more difficult to generalise, since it is obvious that the nature of the references will vary greatly from series to series. However, certain general principles are clear. Firstly, any analysis must take into account the fact that such references are made in a humorous mode, and we have seen how the mechanisms of humour frequently result in ambiguities. Secondly, as a result of this first principle, audiences may well 'read' sitcoms very differently: the dual reaction to *All in the Family* and *Till Death Us Do Part* demonstrates this much if nothing else.

Genre

We have seen that sitcom is based in seriality, and that it uses seriality to deliver a certain style of humour. This may be taken as an example of genre based upon enunciative situation (see chapter 7) insofar as it is the features of a broadcast medium which are responsible for features of the humour (extended familiarity with characters as the precondition of humour, for example). Clearly this is not without impact on the structure of a culture: the earlier institutions of humour (vaudeville, music hall) have been more or less killed by film and television humour (though it is worth noting that in the last decade there has been a great resurgence of nightclub humour, partly out of frustration with the blandness of TV humour). But it is unlikely that genre defined in this way is going to make the same sort of contribution to a culture that we saw in the case of crime fiction, where genre was defined on the basis of an ideology. Arguments to the contrary are based on the centrality of the pseudo-family group which is common to most if not all sitcoms (see Zynda, 1988; Horowitz, 1984).

Notes

Introduction

1 Other central categories of canonical literature which are less relevant for discussion of popular literature are 'character' and 'aesthetic value'; both will be discussed later.
2 The study of sign systems is usually called 'semiotics' (from the Greek 'semeion', a sign). There are many introductory texts available in English; among the most readily comprehensible are Fiske (1982) and Hawkes (1977).

1 Approaches to popular fiction

1 See Hirsch (1980; 1981) and Doob and Macdonald (1979) for detailed reinterpretations of Gerbner's statistical data, which suggest that other causal processes are at work. In crude outline, the authors propose that various social processes create a situation in which certain categories of people who have good reason to be scared of real-life violence (e.g. black women living in the inner city) spend a lot of time at home watching TV. They also point to the anomalous finding in Gerbner's statistics that people who watch no TV at all, or very little, are also very scared of violence; such people, they hypothesise, watch very little TV because they are obliged to be out of the house a lot and as a result are more than averagely exposed to real-life violence. Gerbner and his colleagues advanced many arguments refuting these suggestions; although neither side could be said to have conclusively proved its point, the argument demonstrated that Gerbner's statistical correlations were more ambiguous than had previously been realised. P.M. Hirsch (1980; 1981; also response by Gerbner *et al.* in same volume).
2 It is no accident that a lot of similar research has been carried out on television series – see, for example, Cassata and Skill (1983: 25–37); Vidmar and Rokeach (1974). As Altman (1986) points out, TV programmes are 'menu-driven' rather than 'goal-driven', in the sense that viewers choose which bits of programme they are interested in attending to, whereas traditional narratives (film and novel) leave little scope for such selection. Compare the theory of 'distraction' in Benjamin (1970).

3   For a recent brief overview of literature on TV audiences which stresses these themes, see Gray (1987).

2 Narrative grammar

1   Standard and readily available accounts are: F. Jameson (1972); J. Culler (1975); T. Hawkes (1977); T. Eagleton, (1983).

2   This account of narrative functions and actants omits a series of disagreements between different structuralists over the exact nature of these processes. The most important differences revolve around two problems. Firstly, there is the question of whether actants are derived from an analysis of a limited corpus of stories, as in Propp (1968), or should be composed of universal attributes, as Greimas (1973) and Brémond (1966: 66ff.) proposed – for Greimas, there are only six actants in the whole of literature, that is, six fundamental narrative roles. Secondly, whether narrative functions are to be derived from a limited corpus, so that they become a list of the basic events of the stories, or whether they should be some more basic element to be found in all stories; see, for example, Brémond (1966) and Todorov (1966). Good introductory outlines of these questions are to be found in Rimmon-Kenan (1983: 22–35). Wright is closer to Propp than to the Parisian structuralists here.

3 Narrative and connotative processes

1   Readers familiar with *S/Z* will recognise that this is a very limited selection from Barthes' comments on connotation in these pages, and it will no doubt appear an arbitrary selection; further elements from his commentary will be incorporated into the development of my argument, not always explicitly referring to Barthes' text.

2   See, for example, J. Fiske, *Introduction to Communication Studies*, pp. 91ff.; T. Hawkes, *Structuralism and Semiotics*, pp. 133f.

3   These comments are a summary of aspects of various articles by and on Metz in *Screen*, vol. 14, nos 1–3, and the various essays contained in his *Psychoanalysis and Cinema*.

4   The significance of these four terms (similarity, etc.) is that they refer to traditional debates in linguistics about the nature of fundamental processes, notably metaphor and metonymy, paradigm and syntagm; Metz is trying to demonstrate, via a complex critique of earlier arguments, that the traditional distinctions do not work. For reasons of convenience, I have omitted his critiques, and I am concentrating on his conclusions; this involves some oversimplification of his arguments.

5   For a similar analysis of jokes and gags, see my 1987 publication, ch. 2.

6   Partial summaries of *S/Z* are to be found in Coward and Ellis (1977: ch. 4) and, more abruptly, in Martin (1986: 163ff.) and Eagleton (1983: 137ff.).

7   This distinction is far from original to Genette, who borrowed it from the Russian formalists. But it is Genette's formulation of it that is responsible for its recent influence. Summaries and expansions of the formalists and Genette are to be found in Rimmon-Kenan (1983: ch. 4); Chatman (1978: 29ff. and ch. 2); Martin (1986: ch. 5). It is no accident that Genette's essay is in fact on the treatment of time in Proust. As is well

known, Proust's overall theme is memory and its relation to writing. Genette's aim is to demonstrate that this theme can only be explored in fictional form through the treatment of temporal categories in narrative; thus what he is doing is providing a formalist account of what would otherwise be thought of as individual creativity manifest in words. To this extent his tactics are typically structuralist: to 'disperse' the author into a set of formal characteristics. The significance of such possibilities will become clear when we explore the concept of genre in a later chapter.

8 It has been objected that the distinction story/narrative is false to the extent that the events that compose 'story' must necessarily have been narrated, somewhere, in order to exist as a meaningful sequence. Certainly this is true, but the value of the distinction is heuristic: it allows attribution of different emphases (see B.H. Smith, 1980).

4 The speaking/reading subject

1 This definition is partial, for many reasons. For example, it omits the question of the institutional bases of discourse, and it omits the crucial question of the relationship between signs and their referents in reality; we shall return to these questions. The focus which this partiality produces is the one most apposite at this stage of the argument.

2 What follows leans heavily on material from these sources: A. Culioli (1973); J.-C. Milner (1970); L. Cherchi (1982); J.-M. Rabaté (1982).

3 The distinction statement/utterance derives from Benveniste, who wrote in French. His terms – which have become normal in French – are *énoncé/énonciation*: what is enounced/the act of enouncing it. These terms are notoriously difficult to translate into English: I have adopted 'statement' and 'utterance', in common with others, but clearly they are not entirely satisfactory since 'utterance' conventionally means the same as 'statement'. Henceforth, in this book, 'utterance' will mean 'the act of speaking' as opposed to 'what is said'.

4 This example is taken from Culioli (1973: 87).

5 Focalisation is discussed in Genette (1972: ch. 4, esp. pp. 204ff.); Chatman (1978: ch. 4, esp. pp. 150ff.); Rimmon-Kenan (1983: ch. 6), who presents the best overview of theories to date; Martin (1986: 143ff.).

6 What follows is indebted to Rimmon-Kenan (op. cit.), whose criticisms of Genette's earlier schema seem entirely justified.

5 Narrative and ideology

1 There are many good introductions to the Marxist theory of ideology, and most modern introductory texts to Marxism in general contain a section on the subject. Among the most accessible introductions to the theory of ideology are Lovell (1983), Hall (1977), Larrain (1979); less accessible, but comprehensive, is Hall *et al.* (1977).

2 Althusser's ideas have been summarised and commented upon many times during the last two decades. As well as his own works, good brief presentations are to be found in Callinicos (1976), Hirst (1979), McLennan *et al.* (1977) and Lovell (1983).

6 Hegemony and subject position

1 This traditional term is nowadays used primarily in the sense given it by Gramsci. However, Gramsci's sense is (a) much larger than what is normally encompassed by 'ideology', since it is among other things a theory of the state; (b) somewhat ambiguous because of partial inconsistencies. On the need for caution in interpreting Gramsci, see Nowell-Smith (1985). There is no space here for consideration of such ambiguities, and I am concerned only with the notion of 'hegemony' as it has been used in recent debates about popular fiction and popular culture.

7 Genre

1 This summary of *Thrillers* is extremely condensed. More thorough summaries are to be found in Palmer (1973; 1984) and Glover (1984).

8 Crime fiction: the genre dimension

1 I am aware that this is a very oversimplified account of the classical arguments. I have based this reading on the substantial analysis in Glucksmann (1967).
2 Of course, the way in which criminality and violence occupy a place in the ideological field is by no means reducible to the arguments put forward here and earlier. For other ways of linking the fictional portrayal of violence and crime to ideology, see Palmer (1978), Denning (1987; 1989), and Drummond (1976).

9 Crime fiction: *film noir* and gender

1 See Tompkins (1989), who argues that the Western is fundamentally a rejection of women-dominated domesticity; cf. Fiedler (1968).
2 My analysis of *Looking for Rachel Wallace* has benefited from extensive discussions with Paul Cobley.

10 Soap opera, romance and femininity

1 We should note in passing, in order to return to it in more detail later, that Radway's presentation of how women readers actively seek narrative closure will undermine any attempt to argue a strong connection between soap's lack of narrative resolution and femininity.
2 But see Seiter *et al.* (1989) for a counter-argument.

Bibliography

Abercrombie, N., Hill, S. and Turner, B.S. (1980) *The Dominant Ideology Thesis*, London: Allen and Unwin.

Adorno, T.W. (1975) 'Television and the patterns of culture' in W. Schramm (ed.) *Mass Communications*, Urbana: University of Illinois Press.

Allen, R.C. (1983) 'On reading soaps' in E. Ann Kaplan (ed.), *Regarding Television*, Fredericksburg: University Publications of America, American Film Institute Monograph Series no. 2.

Allen, R.C. (1985) *Speaking of Soap Opera*, Chapel Hill: University of North Carolina Press.

Althusser, L. (1969) 'Ideology and ideological state apparatuses' in *Lenin and Philosophy and Other Essays*, London: New Left Books.

Altman, C.F. (1985) 'Psychoanalysis and cinema' in B. Nichols (ed.) *Movies and Methods* II, Berkeley: University of California Press.

Altman, R. (1986) 'Television/sound' in T. Modleski (ed.) *Studies in Entertainment*, Bloomington: Indiana University Press.

Altman, R. (1989) *The American Film Musical*, Bloomington: Indiana University Press.

Ang, I. (1985) *Watching Dallas*, London: Methuen.

Anon. (1973) *The Arabian Nights*, ed. N.J. Dawood, London: Penguin.

Aristotle (1968) *The Poetics*, ed. Lucas, Oxford: Oxford University Press.

Auden, W.H. (1948) 'The Guilty Vicarage' in *The Dyer's Hand*, London: Faber & Faber.

Badiou, A. and Balmès, F. (1976) *De l'Idéologie*, Paris: Maspéro.

Barker, D. (1984) 'TV production techniques as communication' in H. Newcomb (ed.) *Television, the Critical View*, Oxford: Oxford University Press.

Barthes, R. (1970) *S/Z*, Paris: Editions du Seuil; 2nd edn 1975, R. Miller (trans.), London: Cape.

Barthes, R. (1971) 'Rhetoric of the image', *Working Papers in Cultural Studies* 1 (1): 37–50; (1977) reprinted in R. Barthes, *Image Music Text*, London: Fontana.

Bathrick, S. (1984) '*The Mary Tyler Moore Show*: women at home and at work' in J. Feuer, P. Kerr and T. Vahimagi (eds) *MTM: Quality Television*, London: British Film Institute.

Baym, N. (1978) *Women's Fiction*, Ithaca: Cornell University Press.

Bazin, A. (1955) 'L'évolution du Western', *Cahiers du Cinéma* 9, 54: 22–6.

Benjamin, W. (1970) 'The Work of Art in the age of mechanical reproduction', in *Illuminations*, London: Fontana.

Bennett, D. (1979) 'The detective story: towards a definition of genre', *PTL: a Journal for Descriptive Poetics and the Theory of Literature* 4, 233–66.

Bennett, T. (ed.) (1981) *Popular Culture (U203)*, Milton Keynes: Open University Press.

Bennett, T. (1982) 'Theories of the media, theories of society', in M. Gurewitch, T. Bennett, J. Curran, and J. Woollacott (eds), *Culture, Society and the Media*, London: Methuen.

Bennett, T. (1986a) 'Popular culture and "the turn to Gramsci"', in T. Bennett, C. Mercer and J. Woollacott, *Popular Culture and Social Relations*, Milton Keynes: Open University Press.

Bennett, T. (1986b) 'The politics of the "popular" and popular culture', in T. Bennett *et al.* (eds) *Popular Culture and Social Relations*, Milton Keynes: Open University Press.

Bennett, T. (1986c) 'Hegemony, ideology, pleasure: Blackpool', in T. Bennett *et al.* (eds) *Popular Culture and Social Relations*, Milton Keynes: Open University Press.

Bennett, T. (1987) 'Really useless knowledge: a political critique of aesthetics', *Literature and History* 13: 38–57.

Bennett, T., Martin, G., Mercer, C. and Woollacott, J. (eds) (1981a) *Culture, Ideology and Social Process*, Milton Keynes: Open University Press.

Bennett, T., Boyd-Bowman, S., Mercer, C. and Woollacott, J. (1981b) *Popular Television and Film*, London: British Film Institute and Open University Press.

Bennett, T., Mercer C. and Woollacott, J. (eds) (1986) *Popular Culture and Social Relations*, Milton Keynes: Open University Press.

Bennett, T. and Woollacott, J. (1987) *Bond and Beyond*, London: Macmillan.

Benveniste, E. (1971) *Problems in General Linguistics*, Miami: University of Miami Press.

Blank, D. (1977) 'Gerbner's violence profile' and 'Final comments on the violence profile', in *Journal of Broadcasting*, 21 (3): 272–9 and 287–96.

Boccaccio, G. (1972) *The Decameron*, London: Penguin.

Boorstin, D. (1962) *The Image*, London: Penguin.

Borde, R. and Chaumeton, E. (1955) *Panorama du film noir américain*, Paris: Editions de Minuit.

Bordwell, D., Staiger, J. and Thompson, K. (1985) *The Classical Hollywood Cinema*, London: Routledge & Kegan Paul.

Bourdieu, P. (1979) *La Distinction*, Paris: Editions de Minuit.

Bowen, J. (ed.) (1990) *Masculinity*, Manchester: Manchester University Press.

Bramson, L. (1967) *The Political Context of Sociology*, Princeton: Princeton University Press.

Brémond, C. (1966) 'La logique des possibles narratifs', *Communications* 8: 60–76.

Bromley, R. (1986) 'Hegemony and popular fiction' in P. Humm (ed.) *Popular Fictions*, London: Methuen.

Brooke-Rose, C. (1981) *A Rhetoric of the Unreal*, Cambridge: Cambridge University Press.

Brooks, P. (1976) *The Melodramatic Imagination*, New Haven: Yale University Press.

Brunsdon, C. (1981) '*Crossroads* – notes on soap opera', *Screen* 22 (4): 32–7.

Buckingham, D. (1987) *Public Secrets*, London: British Film Institute.

Burnett, W.R. (1929 1st edn) *Little Caesar*; 5th edn 1987, London: Zomba Books.

Callinicos, N. (1976) *The Revolutionary Ideas of Karl Marx*, London: Pluto Press.

Cantor, M. and Pingree, S. (1983) *The Soap Opera*, Beverly Hills: Sage.

Cantril, H., Gaudet, S. and Herzog, H. (1940) *Invasion from Mars*, Princeton and London: Princeton University Press.

Carey, J.W. (ed.) (1988) *Media, Myth and Narrative*, Beverly Hills: Sage.

Cassata, M. and Skill, T. (1983) *Life on Daytime Television*, Lexington: Ablex.

Cassidy, M.F. (1989) '*Dallas* refigured' in G. Burns and R.J. Thompson (eds) *Television Studies: Textual Analysis*, New York and London: Praeger.

Cawelti, J.G. (1976) *Mystery, Adventure and Romance*, Chicago: University of Chicago Press.

Cawelti, J.G. (1978) '*Chinatown* and generic transformation in recent American films', in G. Mast and M. Cohen (eds) *Film Theory and Criticism*, New York and London: Oxford University Press.

Cegarra, M. (1973) 'Cinema and semiology', *Screen* 14 (1–2): 129–87.

Chandler, R. (1948) *The Big Sleep*, London: Penguin.

Chandler, R. (1952) *The Lady in the Lake*, London: Penguin.

Chandler, R. (1959) *The Long Goodbye*, London: Penguin.

Chase, J.H. (1977) *No Orchids for Miss Blandish*, 3rd edn, London: Corgi.

Chatman, S. (1978) *Story and Discourse*, Ithaca: Cornell University Press.

Chatman, S. (1980) 'What films can do and novels can't', in W.J.T. Mitchell (ed.) *On Narrative*, Chicago: University of Chicago Press.

Cherchi, L. (1982) 'Sujet de l'énonciation et sujet de l'énoncé', unpublished mimeo, Dijon: Université de Bourgogne.

Cherry, C. (1980) 'What is communication?' in J. Corner and J. Hawthorn (eds) *Communications Theory*, London: Edward Arnold.

Christie, A. (1967) *The Murder of Roger Ackroyd*, London: Collins.

Clarens, C. (1980) *Crime Movies*, London: Secker & Warburg.

Clark, T. (1980) 'Manet's *Olympia* in 1865', in *Screen* 21: 18–42.

Clavell, J. (1981) *Noble House*, London: Coronet Books.

Compaine, B. (1978) *The Book Industry in Transition*, White Plains, NY: Knowledge Industry Publications.

Comstock, G. (1983) 'Introduction', in M. Cassata and T. Skill, *Life on Daytime Television*, Lexington: Ablex.

Cook, J. (ed.) (1982) *Television Sitcom*, London: British Film Institute.

Coward, R. and Ellis, J. (1977) *Language and Materialism*, London: Routledge & Kegan Paul.

Cowie, E. (1979) 'The popular film as a progressive text – a discussion of *Coma*', *M/F* 3: 59–81.

Cowie, E. (1980) 'Discussion of *Coma* – part 2', *M/F* 4: 57–69.

Culioli, A. (1973) 'Sur quelques contradictions en linguistique', *Communications* 20: 83–91.

Culler, J. (1975) *Structuralist Poetics*, London: Routledge & Kegan Paul.

Culler, J. (1983) *On Deconstruction*, London: Routledge & Kegan Paul.

Curran, J., Gurevitch, M. and Woollacott, J. (eds) (1977) *Mass Communication and Society*, London: Edward Arnold.

Davies, T. (1981) 'Education, ideology and literature' in T. Bennett *et al.* (eds) *Culture, Ideology and Social Process*, Milton Keynes: Open University Press.

Dayan, D. (1976) 'The tutor-code of classical cinema' in B. Nichols (ed.), *Movies and Methods I*, Berkeley: University of California Press.

Deighton, L. (1986) *London Match*, London: Grafton Books.

Denning, M. (1987) *Cover Stories*, London: Routledge & Kegan Paul.

Denning, M. (1989) *Mechanic Accents*, London: Verso.

Doane, M.A., Mellencamp, P. and Williams, L. (1984) (eds) *Re-Vision: Essays in Feminist Film Criticism*, Fredericksburg: University Publications of America, American Film Institute Monograph series no. 3.

Docherty, D., Morrison, D. and Tracey, M. (1986) 'Who goes to the cinema?', *Sight and Sound*, Spring: 81–5.

Dominick, J. and Rauch, G. (1972) 'The image of women in network TV commercials', *Journal of Broadcasting* 16: 259–65.

Doob, A. and Macdonald, G. (1979) 'Television viewing and fear of victimization', *Journal of Personality and Social Psychology* 37 (2): 170–9.

Douglas, A. (1980) 'Soft-porn culture', *New Republic*, 30 August: 25–9.

Douglas, M. (1968) 'The social control of cognition', *Man* (new series) 3, 361–76.

Drotner, K. (1989) 'Intensities of feeling: emotion, reception and gender in popular culture', in M. Skovmand (ed.) *Media Fictions, The Dolphin*, Arhus: Arhus University Press.

Drummond, P. (1976) 'Structural and narrative constraints in *The Sweeney*', *Screen Education* 20: 15–36.

Dworkin, A. (1981) *Pornography*, London: The Women's Press.

Dyer, R. (1979) *Stars*, London: British Film Institute.

Dyer, R. (ed.) (1981) *Coronation Street*, London: British Film Institute.

Eagleton, T. (1983) *Literary Theory*, Oxford: Blackwell.

Easthope, A. (1988) *British Post-Structuralism*, London: Routledge.

Eaton, M. (1981) 'Laughter in the dark', *Screen* 22 (2): 21–8.

EBU (1985) European Broadcasting Union seminar on soap opera production, transcript in *European Broadcasting Review* 36 (6).

Eisenstein, E.L. (1979) *The Printing Press as an Agent of Change*, Cambridge: Cambridge University Press.

Eisner, L.H. (1973) *The Haunted Screen*, London, Secker & Warburg.

Eliot, G. (1876) *Daniel Deronda* (reprinted 1967, London: Penguin).

Ellis, J. (1975) 'Made in Ealing', *Screen* 16 (1): 78–127.

Elsaesser, T. (1972) 'Tales of Sound and Fury. Observations on the family melodrama', *Monogram* 4: 2–15; reprinted in C. Gledhill (ed.) (1987) *Home Is Where The Heart Is*, London: British Film Institute.

Escarpit, R. (1966) *The Book Revolution*, London: Harrap.

Farber, S. (1974) 'Violence and the bitch goddess', *Film Comment* 10,

6: 6–33.

Fenton, D. (1989) Unpublished final year undergraduate project, City of London Polytechnic.

Feuer, J. (1984) 'Melodrama, serial form and TV today', *Screen* 25 (1): 4–16.

Feuer, J. (1986) 'Narrative form in American network television', in C. MacCabe (ed.) *High Theory, Low Culture*, Manchester: Manchester University Press.

Feuer, J., Kerr, P. and Vahimagi, T. (eds) (1984) *MTM: Quality Television*, London: British Film Institute.

Fiedler, L. (1968) *The Return of the Vanishing American*, London: Cape.

Fiske, J. (1982) *Introduction to Communication Studies*, London: Methuen.

Fleming, I. (1961) *Thunderball*, London: Pan Books.

Forsyth, F. (1971) *The Day of the Jackal*, London: Hutchinson.

Frayling, C. (1981) *Spaghetti Westerns*, London: Routledge & Kegan Paul.

French, M. (1977) *The Women's Room*, London: Sphere Books.

Frye, N. (1971) *The Anatomy of Criticism*, Princeton: Princeton University Press.

Garnham, N. and Williams, R. (1980) 'Pierre Bourdieu and the sociology of culture', *Media, Culture and Society* 2 (3): 209–23.

Genette, G. (1966) 'Frontières du récit', *Communications* 8: 152–63.

Genette, G. (1972) *Figures III*, Paris: Editions du Seuil.

Genette, G. (1986) *Théorie des genres*, Paris: Editions du Seuil.

Geraghty, C. (1981) 'The continuous serial – a definition', in R. Dyer (ed.), *Coronation Street*, London: British Film Institute.

Geraghty, C. (1991) *Women and Soap Opera*, Cambridge: Polity Press.

Gerbner, G. and Gross, L. (1976) 'Living with television: the violence profile', *Journal of Communication* 26 (2): 173–99.

Gerbner, G. *et al.* (1977) 'TV violence profile no. 8: the highlights', *Journal of Communication* 27 (2): 171–80.

Gerbner, G. *et al.* (1978) 'Cultural indicators: violence profile no. 9', *Journal of Communication* 28 (3): 176–207.

Gerbner, G. *et al.* (1979) 'The demonstration of power: violence profile no. 10', *Journal of Communication* 29 (3): 177–96.

Gerbner, G. *et al.* (1980) 'The mainstreaming of America: violence profile no. 11', *Journal of Communication* 30 (3): 10–29.

Giner, S. (1976) *Mass Society*, London: Martin Robertson.

Gledhill, C. (1984) 'Developments in feminist film criticism', in M.A. Doane *et al.* (eds) *Re-Vision: Essays in Feminist Film Criticism*, Fredericksburg: American Film Institute Monograph Series no. 3.

Gledhill, C. (ed.) (1987) *Home Is Where The Heart Is*, London: British Film Institute.

Glover, D. (1984) *The Sociology of the Mass Media*, Ormskirk: Causeway Press.

Glover, D. (1989) 'The stuff that dreams are made of: masculinity, femininity and the thriller', in D. Longhurst (ed.) *Gender, Genre and Narrative Pleasure*, London: Unwin Hyman.

Glucksmann, A. (1967) *Le Discours de la guerre*, Paris: L'Herne.

Glucksmann, A. (1971) *Violence on the Screen*, London: British Film Institute.

Goodis, D. (1983) *Down There* (1st edn 1956), London: Zomba Books.

Gramsci, A. (1985) *Selection from Cultural Writings*, London: Lawrence & Wishart.

Gray, A. (1987) 'Reading the audience', *Screen* 28 (3): 24–35.

Gray, R. (1981) 'Hegemony in Victorian Britain', in T. Bennett *et al.*, (eds) *Culture, Ideology and Social Process*, Milton Keynes: Open University Press

Greimas, A.J. (1973) 'Les actants, les acteurs et les figures' in C. Chabrol (ed.) *Sémiotique narrative et textuelle*, Paris: Larousse.

Grella, G. (1970) 'Murder and manners: the formal detective story', *Novel* 4 (1).

Grote, D. (1983) *The End of Comedy: The Sitcom and the Comedic Tradition*, Hamden: Archon Books.

Groves, G. (1954) *Dictionary of Music and Musicians*, ed. E. Blom, 5th edn, London: Macmillan.

Guérif, F. (1979) *Le Film noir*, Paris: Editions Henri Veyrier.

Hackett, A.P. and Burke, J.H. (1977) *Eighty Years of Bestsellers*, New York: Bowker.

Hall, S. (1977) 'Culture, the media and the "ideological effect"', in J. Curran, M. Gurevitch and J. Woollacott (eds) *Mass Communication and Society*, London: Edward Arnold.

Hall, S. (1986) 'Popular culture and the state', in T. Bennett, C. Mercer and J. Woollacott, *Popular Culture and Social Relations*, Milton Keynes: Open University Press.

Hall, S., Lumley, B. and McLennan, G. (1977) 'Politics and ideology: Gramsci', in S. Hall *et al.*, (eds) *On Ideology, Working Papers in Cultural Studies* 10; 2nd edn 1978, London: Hutchinson.

Hall, S., Critcher, C., Jefferson, T., Clarke, J. and Roberts, B. (1978) *Policing the Crisis*, London: Macmillan.

Hammett, D. (1930) *The Maltese Falcon*, London: Cassell.

Hammett, D. (1966) *The Glass Key*, London: Penguin Books.

Handelman, D. and Kapferer, B. (1972) 'Forms of joking activity: a comparative approach', *American Anthropologist* 74: 484–517.

Haskell, M. (1974) *From Reverence to Rape: the Treatment of Women in the Movies*, New York: Holt, Rinehart & Winston.

Hawkes, T. (1977) *Structuralism and Semiotics*, London: Methuen.

Haycraft, H. (1941) *Murder for Pleasure*, New York and London: Appleton-Century.

Heath, S. (1976) 'Narrative space', *Screen* 17 (3): 68–112.

Heath, S. (1979) 'The turn of the subject', *Cine-Tracts* 2 (3–4): 32–48.

Heath, S. and Skirrow, G. (1977) 'Television – a world in action', *Screen* 18 (2): 14–56.

Heller, A. (1976) *The Theory of Need in Marx*, London: Allison & Busby.

Hennessee, J.A. (1978) 'The whole soap catalogue', *Action* 11 (6): 16–22.

Hirsch, E.D. (1967) *Validity in Interpretation*, New Haven: Yale University Press.

Hirsch, F. (1981) *The Dark Side of the Screen: Film Noir*, La Jolla: A.S. Barnes.

Hirsch, P.M. (1980) 'The scary world of the non-viewer and other anomalies', *Communications Research* 7 (4): 403–56.

Hirsch, P.M. (1981) 'The scary world of the non-viewer and other anomalies', *Communications Research* 8 (1): 3–37.

Hirst, P.Q. (1979) *On Law and Ideology*, London: Macmillan.

Hobson, D. (1982) *Crossroads. The Drama of a Soap Opera*, London: Methuen.

Hohendahl, P.U. (1977) 'Introduction to reception aesthetics', *New German Critique* 10: 29–63.

Holloway, J. (1979) *Narrative and Structure*, Cambridge: Cambridge University Press.

Holsti, O. (1969) *Content Analysis for the Social Sciences and Humanities*, Reading, MA: Addison-Wesley.

Horowitz, S. (1984) 'Sitcom Domesticus: a species endangered by social change', in H. Newcomb (ed.), *TV: The Most Popular Art*, Garden City, NJ: Anchor.

Horton, D. and Wohl, R.R. (1956) 'Mass communication and para-social interaction', *Psychiatry* 19, 4: 215–29.

Hurd, G. (1981) 'The television presentation of the police', in T. Bennett, S. Boyd-Bowman, C. Mercer and J. Woollacott (eds) *Popular Television and Film*, London: British Film Institute and Open University Press.

Iles, F. (1979) *Malice Aforethought*, London: Pan.

Iser, W. (1978) *The Act of Reading*, London: Routledge.

Iser, W. (1980a) 'The reading process' in J. Tompkins (ed.) *Reader Response Criticism*, Baltimore: Johns Hopkins University Press.

Iser, W. (1980b) 'Interaction between text and reader' in S. Suleiman and I. Crossman (eds) *The Reader in the Text*, Princeton: Princeton University Press.

Jameson, F. (1971) *Marxism and Form*, Princeton: Princeton University Press.

Jameson, F. (1972) *The Prison-House of Language*, Princeton: Princeton University Press.

Jameson, F. (1977) 'Ideology, narrative analysis and popular culture', *Theory and Society* 4: 543–59.

Jameson, F. (1979) 'Reification and Utopia in popular culture', *Social Text* 1 (1): 130–48.

Jameson, F. (1983) *The Political Unconscious*, London: Methuen.

Jauss, H.R. (1974) 'Levels of identification of hero and audience', *New Literary History* 5: 283–317.

Jefferson, G. (1979) 'A technique for inviting laughter and its subsequent acceptance declination', in G. Psathas (ed.) *Everyday Language*, San Francisco: Irvington Publishers.

Johnston, C. and Willemen, P. (eds) (1973) *Frank Tashlin*, Edinburgh: Edinburgh Film Festival.

Jong, E. (1973) *Fear of Flying*, New York: Holt, Rinehart & Winston.

Kaplan, C. (1986) 'An unsuitable genre for a feminist?', *Women's Review* 8: 18–19.

Kaplan, E.A. (1974) 'The importance and ultimate failure of *Last Tango in Paris*', *Jump Cut* 4: 1, 9–11.

Kaplan, E.A. (ed.) (1983) *Regarding Television*, Fredericksburg: University Publications of America, American Film Institute Monograph Series no. 2.

Kerbrat-Orecchioni, C. (1980) *L'Enonciation de la subjectivité dans le langage*, Paris: Presses Universitaires Françaises.

Krippendorff, K. (1980) *Content Analysis. An Introduction to its Methodology*, Beverly Hills: Sage.

Lacan, J. (1949) 'Le Stade du Miroir comme formateur de la fonction du Je', in *Ecrits*, Paris: Editions du Seuil.

Lacan, J. (1966) *Ecrits*, Paris: Editions du Seuil.

Laclau, E. (1977) *Politics and Ideology in Marxist Theory*, London: New Left Books.

Langer, S. (1953) *Feeling and Form*, London: Routledge & Kegan Paul.

Laplanche, J. and Pontalis, J.B. (1967) *Vocabulaire de la psychanalyse*, Paris: Presses Universitaires Françaises. (*The Language of Psychoanalysis* (1973) trans. D. Nicholson-Smith, London: Hogarth Press.)

Larrain, J. (1979) *The Concept of Ideology*, London: Hutchinson.

Lauretis, T. de (1984) *Alice Doesn't*, Bloomington: Indiana University Press.

Leach, E. (1980) 'Problems of terminology', in J. Corner and J. Hawthorn (eds) *Communication Studies*, London: Edward Arnold.

Leavis, Q.D. (1932) *Fiction and the Reading Public*, London: Chatto & Windus.

Le Carré, J. (1987) *A Perfect Spy*, London: Hodder & Stoughton.

Lemon, J. (1977) 'Women and blacks on prime-time TV', *Journal of Communication* 27 (4): 70–9.

Lemon, J. (1978) 'Dominant or dominated? Women on prime-time TV', in G. Tuchman *et al.* (eds) *Hearth and Home: Images of Women in the Mass Media*, London: Oxford University Press.

Leonard, E. (1984) *Swag*, London: Penguin Books.

Leonard, E. (1988) *Freaky Deaky*, London: Penguin Books.

Liebes, T. and Katz, E. (1986) 'Patterns of involvement in television fiction', *European Journal of Communication* 1: 151–71.

Lodge, D. (1981) '*Middlemarch* and the idea of the classic realist text', in A. Kettle (ed.), *The Nineteenth-Century Novel, Critical Essays and Documents* (rev. edn), London: Heinemann.

Longhurst, D. (ed.) (1989) *Gender, Genre and Narrative Pleasure*, London: Unwin Hyman.

Lovell, T. (1981) 'Ideology and *Coronation Street*', in R. Dyer (ed.), *Coronation Street*, London: British Film Institute.

Lovell, T. (1982) 'A genre of social disruption?' in J. Cook (ed.) *Television Sitcom*, London: British Film Institute.

Lovell, T. (1983) *Pictures of Reality*, London: British Film Institute.

Lovell, T. (1984) 'The novel and the commodification of literature', paper given to the British Sociological Association, Bradford, April.

Ludlum, R. (1980) *The Bourne Identity*, London: Granada.

Lukow, G. and Ricci, S. (1984) 'The "audience" goes public: intertextuality, genre, and the responsibilities of film literacy', *On Film* 12: 29–36.

Lyons, J. (1977) *Semantics*, Cambridge: Cambridge University Press.

Lyons, J. (1981) *Language, Meaning and Context*, London: Fontana.

MacCabe, C. (1974) 'Realism and the cinema', *Screen* 15 (2): 7–27.

MacCabe, C. (1978) 'The discursive and the ideological in film', *Screen* 19 (4): 29–44.

MacCabe, C. (1979) 'On discourse', *Economy and Society* 8 (4): 279–307.

MacCabe, C. (ed.) (1986) *High Theory/Low Culture*, Manchester: Manchester University Press.

McLennan, G., Molina, V. and Peters, R. (1977) 'Althusser's theory of ideology', in S. Hall *et al.*, (eds) *On Ideology, Working Papers in Cultural Studies* 10.

McQuail, D., Blumler, J. and Brown, R. (1972) 'The television audience: a revised perspective', in D. McQuail (ed.) *The Sociology of Mass Communications*, London: Penguin Books.

Martin, W. (1986) *Recent Theories of Narrative*, Ithaca: Cornell University Press.

Mast, G. and Cohen, M. (1974) *Film Theory and Criticism*, New York and London: Oxford University Press.

Marx, K. and Engels, F. (1965) *The German Ideology*, London: Lawrence & Wishart.

Marx, K. (1961) *Capital*, vol. I, Moscow: Foreign Languages Publishing House.

Mellencamp, P. (1986) 'Situation comedy, feminism and Freud', in T. Modleski (ed.) *Studies in Entertainment*, Bloomington: Indiana University Press.

Melville, H. (1972) *Moby-Dick*, London: Penguin Books.

Merrington, J. (1968) 'Theory and practice in Gramsci's Marxism', *Socialist Register*: 145–76.

Metz, C. (1973a) 'Current problems in film theory', *Screen* 14 (1–2): 40–88.

Metz, C. (1982) *Psycho-Analysis and Cinema*, London: Macmillan.

Michaels, W.B. (1980) 'The interpreter's self: Peirce on the Cartesian subject' in J.M.S. Tompkins (ed.), *Reader-Response Criticism*, Baltimore: Johns Hopkins University Press.

Miller, J.-A. (1968) 'Action de la structure', *Cahiers de l'Analyse* 9.

Milner, J.-C. (1970) *L'Amour de la langue*, Paris: Editions du Seuil.

Mintz, L. (1985) 'Situation comedy' in B. Rose (ed.), *TV Genres*, Westport: Greenwood Press.

Modleski, T. (1979) 'The search for tomorrow in today's soap operas', *Film Quarterly* 33 (1): 12–21.

Modleski, T. (1980) 'The disappearing act: a study of Harlequin romances', *Signs* 5: 435–48.

Modleski, T. (1982) *Loving With a Vengeance*, Hamden: Archon Books.

Modleski, T. (1983) 'The rhythms of reception: daytime television and women's work', in E.A. Kaplan (ed.) *Regarding Television*, Fredericksburg: University Publications of America, American Film Institute Monograph Series no. 2, 67–75.

Modleski, T. (ed.) (1986) *Studies in Entertainment*, Bloomington: Indiana University Press.

Moers, E. (1976) *Literary Women*, New York: Doubleday.

Moi, T. (1985) *Sexual/Textual Politics*, London: Methuen.

Morley, D. (1986) *Family Television: Cultural Power and Domestic Leisure*, London: Comedia.

Mott, F.L. (1947) *Golden Multitudes*, New York: Macmillan.

Mouffe, C. (1981) 'Hegemony and ideology in Gramsci', in T. Bennett *et al.*, (eds) *Culture, Ideology and Social Process*, Milton Keynes: Open University Press.

Mulhern, F. (1979) *The Moment of Scrutiny*, London: Verso.

Mulvey, L. (1986) 'Melodrama in and out of the home', in C. MacCabe (ed.) *High Theory/Low Culture*, Manchester: Manchester University Press.

Mulvey, L. (1987) 'Notes on Sirk and melodrama' in C. Gledhill (ed.) *Home Is Where The Heart Is*, London: British Film Institute.

Neale, S. (1979) 'Stereotypes', *Screen Education* 32/3: 33–38.

Neale, S. (1981a) 'Genre and cinema' in T. Bennett, S. Boyd-Bowman, C. Mercer, and J. Woollacott (eds) *Popular Television and Film*, London: British Film Institute.

Neale, S. (1981b) 'Psycho-analysis and comedy', *Screen* 22 (2): 29–43.

Neale, S. (1990) 'Genre: current issues and questions', *Screen* 30.

Negri, T. (1988) *Revolution Retrieved: Selected Writings*, London: Red Notes.

Newcomb, H. (1974) *TV: The Most Popular Art*, Garden City: Anchor.

Newcomb, H. (ed.) (1984) *Television: The Critical View*, London: Oxford University Press.

Newcomb, H, (1988) 'One night of prime time' in J.W. Carey (ed.) *Media, Myth and Narrative*, Beverly Hills: Sage.

Nichols, B. (1976) *Movies and Methods*, Berkeley: University of California Press.

Nichols, B. (1985) *Movies and Methods II*, Berkeley: University of California Press.

Nicoll, A. (1931) *Masks, Mimes and Miracles*, London: Harrap.

Nicoll, A. (1963) *The World of Harlequin*, Cambridge: Cambridge University Press.

Nowell-Smith, G. (1985) 'Introduction' in A. Gramsci, *Selection from Cultural Writings*, London: Lawrence & Wishart.

Nowell-Smith, G. (1987) 'Minnelli and melodrama' in C. Gledhill (ed.) *Home Is Where The Heart Is*, London: British Film Institute.

Oakley, G. (1982) '*Yes Minister*' in J. Cook (ed.) *Television Sitcom*, London: British Film Institute.

Ong, W.J. (1982) *Orality and Literacy: The Technologising of the Word*, London: Methuen.

Palmer, J. (1973) 'Thrillers: the deviant behind the consensus', in I. Taylor and L. Taylor (eds) *Politics and Deviance*, London: Pelican Books.

Palmer, J. (1976) 'Evils merely prohibited. Conceptions of property and conceptions of criminality in the criminal law reform of the English Industrial Revolution', *British Journal of Law and Society* 3 (1): 1–16.

Palmer, J. (1978) *Thrillers*, London: Edward Arnold.

Palmer, J. (1984) 'Thrillers', in C. Pawling (ed.) *Popular Literature and Social Change*, London: Macmillan.

Palmer, J. (1987) *The Logic of the Absurd: on Film and TV Comedy*, London: British Film Institute.

Palmer J. (1988) 'Humor in Great Britain' in A. Ziv (ed.) *National Styles of Humor*, Westport: Greenwood Press.

Palmer, J. (1990) 'Masculinity and humour' in J. Bowen (ed.) *Masculinity*, Manchester: Manchester University Press.

Palmer, J. (1991) *Taking Humour Seriously*, London: Routledge.

Paretsky, S. (1982) *Indemnity Only*, London: Penguin Books.

Parker, R.B. (1978) *The Promised Land*, London: Penguin Books.

Parker, R.B. (1980) *Looking for Rachel Wallace*, New York: Dell Books.

Parsons, T. (1959) 'A Rejoinder to Ogles and Levy', *American Sociological Review* 24 (2).

Paterson, R. (1980) 'Programming the family: the art of the TV schedule', *Screen Education* 35: 79–85.

Paterson, R. (1981) 'The production context of *Coronation Street*' in R. Dyer (ed.) *Coronation Street*, London: British Film Institute.

Pêcheux, M. (1975) *Les Vérités de La Palice*, Paris: Maspero; (1982) H. Nagpal (trans.) as *Language, Semantics, Ideology. Stating the Obvious*, London: Macmillan.

Place, J.A. and Peterson, L.S. (1974) 'Some visual motifs in film noir', *Film Comment* 10 (1): 30–3.

Podmore, B. (1984) 'Popular serials' in *European Broadcasting Review* 35 (6).

Propp, V. (1968) *Morphology of the Folktale*, Austin: University of Texas Press.

Puzo, M. (1969) *The Godfather*, Greenwich: Fawcett Publications.

Puzo, M. (1972) *The Godfather Papers*, London: Heinemann.

Rabaté, J.-M. (1982) 'Enunciation in the field of psychoanalysis', unpublished mimeo, Université de Bourgogne.

Radin, P. (1976) *The Trickster*, 2nd edn, New York: Schocken Books.

Radway, J. (1981) 'The utopian impulse in popular literature: Gothic romances and "feminist" protest', *American Quarterly* 33: 140–62.

Radway, J. (1984) *Reading the Romance*, Chapel Hill: University of North Carolina Press.

Rancière, J. (1974) *La Leçon d'Althusser*, Paris: Gallimard.

Rimmon-Kenan, S. (1983) *Narrative Fiction*, London: Methuen.

Rosenberg, B. (1971) 'Mass culture revisited', in Rosenberg, B. and Manning White, D. (eds) *Mass Culture Revisited*, New York: Van Nostrand Reinhold.

Saussure, F. de (1974) *Course in General Linguistics*, London: Fontana.

Schaeffer, J.-M. (1989) *Qu'est-ce qu'un genre littéraire?* Paris: Editions du Seuil.

Schick, F.L. (1958) *The Paperbound Book in America*, New York: Bowker.

Schrader, P. (1972) 'Notes on Film Noir', *Film Comment* 8 (1): 8–13.

Schramm, W. (1975) *Mass Communications*, Urbana: University of Illinois Press.

Seiter, E. (1982) 'Promise and contradiction – the daytime TV serial', *Film Reader* 5: 150–63.

Seiter, E. (1983) 'Men, sex and money in recent family melodramas', *Journal of the University Film and Video Association* 35 (1): 17–27.

Seiter E., Warth E.-M., Borchers, H. and Kreutzner, G. (1989) 'Towards an ethnography of soap opera views', in E. Seiter *et al.*, *Remote Control*, London: Routledge.

Shadoian, J. (1977) *Dreams and Dead Ends: The American Gangster/Crime Film*, Cambridge: MIT Press.

Showalter, E. (1978) *A Literature of Their Own*, Princeton: Princeton University Press.

Silbermann, A. (1968) 'A definition of the sociology of art', *International Social Science Journal* 20 (4): 567–88.

Sklar, R. (1980) *Prime-Time America*, London: Oxford University Press.

Skovmand, M. (1989) 'Sherlock Holmes and the sudden death of the three volume novel' in M. Skovmand (ed.) *Media Fictions, The Dolphin* 17, Arhus: Arhus University Press.

Skvorecky, J. (1986) *The Engineer of Human Souls*, London; Picador.

Smith, B.H. (1980) 'Narrative versions, narrative theories', in W.J.T. Mitchell (ed.) *On Narrative*, Chicago: University of Chicago Press.

Smith, N. and Wilson, D. (1979) *Modern Linguistics*, London: Pelican Books.

Snitow, A.B. (1979) 'Mass market romance: pornography for women is different', *Radical History Review* 20: 141–61.

Sophocles (1947) *Oedipus the King*, London: Penguin Books.

Speight, J. (1973) *Till Death Us Do Part*, London: Woburn Press.

Steiner, G. (1967) *Language and Silence*, London: Faber.

Stocking, S.H., Sapolsky, B. and Zillman, D. (1977) 'Sex discrimination in prime-time humor', *Journal of Broadcasting* 21 (4): 447–55.

Sutherland, J. (1981) *Bestsellers*, London: Routledge & Kegan Paul.

Swanson, G. (1981) '*Dallas*', *Framework* 14: 32–5 and 15/17: 81–5.

Taylor, H. (1989) *Scarlett's Women. Gone With the Wind and its Female Fans*, London: Virago.

Terry, J. (1989) Unpublished undergraduate essay, City of London Polytechnic.

Todorov, T. (1966) 'Les catégories du récit littéraire', *Communications* 8: 125–51.

Todorov, T. (1970) *Introduction à la littérature fantastique*, Paris: Editions du Seuil; 2nd edn. 1975, Ithaca: Cornell University Press.

Tompkins, J. (1980) *Reader Response Criticism*, Baltimore: Johns Hopkins University Press.

Tompkins, J. (1989) 'West of everything', in D. Longhurst (ed.) *Gender, Genre and Narrative Pleasure*, London: Unwin Hyman.

Took, B. (1976) *Laughter in the Air*, London: Robson Books.

Torgovnick, M. (1981) *Closure in the Novel*, Princeton: Princeton University Press.

Tudor, A. (1974) *Image and Influence*, London: Allen & Unwin.

Tulloch, J. and Alvarado, M. (1983) *Dr Who: The Unfolding Text*, London: Macmillan.

Vernet, M. (1978) 'Genre', *Film Reader* 3: 13–17.

Vidmar, N. and Rokeach, M. (1974) 'Archie Bunker's bigotry: a study in selective perception and exposure', *Journal of Communication* 24 (1): 36–47.

Waites, B. (1981) 'The Music Hall' in T. Bennett (ed.), *Popular Culture*, Milton Keynes: Open University Course U203.

Warshow, R. (1974) 'Movie chronicle: the Westerner', in G. Mast and M. Cohen (eds) *Film Theory and Criticism*, New York and London: Oxford University Press.

White, H.V. (1973) *On Metahistory: The Historical Imagination In Nineteenth Century Europe*, Baltimore: Johns Hopkins University Press.

White, H.V. (1980) 'The value of narrativity in the representation of reality', in W.J.T. Mitchell (ed.) *On Narrative*, Chicago: University of Chicago Press.

Whitehouse, M. (1971) *Who Does She Think She Is?*, London: New English Library.
Wilden, A. (1972) *System and Structure*, London: Tavistock.
Willemen, P. (1978) 'Notes on subjectivity', *Screen* 19 (1): 41–69.
Williams, R. (1958) *Culture and Society*, London: Pelican Books.
Williams, R. (1961) *The Long Revolution*, London: Pelican Books.
Williams, R. (1974) *Television: Technology and Cultural Form*, London: Fontana.
Wilson, B. (1984) *Murder in the Collective*, London: Women's Press.
Wilson, B. (1987) *Sisters of the Road*, London: Women's Press.
Wober, M. (1984) 'Cinderella comes out', *Media, Culture and Society* 6 (1): 65–71.
Wolff, J. (1981) *The Social Production of Art*, London: Macmillan.
Woodiwiss, K. (1972) *The Flame and the Flower*, New York: Avon Books.
Woolrich, C. (1983) *Phantom Lady* (1st edn 1942), London: Zomba.
Worpole, K. (1983) *Dockers and Detectives*, London: Verso.
Wright, W.P. (1975) *Six Guns and Society*, Berkeley: University of California Press.
Zeman, J. (1977) 'Peirce's theory of signs', in T. Sebeok (ed.) *A Perfusion of Signs*, Bloomington: Indiana University Press.
Zinneman, F. (1990) Interview on *Arena*, BBC2, 9th March.
Zynda, T.H. (1988) '*The Mary Tyler Moore Show* and the transformation of situation comedy', in J.W. Carey (ed.) *Media, Myth and Narrative*, Beverly Hills: Sage.

Index